The Christian Voter: 7 Non-Negotiables for Voting For, Not Against, Your Values

The Christian Voter: 7 Non-Negotiables for Voting For, Not Against, Your Values

Craig A. Huey

Media Specialists

The Christian Voter: 7 Non-Negotiables for Voting For, Not Against, Your Values

Media Specialists, 1313 4th Ave N., Nashville, TN 37208, USA

I want to thank my wife, Shelly, who has powerfully encouraged, challenged and refined the vision of this book to transform our culture and politics.

A very special thank you to Phil Bailey, the wordsmith of content. For the past few years, Phil has helped create my newsletters with great clarity and stronger content.

His work on this book has been invaluable. Without Phil's insight, skills and tenacity this book would not have been possible.

I would also like to thank Kent Barry, whose editorial comments and trusted opinions molded this project into a quality book.

And my talented staff at my company must be acknowledged. For their commitment to their work and flexibility with deadlines, I will be forever grateful.

And of course, the lessons I have learned from my kids – Asher, Julia, Kelly, Caleb and Cory have helped to shape my passion for wanting to see a culture that loves freedom, justice and equality.

Finally, I want to thank the Lord Jesus Christ for opening doors. As He opened, I walked through with the mission to help pastors, church leaders and Christians have a better understanding of the Word of God and its application to politics and culture.

Craig A. Huey

Craig A. Huey, Author

Table of Contents

CHAPTER 1

Should Christians Vote?
A Biblical View of Politics

It's been said that the two topics that should never be discussed in family gatherings or in other social groups are religion and politics. These two topics stir the emotions more than most other subject matter.

As a former singles and youth pastor, I've been told to be silent about moral issues when teaching. And I've talked to people who have attended Bible studies in my home who have said they would never have come back if any political issues had been discussed – even if they were part of Scripture.

In this book we will attempt to discuss both Christianity and politics together, using Scripture to outline a biblical view of politics and government – and a biblical view of the Christian's responsibility to participate in those areas of society.

There are several myths about politics and Christianity that Christians on both sides of the political spectrum often believe. Let's start by stating and addressing these myths:

Myth #1. Politics is evil.

For the purpose of this discussion, we are defining politics as simply the *management* of the affairs of the government – whether local, state or federal.

Notice the differences between politics and government. Government is basically the rule or jurisdiction of one person or group of people over others. Politics consists of the rules and policies that control the operation and function of the jurisdiction.

Some guidelines, rules and limitations pertaining to the operation of government are specified in the U.S. Constitution. But not all the necessary guidelines and rules are spelled out in every detail. That's why politics is necessary for government to function – and hopefully to function efficiently.

Politics has existed for as long as there have been people groups living together and agreeing to some form of corporate government. Its existence is suggested in the creation mandate given to Adam and Eve – and through them to all of mankind – to steward and exercise dominion over the entirety of the created order:

God blessed them; and God said to them, "Be fruitful and multiply, and fill the earth, and subdue it; and rule over the fish of the sea and over the birds of the sky and over every living thing that moves on the earth." (Genesis 1:28)

If a system of government –and the political management of that government – was necessary for mankind to rule over God's creation, it became even more necessary after the fall of Adam in the Garden of Eden.

Why?

Because a system of checks and balances is necessary to restrain sin and the evil that exists inside the hearts of people living in rebellion against God. And that includes all of us – every man, woman, and child.

That's why the framers of our Constitution set up a Constitutional Republic – a representative form of government with checks and balances – and not a pure democracy in which a majority of just one can dictate laws and policies to everyone else.

It's clear then that intrinsically, all men and women at their core are evil – and that although men and women participate in politics, that doesn't make politics evil. Politics is not a personal entity – it's a thing, a process, a tool. It is therefore amoral – neither good nor evil in and of itself.

Myth #2. Jesus didn't deal with politics.

In Mark 12:13-17, a group of religious and secular leaders attempted to trick Jesus with a question: "Is it lawful to pay a poll-tax to Caesar, or not? Shall we pay or shall we not pay?"

Jesus responded, "Why are you testing me? Bring me a denarius to look at."

They handed him the coin. The inscription read, "Tiberius King, Son of the God Augustus Maximus, High Priest." The Roman Emperor – Tiberius Caesar Augustus – was claiming deity and absolute authority over all people in the empire. Rome was a totalitarian regime in which those who refused to bow to the absolute power and authority of the Roman State would be executed on a cross.

Jesus held up the denarius and asked rhetorically, "Whose likeness and inscription is this?"

"Caesar's," they replied. "Then render to Caesar what belongs to Caesar, and to God what belongs to God," Jesus responded.

While acknowledging the legitimacy and the necessity of government and politics, Jesus clearly declared the sovereignty of God over mankind AND politics. The coin imprinted with Caesar's image and inscription fell under his authority. But people – created by God and made in His image – rightfully belong to God.

Matthew Lee Anderson, founder and lead writer for Mere Orthodoxy, adds, "It's pretty much impossible to understand the message of Jesus without understanding the political context.... We have to understand the context into which Jesus proclaimed the Gospel and its deeply politicized idolatry."[1]

Myth #3. It is always easy to discern the biblical view of political policy.

While some policy positions are made clear in Scripture – such as the value of human life – others aren't as clear.

For example, determining corporate and individual tax policy, or what should be cut from the federal budget, requires open and honest discussion and debate of biblical principles.

Politicians who claim to be following biblical principles – and who may even quote Scripture to support their positions – may come to conflicting conclusions on specific policies or actions.

It's not easy to discern God's will in every circumstance. It takes much prayer, consulting godly counsel and a lifetime of biblical study – and even with all of that, there are still areas of truth we cannot completely understand in our finite wisdom.

"Where no wise guidance is, the people fall, but in the multitude of counselors there is safety."
(Proverbs 11:14)

Myth #4. Christians should only teach the Bible.

All truth is God's truth, whether it comes from the Bible or from nature or from the discoveries of mathematicians, astronomers or scientists.

God has revealed Himself to mankind in two primary ways:

- Through His creation – the world and universe
- Through His Son Jesus Christ

Most Christians are aware – at least somewhat – of the revelation from God through Jesus Christ that is contained in the Bible. But we should also be familiar with what God is revealing about Himself through His creation:

"The heavens declare the glory of God; and the firmament shows and proclaims His handiwork. Day after day pours forth speech, and night after night shows forth knowledge. There is no speech nor spoken

word [from the stars]; their voice is not heard. Yet their voice [in evidence] goes out through all the earth, their sayings to the end of the world."
(Psalm 19:1-4, Amplified Bible)

If we Christians want to produce followers of Christ who acknowledge and embrace the Lordship of Christ over all things – and we are commanded in Matthew 28 to do just that – we must teach more than the Bible. We must teach from the book of nature ... we must teach world and U.S. history – and we must teach our nation's founding documents: the Declaration of Independence and the United States Constitution.

Myth #5. Christians should stay away from politics because the Rapture is coming soon.

A corollary of this myth is a statement that became popular in the 1970s in some quarters of the "Jesus Movement." The saying was something along the lines of this: "Don't waste your time polishing the brass on a sinking ship."

The idea was that the U.S. was deteriorating morally and going downhill fast and there was no hope of salvaging the government or the country.

Fifty years have passed since then and we're still here.

The Rapture could happen today or tomorrow ... and it may not happen for another hundred years or more.

We just don't know. But regardless, there is nothing in Scripture that indicates we should not be involved in politics because the Rapture ***may*** occur soon. In fact, we are told just the opposite.

In Luke 19, Jesus told a parable to His followers because they believed He was about to set up a political kingdom in Jerusalem. The parable begins like this:

"A nobleman went to a distant country to receive a kingdom for himself, and then return. And he called ten of his slaves and gave them ten minas and said to them, 'Do business with this until I come back.'"
(Luke 19:12-13)

A mina was a unit of weight and monetary value in silver equal to 60 shekels. The point of the parable is that the nobleman in the story – who is symbolic of Christ – expected his servants to be diligent and responsible in handling their master's money and not sit around doing nothing because they expected their master to return soon.

When the nobleman returned to his servants, he rewarded those who had invested the funds they had been entrusted with, and severely punished the servant who had done nothing.

God has entrusted us with life, talents, skills, and responsibilities. He expects us to follow His instructions and be fruitful right up to the time when He either calls us to join Him in heaven or returns to earth to gather us to Himself. Some of those responsibilities include exercising governing authority over ourselves, our families, our churches, our schools, our businesses and our civil society.

Myth #6. If pastors get involved in politics, churches will lose their tax-exempt status.

The possible but unlikely loss of funding that might occur if churches were to have their tax-exempt status revoked by the IRS is a poor excuse for failing to declare God's truth in every area of life and thought.

Jesus Christ is Lord over every area of life, including civil government and politics. If pastors avoid talking from the pulpit about how biblical principles should inform our voting decisions, because they fear reprisals from the IRS, they are fearing man more than they are fearing and revering God.

Pastors should ask themselves whether any of the following Bible verses have any application to their churches' relationship to the IRS:

"The fear of man brings a snare, but he who trusts in the Lord will be exalted." (Proverbs 29:25)

"It is better to take refuge in the Lord than to trust in man." (Psalm 118:8)

"But Peter and the apostles answered, 'We must obey God rather than men.'" (Acts 5:29)

One of the most famous and familiar teachings of Jesus in the New Testament Gospels is the incident – mentioned earlier in this chapter – in which he tells the Pharisees, *"Then render to Caesar the things that are Caesar's, and to God the things that are God's." (Matthew 22:21, Mark 12:17, Luke 20:25)*

If a political candidate who is running for elected office advocates taking children from the custody of parents and turning them over to the government for their education and upbringing, should pastors not warn their congregations to vote against that candidate because he/she is clearly advocating an action that violates a command in Scripture?

God will bless and support and fund any faithful and believing ministry that honors and obeys Him, whether or not that ministry is an IRS-approved tax-exempt ministry. Consider the following admonition and warning in Proverbs:

"Deliver those who are being taken away to death, and those who are staggering to slaughter, Oh hold them back. If you say, 'See, we did not know this,' Does He not consider it who weighs the hearts? And does He not know it who keeps your soul? And will He not render to man according to his work?" (Proverbs 24:11-12)

Myth #7. The pastor and church leaders must be neutral.

This is the most evil myth of all because it assumes we live in a neutral world and that neutrality can exist in areas such as education, economics, law and politics.

But just as all *truth* is God's truth, so also all *facts* are God-created facts. Evangelical pastors would certainly agree that the way of salvation is **not** neutral. Nor is the resurrection of Jesus a neutral fact. The narrow path leads to salvation. The wide (neutral) path leads to destruction (Matthew 7:13-14).

If there is no neutrality in the spiritual realm, why do we assume there is neutrality in the physical realm? We do not live in a dichotomy – in a world that's divided between a spiritual compartment and a secular compartment. There is no neutrality anywhere in the universe.[2]

The myth that neutrality exists is an idea that began with Satan's temptation of Eve in the Garden of Eden and has been popularized throughout history by atheistic or agnostic philosophers and writers – and in modern times by the media and by politicians.

For example, we are constantly told that the law and the courts are neutral and impartial. But if you stop to think about it, this is nonsense. No law is ever neutral. The law distinguishes between right and wrong, good and evil. Judges and courts do the same thing.

Pastors and church leaders – as well as all Christians who believe that all truth is God's truth – can only be "neutral" – that is, non-committal – to the extent that they do not know the facts and the truth of a matter. Once they know the facts and the truth, they must be bound by it and committed to it.

Why Christians Are Politically Inactive

One of the primary reasons why so many Christians are politically inactive is that they don't know or understand the biblical and historical heritage of the United States. Most are unfamiliar with the stories of Samoset and Squanto – native American Indians who befriended and helped the early Pilgrim settlers in Plymouth, Massachusetts. And most are unfamiliar with the many miraculous ways God protected and provided for the struggling settlers and colonists.

They also don't realize that as Christians, we all are accountable to God for all that He has done throughout history to bring to pass a society in which liberty and justice is available for all ... and in which an economic system based on the biblical principles of individual responsibility and free enterprise is able to thrive.

Many Christians do not realize that freedoms and rights come from God, not government. If there is no God, there are no inherent rights. If the government doesn't recognize that rights are granted by God – by virtue of our being created in the image of God – then there are no unalienable rights because the government can take away at any time any individual rights it wishes to deny.

This is why our country's Founders wrote in the Declaration of Independence:

"We hold these truths to be self-evident, that all men are created equal, that they are endowed by their Creator with certain unalienable Rights, that among these are Life, Liberty and the pursuit of Happiness..."

They knew what it was like to live under a monarch and under an aristocracy that dictated to the subjects which rights they were or were not allowed to have. They wanted to create a different form of government – a government that would be "***of*** the people, ***by*** the people, and ***for*** the people."

What has happened in the past 80 to 100 years, however, is that our government bureaucracy has grown so large and inefficient and unresponsive to the people that it has departed from the principles of the Declaration of Independence.

And because Christians have stood silent while non-

Christians have taken control of government agencies and institutions, we now have a federal government that is of the government, by the government, and for the preservation of the government. We have a government that is attempting to declare immunity and independence from God's sovereignty.

When man lives by the idea that he has the right to determine good and evil for himself, he begins to believe he is autonomous from God, his Creator. The logical conclusion of this way of thinking is that God becomes obsolete, and belief in Him becomes old fashioned, out of date and unnecessary.

Therefore, God no longer exists. This is the basis of the philosophy – first proclaimed by atheist philosopher Friedrich Nietzsche more than 100 years ago – that sparked the "God is dead" movement that began in the 1960s.

For many in secular society, the government or the "state" is their god. Politicians, elections and the creation and enforcement of government policies are their religion. They have denied or abandoned the salvation and redemption offered by their Creator, and instead look to the government for their salvation. They subscribe to the declaration of the philosopher Georg Hegel that the state is God walking on earth.

This all has nothing to do with the so-called

"separation of church and state" by the way. It is rather mankind's attempt to separate his entire existence from the sovereign, all-powerful God of creation.

But since man cannot eliminate God completely, he erects a wall of illusion – a dichotomy of artificial divide between "sacred" subjects (i.e., religion) and "secular" subjects (everything else). Government is seen as neutral – devoid of religion and separated from God's sovereignty and control. John W. Whitehead addresses this issue in his book, *The Separation Illusion.*[3]

Here are just a few of those responsibilities: life and separate so-called "sacred" subjects from "secular" subjects, result in four misguided behaviors:

1. Many Christians don't vote at all (see Chapter Six).
2. Many Christians vote against, not for, what they believe in (see Chapter Three).
3. Christians don't run for office (see Chapter Seventeen)
4. Pastors and church leaders don't lead, encourage or speak out on the Lordship of Christ over every area of life (see Chapter Fifteen).

The central theme of all of Scripture is that there is no escape anywhere in the universe from the sovereignty of God. There is no neutrality – no area or subject that can be separated from Him:

"Yours, O Lord, is the greatness and the power and the glory and the victory and the majesty, for all that is in the heaven and in the earth is Yours. Yours is the kingdom, O Lord, and You are exalted as head above all. Both riches and honor come from You, and You reign over all, and in Your hand is power and might, and in Your hand it is to make great, and to give strength unto all." (1 Chronicles 29:11-12)

Why Christians SHOULD Be Involved in Politics

Remember how we defined politics earlier in this chapter? It is the management of government – the organizing and management of the affairs of civil government.

Francis Schaeffer, in his explosive and pivotal book, *A Christian Manifesto*[4], points out that the Lordship of Christ – another way of saying the sovereignty of God – covers ALL of life ... and ALL of life equally. This means that there is nothing concerning reality that is not spiritual.

Christianity therefore is not just a series of truths, but it is Truth itself – Truth about all of reality. And holding to that Truth intellectually – and then in some incomplete way depending on and living that Truth – the Truth of what IS – produces not only certain personal results, but also governmental and legal results.

THIS is why Christians should be involved in politics – and should diligently exercise their right and responsibility to speak their minds in the public sphere about government by voting in every election.

Here is a list and summary of five specific reasons why we as Christians should take our civic duty to vote seriously:

1. Christians should vote because of who God is.

He is the God of nature ... the God of all flesh ... the God of the universe.

He is the Master ... the Sustainer ... and the Lord of all people and of all things.

"The earth is the Lord's, and all it contains, the world, and those who dwell in it." (Psalm 24:1)

He is not to be excluded from any area of life – including politics and government.

"For the Lord is our judge, the Lord is our lawgiver, the Lord is our king; He will save us. (Isaiah 33:22)

2. Christians should vote because of who man is.

Man is created in the image of God (Genesis 1:26). But he is created to be a dependent being – dependent first on his Creator ... and also dependent on others.

But when man rebels against God, he also rebels against his fellow man. He wants to be totally independent and unaccountable.

Proverbs 18:1-2 describes man's drive to be autonomous and isolated:

"He who separates himself seeks his own desire; he quarrels against all sound wisdom. A fool does not delight in understanding, but only in revealing his own mind."

Men and women need other men and women to provide counsel, reason and advice ... and to hold them accountable for their actions. This is where choosing wise leaders and counselors through the electoral process is important.

"Where no wise guidance is, the people fall, but in the multitude of counselors there is safety."
(Proverbs 11:14)

3. Christians should vote because of their biblical calling.

As followers of Jesus, we are given several responsibilities regarding the world we live in, the people we live with ... and the nations we belong to. Here are just a few of those responsibilities:

- We are the salt of the earth and the light of the world (Matthew 5:13-16).
  - *Salt* is a preservative – it prevents corruption and decay.
  - *Light* exposes darkness and evil – it provides clarity and guidance.
- We are commanded to do battle with ideas and to conquer *"speculations and every lofty thing raised up against the knowledge of God..."* (2 Corinthians 10:3-6).
- As members of the body of Christ – the church – we are to attack and conquer the gates of Hell (Matthew 16:18).
- As followers of Christ, we are called to lead others to Christ and to teach them how to follow Christ themselves. (Matthew 28:19-20).

4. Christians should vote because of the God-ordained purpose of government.

Government is established by God but managed by mankind. It is intended to be a minister of God to reward those who do good and to punish those who do evil.

"Every person is to be in subjection to the governing authorities. For there is no authority except from God, and those which exist are established by God. Therefore whoever resists authority has opposed the ordinance of God; and they who have opposed will receive condemnation upon themselves. For rulers are not a cause of fear for good behavior, but for evil. Do you want to have no fear of authority? Do what is good and you will have praise from the same; for it is a minister of God to you for good. But if you do what is evil, be afraid; for it does not bear the sword for nothing; for it is a minister of God, an avenger who brings wrath on the one who practices evil." (Romans 13:1-4)

In a republic such as ours – in which citizens have the privilege of participating in the selection of the governing authorities through the electoral process, it's of the utmost importance that Christians exercise that privilege.

If we fail to do so, what's to prevent the governing authorities from rejecting God and rewarding those who do evil, while punishing those who do good? We already see this happening at the state and local level in many places.

Isaiah the prophet warned the people of God about this very thing:

"Woe to those who call evil good, and good evil; who substitute darkness for light and light for darkness; who substitute bitter for sweet and sweet for bitter! Woe to those who are wise in their own eyes and clever in their own sight! Woe to those who are heroes in drinking wine and valiant men in mixing strong drink, who justify the wicked for a bribe, and take away the rights of the ones who are in the right!" (Isaiah 5:20-23)

God promises judgment even on ***His own chosen people*** for turning His moral laws upside down. Can we expect to escape judgment if we allow our government leaders in the U.S. to do the same?

Plato said, *"One of the penalties for refusing to participate in politics is that you end up being governed by your inferiors."*

And the Irish statesman and philosopher Edmund Burke is famous for saying, *"The only thing necessary for the triumph of evil is for good men to do nothing."*

5. Christians should vote because of the transforming power of salvation.

Because of sin and rebellion against God, the whole person is fallen. Therefore, the whole person is saved by grace – even the mind.

"Therefore if anyone is in Christ, he is a new creature; the old things passed away; behold, new things have come." (2 Corinthians 5:17)

"And do not be conformed to this world, but be transformed by the renewing of your mind, so that you may prove what the will of God is, that which is good and acceptable and perfect." (Romans 12:1)

The wisdom and discernment that God gives to those followers of Jesus who are also students of the word of God cause them to be valuable leaders and counselors in the affairs of politics and government.

"And concerning you, my brethren, I myself also am convinced that you yourselves are full of goodness, filled with all knowledge and able also to admonish one another." (Romans 15:14)

The Living Bible paraphrase of Proverbs 11:11 says this: *"The good influence of godly citizens causes a city to prosper, but the moral decay of the wicked drives it downhill."*

A Final Thought

Please do not construe anything in this chapter as advocating the idea that government and politics are the answers – or contain or provide the answers – to the social issues and problems people face, both as individuals and as members of social, cultural or political groups.

The answer to ALL of the problems of fallen man is Jesus Christ and the salvation and redemption that He and He alone has provided to all who will trust in His substitutionary death on the cross and His bodily resurrection from the dead.

Psalm 146 gives us an excellent summary of this:

"Praise the Lord!

Praise the Lord, O my soul!

I will praise the Lord while I live;

I will sing praises to my God while I have my being.

Do not trust in princes,

In mortal man, in whom there is no salvation.

His spirit departs, he returns to the earth;

In that very day his thoughts perish.

How blessed is he whose help is the God of Jacob,

Whose help is in the Lord his God,

Who made heaven and earth,

The sea and all that is in them;

Who keeps faith forever;

Who executes justice for the oppressed;

Who gives food to the hungry.

The Lord sets the prisoners free.

The Lord opens the eyes of the blind;

The Lord raises up those who are bowed down;

The Lord loves the righteous;

The Lord protects the strangers;

He supports the fatherless and the widow,

But He thwarts the way of the wicked.

The Lord will reign forever,

Your God, O Zion, to all generations.

Praise the Lord!"

(Psalm 146:1-10)

CHAPTER 2

The Christian Vote: The Power to Transform Culture and Politics

It's a sad commentary on the history of American society that we even need to talk about transforming our culture and politics.

Why do our culture and politics need to be transformed? And into what do they need to be transformed?

To answer these questions, we need to go back in time and revisit the culture that existed in the American colonies at the birth of the United States of America.

American Culture as it Once Was

On September 5, 1774, the First Continental Congress met for the first time in Philadelphia.[5] The purpose of the meeting was to coordinate a unified response to Parliament's passage of the Intolerable Acts, which the British had imposed on the colonies in response to the riot in Boston on December 16, 1773 – known as the Boston Tea Party.[6]

The 55 Continental Congress delegates were divided between those who wanted to take immediate action against the British, and those who wanted to give the British government time to come to its senses and peacefully settle their differences with the colonies.[7]

From letters written by John Adams to his wife, Abigail, during the meetings, we know that when the delegates met for the second time on September 7th, they spent two hours praying and then studied four chapters from the Bible.[8] Clearly, the men who penned the Declaration of Independence and the Constitution of the United States shared a biblical worldview and wanted to form a nation and a republican form of government based on biblical principles.

The Second Continental Congress convened on May 10, 1775, after the American Revolution had already begun.[9] This Congress produced several documents, including:

- The Olive Branch Petition, adopted on July 5, 1775 – a personal appeal to King George III to help the colonists settle their differences with the British government.

- The Declaration of the Causes and Necessity of Taking Up Arms – written on July 6, 1775 by John Dickinson of Pennsylvania and Thomas Jefferson of Virginia.

- A proposal for independence – submitted by Virginia delegate Richard Henry Lee on June 7, 1776.

- The Declaration of Independence – written primarily by Thomas Jefferson, with the help of John Adams, Benjamin Franklin, Roger Sherman and Robert Livingston – and approved on July 4, 1776.[10]

Every human right listed in the Declaration of Independence had been preached in churches in the colonies prior to the Second Continental Congress (1763). It's a little-known fact that Jefferson's original draft of the Declaration contained a strong anti-slavery section that was edited out of the final document by the Congress – among some 80 other changes that were made before the vote for final approval was taken.[11]

In addition, each of the 10 Amendments to the Constitution, collectively known as the Bill of Rights, is based on biblical principles contained in Scripture.[12]

As if the foregoing facts aren't enough to show that American culture and politics were originally founded on and influenced by Christianity, consider the following:

- There were 15 calls to prayer among the leaders who attended the Second Continental Congress during the Revolutionary War.

- By 1815, there had been 1,400 government-issued national calls to prayer.

- The first English Bible printed in America – printed 11 months after the Battle of Yorktown – was printed as authorized by Congress for use in schools.[13]

- Andrew Jackson – the seventh U.S. President (1829-1837) – said, *"The Bible is the rock on which this Republic rests."*[14]

George Washington, in his farewell address to the new nation on September 19, 1796, said,

"Of all the dispositions and habits which lead to political prosperity, Religion and morality are indispensable supports. In vain would that man claim tribute of patriotism who should labour to subvert these great Pillars of human happiness ... and let us with caution indulge the supposition, that morality can be maintained without religion. Whatever may be conceded to the influence of refined education on minds of peculiar structure reason and experience both

forbid us to expect that National morality can prevail in exclusion of religious principle."[15]

Zachary Taylor – the 12th U.S. President, said this:

"Especially should the Bible be placed in the hands of the young. It is the best schoolbook in the world. I would that all our people were brought up under the influence of that Holy Book."[16]

Theodore Roosevelt – the first U.S. President of the twentieth century (1901–1909) – said:

"The teachings of the Bible are so interwoven and entwined with our whole civic and social life that it would be impossible for us to figure to ourselves what life would be if these teachings were removed."[17]

After the December 7, 1941 Japanese attack on Pearl Harbor, President Franklin Roosevelt said in one of his popular "fireside chats" that what had happened was a direct attack of anti-Christianity against Christianity.[18]

He also said: "The whole world is divided between ... pagan brutality and the Christian ideal. We choose freedom which is the Christian ideal."

When World War II ended, President Harry S. Truman said the only way the United States could reconstruct the nations that had been defeated was on the basis of Christianity. He believed the only way another world war could be prevented in the future was if world leaders would agree to live by the Ten Commandments and the Sermon on the Mount.[19]

Truman said this about the United States:

"This is a Christian nation. In this great country of ours has been demonstrated the fundamental unity of Christianity and democracy ... The fundamental basis of our Bill of Rights comes from the teachings of ... Exodus and Saint Matthew, from Isaiah and Saint Paul. I don't think we emphasize that enough these days."[20]

Boston Globe columnist Jeff Jacoby wrote, *"This is a Christian country. It was founded by Christians and built on broad Christian principles."*[21] The verdicts of more than 300 court cases – including Supreme Court cases – have included statements declaring that America is a Christian nation.[22]

Many more quotations of presidents and other prominent leaders in other walks of life could be cited to reinforce the idea that American culture and politics were clearly Christian in nature in the beginning – and for more than 150 years following the nation's founding.

Characteristics of a Christian Culture

A Christian culture doesn't mean that the majority of people in a society are Christians. It means only that Christianity has largely shaped and influenced the society. Eight characteristics of American society can be traced to biblical Christian foundations:

1. A Republican form of government.

Monarchy had been the form of government all across Europe for hundreds of years when the Pilgrims and Puritans came to America. The settlers wanted to follow the biblical principle of Exodus 18:21 and create a representative government in which leaders would be elected by the citizens rather than inheriting their positions by birth or by a king's decree.

"Furthermore, you shall select out of all the people able men who fear God, men of truth, those who hate dishonest gain, and you shall place these over them as leaders of thousands, of hundreds, of fifties and of tens."

The first elected legislature in America – the House of Burgesses – was established in1619.

2. Rights of conscience.

No persons should be required by law to act in a way

that violates or contradicts the moral beliefs and convictions that form their conscience. This principle comes from several passages in the New Testament.

One example can be found in Romans 14:

"Now accept the one who is weak in faith, but not for the purpose of passing judgment on his opinions ... Who are you to judge the servant of another? To his own master he stands or falls ... One-man judges one day above another, another regards every day alike. Let each man be fully convinced in his own mind. (Romans 14:1, 4a, 5)

In the Christian culture of early America, personal conviction, not social pressure alone, molded individual behavior. The founders understood that God loves and accepts all people regardless of their personal beliefs.

3. A free-market approach to religion.

In contrast to some other major world religions, Christianity is non-coercive and encourages free and open communication with other religious faiths. For example, Acts 17:16-32 records a debate between the apostle Paul and a group of religious leaders in the city of Athens.

By contrast, Christians cannot openly share their faith in France and several other countries. To do so will result in arrest and serving time in jail due to laws prohibiting "proselytizing."

It's true that Christians **are** urged in Scripture to share their faith with others. For example, in Mark 16:15, Jesus told His disciples to *"Go into all the world and preach the gospel to all creation."*

And in Acts 1:8 Jesus said, *"... but you shall receive power when the Holy Spirit has come upon you, and you shall be My witnesses both in Jerusalem and in all Judea and Samaria, and even to the remotest part of the earth."*

Christians are also commanded to share their faith gently and with sensitivity and respect. As the apostle Paul exhorted Timothy:

"I solemnly charge you in the presence of God and of Christ Jesus ... preach the word; be ready in season and out of season; reprove, rebuke, exhort with great patience and instruction." (2 Timothy 4:1-2)

The apostle Peter admonished believers with these words:

"... but sanctify Christ as Lord in your hearts, always being ready to make a defense to every one who asks you to give an account for the hope that is in you, ***yet with gentleness and reverence.****" (2 Peter 3:18)*

4. Institutional separation of church and state.

God made a clear distinction among His chosen people between the civil government and the religious government.

During the 40 years that the Israelites wandered in the Judean wilderness, after their exodus from Egypt, Moses was in charge of the civil government, and Aaron was in charge of the priesthood and religious government.

Whenever a king would decide to go into the seat of the religious government – the Jewish tabernacle or temple – and perform a function reserved only for the Jewish Priests, things would go badly for that king.

A good example is King Uzziah, who decided to go into the Jewish temple and offer incense – an activity reserved only for the priests. As a result of his usurpation of institutional "church" authority, God struck him with leprosy. (2 Chronicles 26:16-21.)

5. An emphasis on Christian education.

The influence of Christianity on education in America – particularly higher education – was profound and significant during the first hundred years of the Republic. Consider the following statistics regarding the 246 colleges that existed in the U.S. in 1860:

- 229 of the 246 colleges were affiliated with a Christian denomination.
- 224 of the 246 colleges had presidents who were ordained ministers of the gospel.

By 1884, there were 370 colleges, 307 (83%) of which were church-affiliated. Even the University of Michigan – not a church-affiliated university – still required mandatory chapel attendance in 1884. If Christianity had not been a prominent fixture in early American culture, there would have been very little, if any, higher education before 1800.

6. A free-market economy.

A free-market economic system is based on two biblical principles:

> **1. Provide for yourself and your own family first.**
> *"But if any one does not provide for his own, and especially for those of his household, he has denied the faith, and is worse than an unbeliever." (1 Timothy 5:8)*
>
> **2. If you refuse to work, don't expect to eat.**
> *"For even when we were with you we used to give you this order: If anyone will not work, neither let him eat." (2 Thessalonians 3:10)*

The early settlers had experimented with a socialist economic system in which all the production of everyone in the community was pooled together and then divided equally among the families. But they soon learned that expecting the hard workers to receive less while producing enough to support the non-workers results in the hard workers producing less.

It's natural for people to expect to receive the fruits of their own labors and not be forced to subsidize those who refuse to work, or who are lazy and produce very little. Taking care of widows and orphans and the poor was always a responsibility of those who followed God's principles. But such charitable giving was always voluntary and according to each person's choice and personal convictions. The biblical principles regarding sharing one's wealth with others are these:

"Now this I say, he who sows sparingly shall also reap sparingly, and he who sows bountifully shall also reap bountifully. Let each one do just as he has purposed in his heart, not grudgingly or under compulsion; for God loves a cheerful giver." (2 Corinthians 9:6-7)

"Give, and it will be given to you, a good measure, pressed down, shaken together and running over, they will pour into your lap. For whatever measure you deal out to others, it will be dealt to you in return."

(Luke 6:38)

7. A spirit of charity.

The U.S. is the most generous country on the planet.[23]

Why? Because Christianity teaches that people should help their neighbors who are in need. Voluntary giving, without expecting anything in return, is one of the characteristics of a Christian culture.

Here is one example: On December 26, 2004, a 9.0 magnitude earthquake occurred under the Indian Ocean near the west coast of Sumatra. The quake caused a massive tsunami "wave train" – the largest ever recorded – which struck the coastlines of 11 countries, killing more than 227,000 people[24] and leaving 1.7 million homeless and displaced.[25]

The hardest-hit country was Indonesia – a Muslim nation. You might expect that Muslim nations around the world would have sprung into action, sending both people and humanitarian aid to Indonesia in large quantities. But this didn't happen.

Instead, U.S. citizens and corporations voluntarily contributed more than $700 million to the tsunami relief effort within six weeks of the event. This was in addition to massive U.S. government assistance totaling more than $1.3 billion.[26]

The Parable of the Good Samaritan in Luke 10:30-37 illustrates three principles of voluntary charity, which are unique to Christianity and to a Christian culture:

1. Voluntary charity is motivated by compassion. (Luke 10:33).

2. Voluntary charity is not driven by convenience. The Samaritan was on a journey when he encountered the injured man. It wasn't convenient for him to stop and help, but he did it anyway.

3. Voluntary charity isn't determined by the race or religion of the one needing help. In Jesus' day, Jews and Samaritans hated each other and had no dealings with one another. Yet the Samaritan helped a person in need who, in effect, was an enemy.

The first hospital in the American colonies was founded on May 11, 1751 by Dr. Thomas Bond and Benjamin Franklin. The purpose of the hospital was to help the poor and sick – both physically and mentally – in the city of Philadelphia.[27]

The hospital seal contains an image of the Good Samaritan along with these words from Luke 10:35: *"Take care of him and I will repay thee."*

8. The concept of God-given unalienable rights.

"We hold these truths to be self-evident, that all men are created equal, that they are endowed by their Creator with certain unalienable Rights, that among these are Life, Liberty and the pursuit of Happiness ..."

These inspiring words in the Declaration of Independence are unique to Christianity and to a Christian culture. In most countries in the world today – and in the countries that existed in the 18th century, when these words were written – human rights are granted by the government. They are neither unalienable – meaning unchangeable – nor are they seen as granted by God.

Notice also that the Declaration of Independence says there are more unalienable God-given rights than just life, liberty, and the pursuit of happiness – which, to the founders, meant the pursuit of property and prosperity. These three rights are ***among*** our unalienable, God-given rights – but they are not all of them.

Other unalienable rights are contained in the first 10 Amendments to the Constitution – the Bill of Rights.

The Steady Erosion of Christian Cultural Influence

The above eight characteristics of a Christian culture have been under relentless attack over the past hundred years or so – since the early 1900s at least. The attacks have become so extensive and severe in recent years that the Christian cultural influences of the past are disappearing before our eyes.

Some Christian authors, philosophers, theologians, and leaders have even gone so far as to say we are living in a post-Christian society and culture today.

Consider the following evidence:

1. Representative government is under attack.

More and more of our federal and state government functions are no longer controlled by representatives elected by the people. Instead, a massive "alphabet soup" of government agencies staffed by unelected career bureaucrats now control most of our government at all levels – local, state and federal.

They crank out endless government regulations and rules that carry the same authority to force compliance and punish disobedience as the laws enacted by Congress and state legislatures. Yet we, the people, cannot fire these bureaucrats, we cannot hold them accountable and we cannot vote them out of office. They are permanent fixtures in both Democrat and Republican administrations, known as The Deep State – and they rule and control nearly every aspect of our lives.[28]

2. Rights of conscience are under attack.

Lawsuit after lawsuit and court case after court case constantly attack and demean Christians who simply want to use their First Amendment right to freely exercise their religious faith without government interference.

Some examples of rights of conscience that are being attacked and threatened are:

- The right to not be forced to work on the day of the week set aside as the Sabbath.
- The right of healthcare workers to not be forced to perform or assist in abortions.
- The right to not be forced by law to support and celebrate same-sex marriage or so-called gender transformation.

We will cover some of the specific legal actions and court cases regarding rights of conscience in a later chapter of this book regarding protecting Christian liberty.

3. The concept of a free-market approach to religion is eroding.

As a nation, we've largely lost the ability to communicate with one another in a civil manner or to carry on open debates about ideas. Any attempt to have a rational discussion about differences of opinion often degenerates quickly into name-calling and personal attacks on one's character or motivations.

Christians are called bigots and other derogatory names because they disagree with those who believe in other gods or in no god. People no longer understood how to separate their ideas and beliefs from the people who hold other views.

Another cause for the erosion of a free-market approach to religion is the so-called post-modern idea that absolute truth does not exist. For those who deny that there is any truth that is true for everyone, discussing and debating religion is meaningless or oppressive.

If truth is only relative, then what's true for you is true for you, and what's true for me is true for me and there's no point in debating the differences because everyone's truth is right and no one's truth is wrong.

4. The separation of church and state is being blurred.

Biblical separation of church and state is an *institutional* separation, not a *religious* separation. There's a difference between the two.

In Old Testament Bible times, there was only one

"church" for the Jewish people. It consisted of the wilderness tabernacle and also the temple in Jerusalem, with a hierarchy of priests and other religious leaders, and a set of operating procedures and responsibilities. The civil government was completely separate. But both institutions were subject to the laws and commandments of God. In other words, both institutions were religious – they followed Judaism.

The idea of "a wall of separation" between church and state, that was introduced by Thomas Jefferson in 1805, was never intended to mean a wall of separation between *religion* and state – it was meant to be a separation between the church *as an organized institution* and the state as an organized civil government.

This distinction, combined with an understanding of religious commonality, prevailed in colonial America in the first 200 years of the Republic's existence. But things have changed drastically in the last 30 or 40 years.

Executive and legislative branches of state governments – and especially the judicial branch – are interpreting the separation of church and state to mean the *secularization* of church and state. Increasingly, state and local governments are hostile to both religion and churches, rather than being supportive of their right to exist and their special place in our society, while being neutral toward them.

5. The influence of Christianity in education is disappearing.

In 1963, the U.S. Supreme Court banned organized prayer and Bible reading in the nation's public schools. Since then:

- Premarital sex has increased 500%
- Pregnancy outside of marriage has risen 400%
- Sexually transmitted diseases have risen 200%
- Suicide is up by more than 400%
- Violent crime has increased by 500%[29]

In higher education, most college professors espouse liberal or far-left ideology. They regularly preach Marxism, identity politics and other anti-American and anti-Christian ideas to their students. Aside from staunchly Christian liberal arts colleges and universities, there are very few professors, on today's campuses, who still hold to a biblical worldview.

Christian writer and speaker, Gabe Lyons – author of *UnChristian* – describes the decline of Christian influence this way:

"America was practically Christian just a handful of years ago, but in the past several decades, our country's predominant self-perceptions have been challenged and replaced ... So, although many of us still feel like we reside in Christian America, that reality is dead."[30]

Another indication of the declining Christian influence in America over the past 40 years has been the increase in the U.S. prison and jail population compared to other countries.

In 1980, the U.S. had a prison and jail incarceration rate of 100 prisoners per 100,000 residents – the same as the average per capita prison population in the rest of the world. But by 2016, the incarceration rate in the U.S. had risen to 655 per 100,000 – by far the highest rate in the world. In addition, the U.S. held 21% of the world's prisoners in 2015 while having only 4.4% of the world's population.[31]

6. Our free-market economy is under attack.

The free-market economy of Christian America has become more and more of a government-controlled, socialist-style economy.

In spite of the recent federal regulatory rollbacks under President Trump, business regulations in some states still stifle entrepreneurs and innovators and make it increasingly difficult to sustain new business start-ups. High state business taxes and anti-minority minimum wage laws have forced many small businesses to fire full-time employees (especially minority youth), slow expanding operations and cutback on new investment.

Thomas Jefferson once said, *"The pillars of our prosperity are the most thriving when left most free to individual enterprise."*[32]

That is not what's happening in our economy today. Our current tax and welfare systems are striking examples of the declining influence of Christianity.

Instead of rewarding those who work hard to provide for themselves and for their families (1Timothy 5:8), our tax and welfare systems do just the opposite. They reward those who do **not** work, by confiscating a large portion of the income of hard-working Americans and redistributing the fruits of their labor by giving free handouts to those who refuse to work!

These outrageous government policies make it more profitable for people to stay at home and collect free welfare! They would rather take your hard-earned money in government handouts than get a job and work.

7. Government assistance programs discourage voluntary charity.

There was a time in America when assistance to the

poor and needy was provided by churches and by nonprofit "tithe agencies" – organizations funded by the voluntary contributions of caring citizens. The first orphanages, the first hospitals, the first school, and the first homeless shelters were all founded by Christians.

There are still a substantial number of nonprofit charitable organizations in the United States, and 22 of them were ranked in the top 100 U.S. nonprofits for financial integrity, in 2007, by The Nonprofit Times.[33]

But despite the large amount of charitable giving by U.S. citizens – and despite the fact that the United States is by far the most generous country in the world when measured by total charitable donations as a percentage of GDP[34] – a smaller percentage of Americans donate to charity than do the citizens of 12 other countries.[35]

The reason fewer Americans as a percentage of the country's population donate to charity stems from two factors:

- A high tax burden.
- The fact that government agencies continue to usurp the biblically-mandated responsibilities of individual believing churches and the broader Christian community.

More and more Christians rationalize that since they pay their taxes, which fund government welfare programs, they are doing their part to take care of the poor and needy.

8. Unalienable God-given rights are under attack.

The most obvious unalienable right that is being attacked and abrogated today is the right to life of the unborn. A later chapter in this book deals at length with the importance of protecting unborn human life.

Not only are the rights of the unborn under siege, but the right to life of all people is under threat of extinction by gangs, hate groups and other individuals who dehumanize life in general and think of human life as worthless. Increased murder and disregard for human life are the consequences of American society turning away from God and rejecting Christian teaching and value.

Consider these words from Psalm 10:

"In pride the wicked hotly pursue the afflicted; let them be caught in the plots which they have devised. For the wicked boasts of his heart's desire, and the greedy man curses and spurns the Lord. The wicked, in the haughtiness of his countenance, does not seek Him. All his thoughts are, 'There is no God.'...

"He sits in the lurking places of the villages; in the

hiding places he kills the innocent; his eyes stealthily watch for the unfortunate ... He says to himself, 'God has forgotten; He has hidden His face; He will never see it.'" (Psalm 10:2-4, 8, 11)

Liberty is another unalienable right that is under attack in today's culture. In a later chapter, we will also cover the importance of protecting liberty.

How Christians Can Transform Culture

There are many actions Christians can take – both individually and working together with other Christians – to help transform American culture and politics and restore them to a sound Christian foundation. In a future book, I will list and develop a full array of those actions.

For the purpose and scope of this book, the primary action that Christians can take to have a significant and powerful effect on our culture and politics is to exercise their civic duty to **vote** in every election. That must include the national presidential elections every four years, state and local primary elections, school board elections, referendum elections – ALL elections.

While the ancient Jews were living in Babylon – a foreign country with a different history, a different culture and a different language – God told His people, through Jeremiah the prophet, *"Seek the welfare of the city where I have sent you into exile, and pray to the Lord on its behalf; for in its welfare you will have welfare." (Jeremiah 29:7)*

This command is unmistakable in its application for us today: We Christians should seek the welfare of the city, the state and the nation in which we live. Why? Because our welfare is dependent on the welfare of the people with whom we live – and the welfare of the government under which we live.

President James Garfield said, *"Now more than ever the people are responsible for the character of their Congress. If that body be ignorant, reckless and corrupt, it is because the people tolerate ignorance, recklessness and corruption."*[36]

The Power of Evangelical Christian Voters

There are about 80 million potential evangelical Christian voters in the United States. Of those voters, only 38.4 million (48%) voted in the 2016 presidential election. That means that 41.6 million evangelical Christians didn't vote for either presidential candidate in 2016! And 12 million of those 41.6 million are not even registered to vote!

In California, 7,280,000 out of the state's 14 million evangelical Christian voters did not bother to vote in 2016. Imagine if those seven million plus Christians had voted. The following most likely would have happened:

- Donald Trump would have won the national popular vote.
- He would have carried the state of California.
- There wouldn't be a huge push on the part of far-left liberals and socialists to eliminate the Electoral College, since the popular vote and the Electoral College vote would have yielded the same results.

And if those seven million California evangelical Christians had voted in the 2018 midterm elections, the state would have elected a conservative rather than a liberal, governor ... and several conservative, Orange County, California, state legislators would not have lost to their Democrat opponents in the days following election day due to the blatantly corrupt so-called "ballot harvesting" by vote-stealing Democrats.

The evangelical Christian vote is critical in any election. The participation of evangelical Christian voters will determine the outcome of the 2020 national election. A strong turnout by evangelical Christians will result in a strengthening of the eight characteristics of a Christian culture. A low turnout by evangelical Christians will result in the further erosion and deterioration of those Christian influences.

James 4:17 reminds us about the importance of fulfilling our responsibility and duty to vote:

"Therefore, to one who knows the right thing to do, and does not do it, to him it is sin."

If the Christian foundations of our nation and our culture continue to crumble, we will be in deep and potentially irreversible trouble:

"If the foundations are destroyed, what can the righteous do?" (Psalm 11:3)

But things don't have to reach that point.

A Call to Action

Christians can and must work to restore and rebuild the foundations of our Republic. We are commanded to do no less:

"And if you give yourself to the hungry and satisfy the desire of the afflicted, then your light will rise in darkness and your gloom will become like midday. And the Lord will continually guide you, and satisfy your desire in scorched places, and give strength to your bones; and you will be like a watered garden, and like a spring of water whose waters do not fail. Those from among you will rebuild the ancient ruins; ***you will***

raise up the age-old foundations; and you will be called the repairer of the breach, the restorer of the streets in which to dwell. *" (Isaiah 58:10-12)*

Here's an action plan:

1. Pray for revival among Christians. Why a revival among Christians? Because when non-Christians start seeing Christians loving each other – and the world – instead of fighting with each other and complaining about all that's wrong with the world, they will become attracted to Christianity and the revival will spread. But revival has to start with all of us who are Christians.

Jesus said to His disciples the night before His crucifixion, *"A new commandment I give to you, that you love one another, even as I have loved you ... By this all men will know that you are My disciples, if you have love for one another." (John 13:34-35)*

2. Be a part of the Christian revival yourself. How? Begin to serve the hungry and satisfy the desires of the afflicted by joining a group of like-minded Christians through your church or through another voluntary nonprofit organization.

3. Pray for revival and changed hearts among non-Christians. Remember that we are called as Christians to pray for all, regardless of nationality, race, ethnicity, religion, color or gender.

"First of all, then, I urge that entreaties and prayers, petitions and thanksgivings, be made on behalf of all men and women, for kings and all who are in authority, in order that we may lead a tranquil and quiet life in all godliness and dignity." (1 Timothy 2:1-2)

"The Lord is not slow about His promise, as some count slowness, but is patient toward you, not wishing for any to perish, but for all to come to repentance."
(2 Peter 3:9)

4. Begin educating yourself now in preparation for the November 2020 national election. Research the positions of the candidates who are running for every office. Research the pros and cons of every proposition and local measure on the ballot. Plan to attend one of my Election Forums. Check my Election Forum speaking schedule at this website: electionforum.org/biblical-world-view

5. Plan to vote in the November 2020 election – and in every local, state and national election from now on. Don't let anything stop you from letting your voice be heard at the ballot box!

6. Help educate other Christians and urge them to vote in November also. Encourage your family and friends to attend an Election Forum and consult our voter guides. Perhaps you can help babysit children while their parents go to the polls or collect and turn in the ballots of the shut-ins from your church who are not able to go to the polls.

See the next chapter of this book to learn how to vote according to your Christian values.

CHAPTER 3

Strategically Limiting Evil While Voting For – Not Against – Your Christian Values

As Christian citizens living and working and sharing our faith in a fallen world, we have a moral obligation to vote in elections, and to choose with intelligence and with discretion the candidates for whom we vote.

According to Exodus 18:21, the general character qualities we should be looking for in political candidates are the following:

- Capable men and women who fear God;
- Men and women of truth – committed to speaking the truth and living by the truth; and
- Men and women who hate dishonest gain

If there are political candidates who clearly exhibit these qualities, they are the ones we should support.

But often it's not possible to know, for example, whether a candidate truly reveres and trusts God in his or her daily life, or just believes in the existence of God. (Revering God and believing in God are not the same things.)

Political candidates, in attempting to appeal to a broad spectrum of the voting public, usually speak in generalities rather than specifics. And then there's the added complication that the news media and social media only communicate what they want us to hear.

So, unless we have the time to read and listen to a variety of news sources every day, and to read and listen to everything that every political candidate says – and no one has that kind of time – we must make our voting decisions based on incomplete and often distorted information.

How do we get around the information maze and make discerning and wise voting decisions? I recommend examining whether candidates agree or disagree with us on the social issues that are most important to us, such as:

- Support for abortion vs. support for life;
- Support for the sanctity of heterosexual marriage;
- Support for religious liberty;
- Support for Israel;

- Standing up for persecuted Christians around the world – and against governments that persecute Christians and other religious minorities; and

- Support for homeschooling, school choice and for Christian schools.

These are a few of the non-negotiable values and political positions that can help determine our support for a candidate.

Note: The biblical principles regarding each of the above "non-negotiable" issues are covered in separate chapters later in this book.

It's rare to find a candidate who agrees with all of the non-negotiable issues that are important to Christians. This creates a dilemma.

In searching for a solution, it's helpful to consider that one of our moral responsibilities as Christians is to avoid evil in our own lives and to seek to limit evil in the lives of our government leaders by taking a stand against it.

"Do not enter the path of the wicked and do not proceed in the way of evil men. Avoid it, do not pass by it; turn away from it and pass on." (Proverbs 4:14-15)

"When the righteous increase, the people rejoice, but when a wicked man rules, the people groan ... The king

gives stability to the land by justice, but a man who takes bribes overthrows it." (Proverbs 29:2, 4)

Here's a three-step strategy for voting wisely:

1. Pray for wisdom and discernment in voting.

"But if any of you lacks wisdom, let him ask of God, who gives to all generously and without reproach, and it will be given." (James 1:5)

2. Choose candidates who agree with your Christian values. Vote for your values, not against them.

3. Vote strategically with wisdom and prayer, to limit evil. Vote in such a way as to prevent dishonesty and evil in the areas of political "back room" deal-making and government policies.

Let me explain how strategically limiting evil works.

On rare occasions, there may be a really good candidate who aligns with your Christian worldview on every issue. But most often, you will be faced with choices that are not clear.

Consider a typical example of two candidates running for an elected office. Let's call them Candidate A and Candidate B.

Candidate A agrees with your values on some issues

but not on others. And Candidate B agrees with your values on issues that Candidate A disagrees with, but disagrees with your values on issues that Candidate A agrees with!

To complicate matters even more, let's say there's a third-party candidate – an Independent Candidate C – who is more completely aligned with your values. But realistically, Candidate C has no chance of winning the election.

As a Christian, you want to vote according to your Christian values and worldview ... and honor God with your vote. That is your dilemma.

What do you do? How do you cast your vote?

As Christians, our stances on non-negotiable issues are inflexible. They go beyond politics. They are moral issues that will affect the future of our society as well as determine the type of world in which our children will grow up.

Issues of life, building strong families, traditional marriage and pro-job creation and pro-economic growth are fundamental to our belief system and a healthy society.

Other issues important to Christians may include:

- Stop human-trafficking;

- lowering taxes (vs. legalized theft);
- replacing a healthcare rationing system mandated and controlled by bureaucratic government with a fair and comprehensive free-market system;
- Ending budget deficits (generational theft which creates the most immoral tax of all – inflation);
- Eliminating wasteful government spending;
- strengthening national defense;
- supporting persecuted Christians around the world and holding nations accountable for human-rights violations
- Righting wrongs with Justice reform; and
- Strengthening the family.

Against that background, there are two ways Christians can view how to vote:

Christian voter #1: You vote only on principle. You vote ***for*** a candidate, not against one. You vote only for a candidate who agrees with your non-negotiable positions.

You believe this is the only way to have a clear conscience.

So, if Candidate A supports using government funds – taxpayer money – to pay for abortion, you could never vote for that candidate. But what if that candidate supports parental notification and opposes partial-birth abortion while supporting the use of taxpayer dollars to fund abortion? Your vote would still be "No."

Now let's say Candidate B also supports taxpayer-funded abortion, also supports partial-birth abortion, and is against parental notification. You would never vote for that candidate either. Instead, you vote for Candidate C who agrees with your Christian values on abortion, but who clearly has no chance of winning.

If Candidate B—who is for taxpayer-supported abortion, for partial-birth abortion and against parental consent—wins because you, as a Christian, voted for Candidate C who is aligned with your Christian values, that's OK with you.

Why? Because you believe God doesn't measure us by who wins or loses, but by our faithfulness to our values without compromise.

This view believes we honor God by not voting for anyone who disagrees with any of our biblical values, and we then allow Him to do the impossible. We are being faithful to what God has called us to do, and we leave the results in His hands.

By voting for a third-party candidate or write-in, you

are saying the lesser of two evils is still evil.

Christian voter #2: This person votes to strategically limit evil as much as is possible. This voter disagrees with voter #1.

In the case of abortion, voting for Candidate A, who is opposed to partial-birth abortion and for parental consent, even if he is in favor of taxpayer-funded abortion, is a way to restrain evil and save lives.

By saving lives, you are strategically limiting evil.

The principle of strategically avoiding the worst evil means that although you are not voting for a candidate who fully agrees with your views, you are choosing the candidate who is best suited to your values among those candidates who have a legitimate chance of winning the election.

You may not like how the candidate sounds. You may not like their past. You may not like their policies. But, they are better than their opponent. They may not be perfect, but they would stop some evil policies. They may promote school choices, protection of religious freedom, support for Israel. Not perfect, but better than the opponent – you can strategically limit evil.

The dilemma faced by the above two Christian voters accentuates the importance of voting in primary elections. Voting in a primary election sometimes allows you to vote for the "near perfect candidate" because the field is broad, and you have more candidates to choose from.

Voting for a third-party candidate in a general election – or not voting at all – is, in a sense, voting for the worst candidate. You actually are indirectly voting for the candidate who supports the most evil!

Rahab, the prostitute in the ancient city of Jericho, used this principle to protect Jewish spies. You can read her amazing story in Joshua 2:1-21, and 6:1-25.

Death-camp survivor and best-selling writer, Corrie Ten Boom, tells of the Nazis pounding on her family's front door and demanding to know if they are hiding Jews. The higher moral ground was to lie to protect life.

It's not a matter of choosing "the lesser of two evils." As Christians, we must never choose evil. Instead, our vote for the imperfect candidate is strategically used to limit evil—and that, in itself, is a morally sound choice.

There are three key benefits to this approach:

1. **Your vote keeps the worst person from being elected**—and doing even more harm. This is a good moral choice.

2. **You're voting for some good moral and biblical values**—a morally good choice.

3. **You're often voting for more than just the office for which a candidate is running.** For example, a state governor will appoint 300 judges, commissioners, and others to important positions. The candidate most aligned with your values will appoint more people who are acceptable. Other tightly contested races may have other important, though indirect, short- and long-term consequences.

So, you are faced with those two strategic choices as a Christian voter.

Voter guides are essential to helping you vote. Guides like iVoter.Com evaluate each candidate.

In our voter guide we share a list of recommendations, posted at electionforum.org. Some races receive a "2 thumbs-up," or "better than opponent." Other races are graded more specifically, with a rating. The rating could be a 1-star or anything between 2 – 4 stars. The list includes Republican and Democratic candidates who are strategic in restraining evil.

In some races, a third-party candidate for a specific office is given two or three thumbs up – even though that candidate has no legitimate chance of winning the election. That rating is for those who wish to follow the strategy of Christian voter #1. For those who decide to vote this way, you must remember that the lesser of two evils is still evil.

In cases where the third party gets a higher ranking, they won't win. Subscribe and read my newsletter *Reality Alert* **for more information.** Go to ElectionForum.org to sign-up.

CHAPTER 4

A Brief History of Christian Revival and Political Activism in America

Christianity and politics are often pitted against each other and characterized as polar opposites – mutually exclusive activities – by the progressive media and by professional career politicians. Never should they be mixed, they say.

As a Christian who is involved in both business AND politics, I receive frequent requests for interviews. I was once doing a live interview on the air about my Christian faith and politics. I knew the argument that would be used against me: the separation of church and state. It's the standard attack employed against Christians who are involved in politics.

Separation of Church and State?

The so-called "separation of church and state" is usually cited as the reason Christianity and politics should be kept forever separate and never comingled.

But this is faulty thinking and warped logic for three reasons:

1. The concept of "separation of church and state" is not found in the U.S. Constitution. It was a phrase composed and written by President Thomas Jefferson in a letter he wrote in 1802 to the Danbury Baptist Association in Danbury, Connecticut. He was trying to clarify the meaning of a clause in the First Amendment to the U.S. Constitution.

2. The separation of church and state does not mean what many people today think it means. The clause in the First Amendment on which the so-called "separation of church and state" principle is based says this: *"Congress shall make no law respecting an establishment of religion, or prohibiting the free exercise thereof..."*

   Thomas Jefferson drew a comparison in his letter between the words "an establishment of religion" and the word "church" because in the minds of the Framers, the word "church" didn't refer to Christianity in general, it referred to any one of the several denominations of Christianity that were popular at the time.

In other words, "an establishment of religion" meant an establishment of Baptists, or an establishment of Congregationalists, or an establishment of Lutherans, etc. The First Amendment was intended to prohibit Congress from making laws that showed a preference for one denomination of Christianity over the others.

What the Establishment Clause of the First Amendment actually means is that Congress is prohibited from making two kinds of laws:

- Laws that require the ***blending*** of a Christian denomination with the government
- Laws that require the ***separation*** of a Christian denomination from the government

Why?

Because to do so would be to make a law respecting – or concerning – an establishment of religion. Government can't have it both ways.

The First Amendment requires Congress to stay away from religion completely – to avoid creating any restrictions on individual churches or denominations... and to avoid favoring any individual church or denomination.

3. Christianity is not a church. It is the foundational faith of many churches, but it is not in itself an organized church. There are many different Christian denominations with different doctrinal statements and credos. There is no single organized "Christian church" in America with a hierarchy of leadership, doctrinal decrees and policy pronouncements.

The So-Called "Johnson Amendment"

There has been much talk in recent years about a provision that was added to the United States Internal Revenue Code of 1954 that came to be known as the "Johnson Amendment." There are a few unusual things about this amendment – and about its architect, Lyndon B. Johnson:

- The amendment was added to H.R. 8300 – a House bill revising the Internal Revenue Code statutes in the U.S. Code (U.S.C.).

- Lyndon B. Johnson was a Senator representing Texas and was running for his second term as Senator when he introduced his amendment to H.R. 8300. He had won the Democrat primary for his first term in 1948 in a run-off election by a razor-thin margin of 87 votes out of almost a million votes cast. And some believed his victory was based on at least two hundred fraudulent ballots that had been certified as valid by an election judge.[37]

- The amendment revised paragraph (3) of subsection (c) within section 501 of Title 26 (Internal Revenue Code) of the U.S.C. – which describes organizations which may be exempt from federal income tax.

- The amendment was intended to prohibit 501(c)(3) organizations from endorsing or opposing political candidates, and from participating in political campaign activities – especially fundraising activities.

The Johnson Amendment is actually a violation of the free exercise clause of the First Amendment. Why Christian churches capitulated from their God-given responsibility to speak God's word concerning every area of life and thought – and failed to sue the IRS for violating the free exercise clause of the First Amendment – is a mystery.

The First Great Awakening and the War of Independence

The first large-scale revival in America took place in the colonies approximately between the late 1720s and the mid-1740s. It is called in American history The First Great Awakening.

It was because of this revival that the United States of America came into being. Without it, the American Revolution – the War of Independence – would not have happened. All the great social movements in early American history were the products of revival.

The reason the revival was so significant and transformative is because a spiritual apathy had developed among the descendants of the early colonists.

When the Puritans and pilgrims first arrived in America, they had a fervent faith and a vision for establishing a godly society and government. Within a century, their commitment had cooled.

The descendants of the original immigrants became more concerned with building their wealth and living in comfort than with building the Kingdom of God. The same spiritual malaise had spread throughout the American colonies by the early 1700s.

Jonathan Edwards – a Congregationalist pastor in Northampton, Massachusetts, during the 1730s and 1740s – has been called the Father of the Great Awakening. In the 1730s, Edwards began seeing a large number of conversions in Massachusetts. He preached a series of sermons in 1734 on justification by faith alone. Subsequently, he recorded three hundred conversions over a six-month period.[38]

Edwards' most famous sermon – "Sinners in the Hands of an Angry God" – was delivered in Enfield, Massachusetts – on the Connecticut border – in 1741.

George Whitfield – an Anglican evangelist – made an even more significant contribution to the Great Awakening than Edwards. Educated at Oxford, Whitfield became an ordained minister at the age of 22 and began preaching the gospel all over Great Britain.

Between 1738 and 1770, Whitfield made seven evangelistic trips to the American colonies where he drew crowds that were too large for churches to accommodate. On more than one occasion he spoke to an open-air crowd of 30,000.[39]

In New England alone, between 1740 and 1742, church membership doubled from 25,000 to 50,000. Hundreds of new churches sprang up to accommodate the rapid increase in the number of churchgoers.

Perhaps more than any other preacher in America in the 1730s and 1740s, George Whitfield united the various independent movements of the Great Awakening and united the separate colonies into a more cohesive unit under the teachings of Christ.

Benjamin Franklin – who never openly professed a personal faith in Christ – wrote that he was pleased with the changes he noticed in the manners and behaviors of local townsfolk. He commented that one couldn't walk through a town in the evening without hearing psalms sung by different families on every street.[40]

The spiritual revival caused by the First Great Awakening had an especially profound influence on two areas of colonial society: higher education and politics:

- In higher education, Princeton, Rutgers, Brown and Dartmouth universities were all founded and established as a direct result of the Great Awakening.

- Among leading thinkers and social elites, the Christian principles of individual responsibility and liberty in Christ spawned a greater emphasis on individual responsibility and liberty in politics and government.

There were many factors that combined to unite the colonists in such a strong opposition to British rule that they were willing to risk everything in a war of independence from Great Britain.

As the founders proclaimed in their Declaration of Independence, "…for the support of this Declaration, with a firm reliance on the protection of Divine Providence, we mutually pledge to each other our lives, our fortunes, and our sacred Honor."

It was the First Great Awakening that laid the foundations for the Declaration of Independence, the Constitution, and more. Without that revival, the great American experiment in freedom and representative government might never have happened.

Another factor that united the colonies in opposition to foreign rule was taxation of the colonists by the King of England, without any representation or participation in legislative decisions by the colonial governments. And the publishing and distribution of Thomas Paine's *Common Sense* in January of 1776 was also a unifying factor.

Although he was anything but an orthodox Christian, Thomas Paine used religious terminology and connotations in his treatise denouncing the British monarchy. He portrayed all kings as "blasphemous usurpers who claim a sovereign authority over other human beings that rightfully belongs only to God."[41]

Paine likened the decision to support the cause of rebellion from British rule as being similar to that of evangelical conversion to Christianity. Thus, *Common Sense* is one of the best examples of how deeply

Christianity and politics were intertwined in the minds of the men and women of the revolutionary generation.

The Great Awakening resulted in many Christians breaking away from the authoritarian and complacent approach to worship that existed among the established churches in the colonies. These Christians came to realize that they could be bold in confronting religious authority, and that if their churches didn't meet their spiritual needs and expectations, they could break away and form new churches.

This same attitude eventually carried over to the political realm. Many colonists – Deists as well as Christians – came to believe that political power didn't exist only in the hands of the King of England, but it rested in their own hands – and in their own will and capacity for self-governance.

This can be clearly seen in the words of the preamble of the Declaration of Independence:

"We hold these truths to be self-evident, that all men are created equal, that they are endowed by their Creator with certain unalienable rights, that among these are Life, Liberty and the pursuit of Happiness. That to secure these rights, Governments are instituted among Men, deriving their just powers from the consent of the governed. That whenever any Form of Government becomes destructive of these ends, it is

the right of the People to alter or to abolish it, and to institute new government, laying its foundation on such principles and organizing its powers in such form, as to them shall seem most likely to affect their Safety and Happiness."

While the War of Independence was seen as a religious crusade by many pastors and churches, only a minority of Christian denominations enthusiastically supported rebellion against Great Britain.

Anglican pastors in particular struggled with the conflict between loyalty to the emerging independence of the United States and their oath to the King of England, which they viewed as having been sworn before God. By some estimates, more than half of them gave up their ministries rather than go against their promise to serve the British Crown.[42]

Meanwhile, other pastors enthusiastically supported the movement for independence. A few examples:

- James Caldwell – a Presbyterian minister and battlefield chaplain, known as "The Fighting Parson" – helped in the Battle of Springfield, New Jersey, by running to a nearby church and bringing back a pile of hymn books to use for wadding – the paper used to hold the powder in the barrel of a rifle – when the militia ran out of it.[43]

- John Witherspoon – a Scottish Presbyterian

minister – represented New Jersey in the Second Continental Congress from 1776 to 1781. He served on more than 100 committees and was one of the 56 signers of the Declaration of Independence.

- John Peter Gabriel Muhlenberg – Ordained as an Anglican Priest, he later served as a Lutheran pastor, statesman and a Brigadier General in the Continental Army. After war broke out, Muhlenberg is reported to have delivered a sermon to his congregation on Ecclesiastes 3:1 and 3:8 – *"To everything there is a season, and a time to every purpose under the Heaven." And, "A time to love, and a time to hate; a time of war, and a time of peace."*

  The pastor closed his sermon with these words: "In the language of Holy writ, there is a time for all things. There is a time to preach and a time to fight, and now is the time to fight!"[44]

  He then dramatically removed his clerical robe, revealing what he was wearing underneath – the uniform of a Continental Army Colonel. His words were followed by action.

Muhlenberg declined to serve as a chaplain during the Revolutionary War. Instead, he became a line officer and led the First Brigade in Lafayette's Light Division at the Battle of Yorktown. His example inspired 300 men from his congregation and the country to join the Continental Army … and inspired Christians throughout the colonies to fight for their God-given rights to life, liberty, and the pursuit of happiness.

Christianity and the U.S. Constitution

There are ongoing debates about whether the U.S. Constitution is a Christian or secular document … whether the Founders were Christians or Deists … and whether they sought to establish the United States as a Christian or a secular nation. A popular secular view is that "the Constitution was the product of men of the Enlightenment," and that Masonic philosophy and deistic beliefs also influenced the document.[45]

However, an honest look at the following historical documents and accounts reveals an unmistakable Christian and biblical influence on the U.S. Constitution:

- The private letters and other writings of the Framers;
- The delegate discussions pertaining to the wording of the First Amendment;
- The philosophical statements in *The Federalist Papers;* And,

- The concluding words of the U.S. Constitution.

George Washington – in his "Circular to the States" (1783) – said America could never be a happy nation unless its citizens learned to imitate Jesus, "the Divine Author of our blessed Religion."[46]

James Madison – considered to be the leading architect of the Constitution, and who also served as the fourth President of the United States (1809 – 1817), wrote that one's obligations to God supersede his obligations to the government. He said, "Before any man can be considered as a member of Civil Society, he must be considered as a subject of the Governor of the Universe." ...We maintain therefore that in matters of Religion, no man's right is abridged by the institution of Civil Society, and that Religion is wholly exempt from its cognizance."[47]

Even Thomas Jefferson – whom many believe wasn't a Christian – wrote in his proposed Virginia Statute for Religious Freedom (1777) that to force people to believe in religious views they don't share is contrary to the teaching of Almighty God, "the holy author of our religion."[48]

The delegate discussions at the Continental-Confederation Congress, in 1789, pertaining to the final wording of the First Amendment, make clear that by their use of the word "religion," the Framers had in mind the various Christian denominations.[49] Their concern was that Congress would not elevate one denomination – Catholic, Anglican, Presbyterian, etc. – above the others. And by restricting Congress from "prohibiting the free exercise thereof," the Framers meant that the federal government was not allowed to interfere in the free and public practice of the Christian religion.[50]

George Mason – called by historians the "Father of the Bill of Rights" – proposed the following wording for the First Amendment:

"[A]ll Men have an equal, natural, and unalienable Right to the Free Exercise of Religion, according to the Dictates of Conscience; and that no particular Religious Sect or Society of Christians ought to be favored or established by Law in preference to others."[51]

Christian Influences in *The Federalist Papers*

The Federalist Papers were a series of 85 articles and essays written by James Madison, Alexander Hamilton and John Jay between October 1787 and May 1788. They were published in various New York state newspapers for the purpose of convincing New York State to ratify the U.S. Constitution. The Christian influence on the philosophical ideas expressed in these essays is unmistakable.

A Christian view of government is based on a biblical view of human nature – a dual nature of dignity and infinite worth by virtue of being created in the image of God, combined with human depravity caused by each person's fallen, broken and sinful condition.

Madison, in *Federalist #51*, argued that government must be based on a realistic view of human nature:

"But what is government itself, but the greatest of all reflections on human nature? If men were angels, no government would be necessary. If angels were to govern men, neither external nor internal controls on government would be necessary. In framing a government which is to be administered by men over men, the great difficulty lies in this: you must first enable the government to control the governed; and in the next place oblige it to control itself."[52]

The Founders were also concerned about the propensity of sinful men to abuse their power when given authority over others. Their solution was to create a separation of powers between the three branches of government so that ambition would be made to counteract ambition.[53]

Finally, the influence of Christianity on the Constitution is evidenced by the reference to the year of our Lord (based on the birth of Jesus Christ) in the Article VII concluding words of the Constitution itself:

"Done in Convention by the Unanimous Consent of the States present the Seventeenth Day of September in the Year of our Lord one thousand seven hundred and Eighty seven and of the Independence of the United States of America the Twelfth in witness whereof We have hereunto subscribed our Names,"

For a much more complete treatment of the influence of Christianity on the U.S. Constitution, see *Christianity and the Constitution: The Faith of Our Founding Fathers*, by John Eidsmoe (Baker Publishing Group, 1987).[54]

The Declaration of Independence, the War of Independence (also known as the American Revolution), and the U.S. Constitution, were among the most important social and political milestones in history. They transformed all aspects of life – including economics, politics, and the protection of religious freedom. And it all transpired because of the momentous events including the First Great Awakening. Revival often sparks historic social change.

The Second Great Awakening and the Abolition of Slavery

The Second Great Awakening was a religious revival that began in the early 1800s and lasted until the beginning of the Civil War, in 1861.

In contrast with the First Great Awakening, which focused on individual and group conversion, this new revival became focused not only on personal salvation but on combating the social ills of the nation and healing the soul of the entire country.

Charles Finney – the most prominent Presbyterian preacher of the Second Great Awakening, and a man who became known as "The Father of Modern Revivalism," characterized this new evangelistic fervor as "a longing desire for the salvation of the whole world."[55]

As a result of this new revival, many Protestant pastors began supporting the social reform movements that were gaining traction during the first half of the nineteenth century, including prison reform and the abolition of slavery.

Protestant colleges and seminaries also came to reject and inveigh against bigotry and human slavery as being contrary to the will of an all-loving God.[56]

Opposition to slavery actually began, both in Great Britain and in colonial America, even before the First Great Awakening, in the 1700s. This is because slavery had existed in the New World for nearly a century before the first group of 20 or so enslaved Africans were brought to Jamestown, in 1619.[57]

In fact, the majority of African slaves were not brought to the American colonies – as most Americans believe – but to Brazil and the Caribbean Islands. And many slaves originally belonged to Spanish or Muslim Arab – not English – owners.

For example:

- In 1526, African slaves were part of a Spanish expedition to establish a settlement on the Atlantic coast of what is today South Carolina.

- There is evidence that scores of Africans plundered from Spanish explorers were aboard a fleet of ships under the command of Sir Francis Drake, an English sea captain, privateer and naval officer, when he arrived at Roanoke Island, in 1586.

- By May of 1616, African slaves from the West Indies were in Bermuda providing expert knowledge about the cultivation of tobacco.[58]

Thus, long before the English established a settlement in Jamestown, Virginia, Enlightenment philosophers opposed the practice of slavery. But it was Christian activists who initiated and organized abolitionist movements on both sides of the Atlantic.

As early as 1688, Dutch Quakers in Germantown, Pennsylvania, sent an antislavery petition to the

Monthly Meeting of Quakers. By 1727, the Quakers in Great Britain officially declared their opposition to the slave trade.[59]

In the 1730s and 1740s, Anthony Benezet – a Quaker abolitionist who had emigrated from France, or from the Netherlands to Philadelphia – worked to persuade all who would listen that owning slaves was not consistent with Christianity. Eventually, legislation called "An Act for the Gradual Abolition of Slavery" was passed by the Pennsylvania General Assembly on March 1, 1780. It was the first legislation in history adopted by a democracy for the purpose of abolishing slavery.[60]

"It is not for us to enquire why, in the creation of mankind, the inhabitants of the several parts of the earth were distinguished by differences in feature or complexion," read the Abolition Act passed that day in Philadelphia. "It is sufficient to know that all are the work of an Almighty Hand."

By the late 1820s, the Northern states had freed most of their relatively small numbers of slaves. Some of these became active in the abolition movement in the South – some within denominational churches, some outside the churches.

Here are some of the key antislavery events that took place during the 1800s, leading up to the American Civil War:

- 1807 – William Wilberforce – with the support and encouragement of Anglican Priest John Newton (writer of "Amazing Grace") – secured the passage of the Slave Trade Act in the British Parliament.

- 1807 – Congress outlawed the importation of slaves to the United States. It became effective on January 1, 1808.

- 1824 – Elizabeth Coltman Heyrick published a tract, *Immediate, Not Gradual Abolition*. She was the first of many devout women to challenge the American establishment's male leadership in the antislavery movement.[61]

- 1833 – In Great Britain, Parliament passed the Slave Emancipation Act, outlawing slavery in parts of the British Empire.

- 1833 – William Lloyd Garrison, along with brothers, Arthur and Lewis Tappan, New York City evangelical businessmen, founded the American Anti-Slavery Society (AASS). By the end of the decade, more than160,000 church members had joined.[62]

- 1852 – Harriet Beecher Stowe – daughter of Presbyterian pastor Lyman Beecher and wife of Dartmouth Professor of Greek and biblical scholar Calvin Ellis Stowe – published her novel, *Uncle Tom's Cabin* – depicting the harsh living conditions of enslaved African Americans.

During the height of the Second Great Awakening, John Wesley, a founder of the Methodist denomination, with George Whitfield and his brother, Charles Wesley, condemned slavery, calling it "the sum of all villainies."[63]

Charles Spurgeon – the English theologian and preacher – had some of his sermons burned by proslavery critics in the South because of his strong censure of slavery.

Spurgeon famously declared, "I now from my inmost soul detest slavery… and although I commune at the Lord's table with men of all creeds, yet with a slave-holder I have no fellowship of any sort or kind. Whenever a slave-holder has called upon me, I have considered it my duty to express my detestation of his wickedness, and I would as soon think of receiving a murderer into my church… as a man stealer."

Presbyterian pastor and evangelist Charles Finney preached that slavery was a moral sin requiring repentance, and that those who continued to support it would incur "the greatest guilt" upon themselves.[64]

And Jonathan Blanchard – an abolitionist pastor who became the founder of Wheaton College near

Chicago, Illinois – said that while most Protestants believed that salvation was by grace alone, attempting to change society by abolishing slavery was outward proof of being saved.[65]

The Second Great Awakening laid the moral and spiritual foundations for ending slavery in America. And it was all based-on God's Word.

Slavery and the Bible

Those who are familiar with the Bible know that human slavery in different forms was a part of ancient Middle East society, and that it was also common in the Roman Empire during the first century A.D., when New Testament events occurred and were recorded.

Bible readers and scholars have always been able to find what they've considered to be scriptural support for whatever doctrines they wanted to believe, or behaviors they wanted to engage in. And, sadly, that has even included human slavery.

This was no less true of Christians in the North and South in the 19th century years – leading up to the Civil War – also called the War Between the States.

Slavery was also a fact of life in Jewish society under Roman rule during the time of Jesus. It was a major economic institution in the Roman Empire. According to many leading historians, slaves constituted about one-third of the total population of the Roman Empire.[66]

Some spoke out about the mistreatment of slaves, and there were occasional slave revolts that were quickly crushed by the Roman government. But no abolitionist or antislavery movement existed.

The institution of slavery was so much a part of life and culture in the first century that Jesus told several parables in which slaves were the major characters in the stories. However, there is no recorded incident in which his disciples ever asked him what he thought about slavery.

The apostles also gave instructions to both slaves and slave owners (i.e., masters) in various passages of their letters. See Ephesians 6:5-9, Colossians 3:22-24, 1 Timothy 6:1-2, and 1 Peter 2:18-20 for some examples.

And the entire short letters Paul and Timothy co-wrote to Philemon is about Philemon's runaway slave Onesimus!

Should we conclude from these passages that human involuntary servitude is approved and not condemned by God?

Not at all!

For at least five reasons, we cannot make a blind leap to such a false conclusion.

First, the fact that God's word is silent about a behavior doesn't mean that He approves of it:

- The Bible doesn't condemn smoking tobacco, yet we know that it's wrong because our bodies are the temple of God and we are not to desecrate it or destroy it. (1 Corinthians 3:16)

- The Bible doesn't condemn abortion, yet we know that God formed our body in our mother's womb and determined the number of our days "when as yet there was not one of them."
(Psalm 139:13-16)

- The Bible doesn't specifically condemn same-sex marriage or gender transition, but it clearly implies that both are contrary to God's will when Jesus quotes from Genesis 1 where it says that God created two sexes, male and female, and God said, *"For this reason a man shall leave his father and mother and be joined to his wife, and the two shall become one flesh." (Matthew 19:3-6)*

Second, God doesn't violate our free will when we

choose to do our own thing, go our own way and act independently and autonomously as if God doesn't exist. All of us – Christians as well as non-Christians and atheists – are guilty of rebelling against God and acting independently of Him – not seeking His will. (Romans 3:9-18, 23)

Third, God created ALL of mankind in His image. We are ALL equally valuable in His eyes, and Jesus died for the sins of the whole world – ALL races, ALL colors, people of ALL national origins and religions. (Genesis 1:26-27; John 3:16; 1 John 2:2)

As the children's song says, "Red and Yellow, Black and White, they are precious in His sight. Jesus loves the little children of the world."

Fourth, we are commanded as followers of Christ to love our neighbors as ourselves (Leviticus 19:18; Matthew 22:36-40). And when a lawyer asked Jesus, "Who is my neighbor?" Jesus told him the parable of the Good Samaritan (Luke 10:25-37). And by the way, Samaritans were the people shunned and ostracized by the Jews of that time.

Fifth, there were some slaves in the first century who were called bond slaves or bond servants. Bond slaves were slaves by choice – and it was a lifetime commitment. A bond slave would have his ear pierced with an awl to indicate that he wanted to spend the rest of his life serving his master.

The apostle Paul called himself a "bond-servant of Christ Jesus" in Romans 1:1 and Philippians 1:1. And in 1 Peter 2, the apostle Peter says this to all Christians everywhere:

"Submit yourselves for the Lord's sake to every human institution, whether to a king as the one in authority, or to governors as sent by him for the punishment of evildoers and the praise of those who do right. For such is the will of God that by doing right you may silence the ignorance of foolish men. Act as free men, and do not use your freedom as a covering for evil but use it as bond slaves of God. Honor all people, love the brotherhood, fear God, honor the king."
(1 Peter 2:13-17)

Here is one final scripture passage about the importance of loving our neighbors as ourselves, and the dangerous consequences of failing to do so.

"For you were called to freedom, brethren; only do not turn your freedom into an opportunity for the flesh, but through love serve one another. For the whole law is fulfilled in one word, in the statement, 'You shall love your neighbor as yourself.' But if you bite and devour one another, take care that you are not consumed by one another." (Galatians 5:13-15)

If there is one takeaway we should all glean from this brief discussion about the history of Christianity in America and some of the effects Christians have had on politics in general, and on the politics of slavery in particular, it should be this: we each have a duty and a responsibility to become a serious student of Scripture, and to *"Be diligent to present yourself approved to God as a workman who does not need to be ashamed, accurately handling the word of truth." (2 Timothy 2:15)*

We must all study the word of God in its entirety and in its proper context and reach our own conclusions and convictions about how to apply biblical truth in every area of life – in education, in business, in economics, in law, in government ... and in politics.

"Each person must be fully convinced in his own mind." (Romans 14:5b)

Conclusion

It should be clear from this chapter that the Christians who emerged from the First Great Awakening in the 1700s and from the Second Great Awakening in the 1800s believed that following Christ implied that they should be involved in the civic life of the communities in which they lived – and that this entailed being involved in politics.

The idea that Christians should shy away from politics and avoid it as though it entails participation in evil plots and activities is not supported by Scripture.

On the contrary, Scripture makes it clear that we are, in fact, our brother's keeper. And we are commanded to love our neighbors as ourselves.

To the extent that local churches and nonprofit Christian organizations create and operate programs to help the hurting, the downtrodden and the needy within the community in which we live, we should support those efforts.

And to the extent that government seeks to assist the churches and the nonprofits in those programs, we should also seek to influence and counsel the government in its participation in those activities.

How can we do this? By voting for and electing local government officials who understand that welfare assistance – or private charity – is first of all a responsibility of the Christian community.

Local civil government exists primarily to provide protection of citizens, safety and to encourage free enterprise. It should then support and assist the voluntary programs and efforts of the charitable and philanthropic organizations of the community, without seeking to take them over and control them.

As Christians, we have a responsibility to provide advice and counsel to all levels of civil government, and to act as a restraining force to prevent government agencies from overstepping the limits of their authority and continually expanding their power and control.

CHAPTER 5

The Election Danger: What Happens When Christians Don't Vote

There's a popular mindset among many Christians today that says it doesn't matter whether or not Christians vote in elections.

After all, the thinking goes, society is "going to hell in a handbasket," and Christians are powerless to stop it.

In fact, the quicker and the sooner our society and culture deteriorate, the sooner the Rapture will come. And when the Rapture comes, we'll all be rescued from the evils of society anyway, so why try to change anything?

Or Christians may say, it's a waste of time. We should just focus on evangelism and let society self-destruct.

There are two major flaws in this kind of thinking.

First, if Christians don't ensure that God-fearing leaders are elected and appointed to leadership positions in local, state and national government, the freedom to share their faith and evangelize in public may very well be eroded and eventually taken away completely.

Second, Christians are commanded in Scripture not only to evangelize, but also to make disciples. And they cannot make disciples of all believers in their various walks of life unless they – Christian disciple-makers – are willing to go into every area of life and teach others how their Christian faith and the Scriptures apply to them today.

We also cannot assume that all government officials and judges support or approve of Christians having the freedom to share their faith in the workplace and in their businesses. Consider these examples:

- In 2016, Brendan Eich – the CEO of Mozilla-Firefox – was forced to resign after the press revealed that he supported traditional marriage and California's Proposition 8 – which would have defined marriage in the state constitution as being solely a union between one man and one woman,

- Kelvin Cochran – the Fire Chief of Atlanta, Georgia – was fired for teaching biblical views about gender and sexuality during his off-hours.

- Aaron and Melissa Klein – a Christian couple in Gresham, Oregon – were forced to close their bakery business, Sweet Cakes by Melissa, when they were fined $135,000 for refusing to design a wedding cake for a gay wedding.

- Barronelle Stutzman – a florist in Richland, Washington – lost her business and her retirement when she was sued by a gay couple for declining – because of her Christian faith – to prepare the flower arrangements for their same-sex wedding.

These examples are just the tip of the iceberg of what happens when Christians refuse to vote in local elections – or fail to research the moral values of judges and end up voting against their own Christian values instead of voting for their values.

Instead of electing conservative judges who honor and uphold the Constitution … and value the First Amendment guarantees of freedom of speech and freedom of religious worship and expression, they end-up voting for judges who believe Christians should be forced to compromise their values and support lifestyles that go against biblical principles.

One of the latest ways Christians are being forced into compromising their values is through so-called "sexual orientation and gender identity (SOGI) laws."

There are three ways SOGI laws punish Christians for their beliefs and for the actions they take based on those beliefs:

1. SOGI laws demand ideological conformity with the new sexual policies and practices.

A Christian painter respectfully declined to imprint T-shirts with a message promoting a homosexual pride festival – instead referring the client to another T-shirt printer.

The person filed a discrimination complaint against the Christian business owner – and the local human rights commission ordered the owner to undergo diversity training at his own expense.

2. SOGI laws don't allow creative professionals to live out their faith in their businesses.

A Christian wedding photographer politely declined to use her artistic photography talents to celebrate a same-sex wedding ceremony. She had to endure seven years of court proceedings and pay nearly $7,000 in attorney's fees to the woman who sued her.

When the New Mexico Supreme Court ruled against her, one of the justices wrote, "...this case teaches that at some point in our lives all of us must compromise, if only a little, to accommodate the contrasting values of others... it is the price of citizenship." [67]

3. SOGI laws threaten the freedom of churches,

religious nonprofits and Christian schools.

In Iowa and Massachusetts, the state governments tried to force churches to:

- Keep silent on what the Bible teaches about sexuality; and
- Allow members of the opposite sex to use sex-specific facilities such as restrooms and showers.

Government leaders have a duty to protect free speech and religious liberty. But laws that add sexual orientation and gender identity as new protected classes do just the opposite. They allow or even compel the government to override basic freedoms of conscience, speech and religion.

And any so-called exemptions that may exist in current SOGI laws will be subject to removal in future amendments to the laws – especially if, in the future, the terms "sexual orientation" and "gender identity" are given the same legal status as race, ethnicity, and sex in anti-discrimination law.

We get the kind of government we deserve according to how we vote – or do not vote. Samuel Adams, one of the Founding Fathers, said this:

"Let each citizen remember he is offering his vote… that he is executing one of the most solemn trusts in human society for which he is accountable to God and his country."

To Not Vote is to Allow Evil

President James Garfield clearly explained the consequences of Christians not voting when he said, "Now, more than ever before, the people are responsible for the character of their Congress. If that body be ignorant, reckless and corrupt, it is because the people tolerate ignorance, recklessness and corruption."

Non-voting Christians don't escape moral responsibility by doing nothing. In the Old Testament, the Prophet Obadiah rebuked the people of Edom – the southern part of Palestine – when the Babylonians conquered Jerusalem in 606 B.C.: *"On the day that you stood aloof, on the day that strangers carried off his [Jerusalem's] wealth, and foreigners entered his gate and cast lots for Jerusalem – you too were as one of them." (Obadiah 1:11)*

If we stand by and accept and tolerate evil in politics, government, our businesses, our homes – or in any part of our lives – and do not speak or act in opposition to it, then we are accomplices in that evil. Dr. Martin Luther King, Jr. said it this way: "He who passively accepts evil is as much involved in it as he who helps to perpetrate it. He who accepts evil without protesting against it is really cooperating with it."

Discipleship Implies Christians Should Vote

In the New Testament passage called the "Great Commission," in Matthew 28, Jesus focused on discipleship. He says, *"All authority has been given to Me in heaven and on earth. Go therefore and make disciples of all the nations, baptizing them in the name of the Father and the Son and the Holy Spirit, teaching them to observe all that I commanded you; and lo, I am with you always, even to the end of the age."*

(Matthew 28:19-20)

One of the things Jesus commanded his disciples to do was to "render to Caesar the things that are Caesar's, and to God the things that are God's." So, how do we, as Christians, carry out this command if our state or local government attempts to "render to Caesar" – that is, to the government – what belongs to God – ourselves and our children?

We should respond in two ways:

1. We should fight back by taking legal action against any government entity that

attempts to usurp our First Amendment rights or our parental rights to direct the upbringing and training of our children.

2. We should vote out of office those legislators or judges who are attempting to take away any of our God-given rights. And if those legislators or judges were appointed by a state governor or other government official, we should vote those persons out of office, too.

Christians have a moral responsibility to do what is right because we are ultimately accountable to God, not to man or to government. If the government passes so-called "anti-discrimination" laws that require Christians to act in ways that violate their consciences or their faith, the government is, in effect, forcing them to do something that's wrong.

If Christians violate their consciences to obey the law, they are sinning against God; if they follow their consciences and disobey the law, they're sinning against the government. This isn't freedom; it's coercion by intimidation.

The prophet Isaiah warned against governments or spiritual leaders who turn good into evil and evil into good:

"Woe to those who call evil good and good evil; who substitute darkness for light and light for darkness; who

substitute bitter for sweet and sweet for bitter! Woe to those who are wise in their own eyes and clever in their own sight! Woe to those who ... justify the wicked for a bribe, and take away the rights of the ones who are in the right! (Isaiah 5:20-21)

Freedom of conscience is essential in a free society. No one should be forced under a threat of punishment to participate in activities they believe are abhorrent, wrong, or evil.

In a diverse society comprising many different worldviews and moral standards, and which employs democratic voting practices, the only way to preserve freedom of conscience is through the ballot box.

As Christians, we must:

- Develop sound, logical arguments for expressing what we believe;
- Learn how to articulate those arguments;
- Let our voices and our arguments be heard in the public square by writing (Letters to Editors, Op-Ed columns, social media) or speaking – or both;
- Back up our beliefs by living our lives consistently according to our faith; and
- Follow through during elections by researching candidates and issues and then voting according to our beliefs.

This is how representative government **of** the people, **by** the people and **for** the people is designed to work in our Constitutional Republic. The only way it **can** work properly, and safeguard the blessings of liberty for all Americans, is for every Christian to exemplify citizenship at its best – and VOTE!

CHAPTER 6

What Is a Biblical Worldview and How Does it Affect How Christians Vote?

Christians are a very powerful voting bloc in America. And how they think about the world helps determine how they vote.

Christians who have a biblical worldview want to be in agreement with Scripture when they vote. They want to stay true to God's word. They want to be able to vote according to the values they've learned from the Bible and they don't want to vote against those true and eternal teachings.

Yet far too many Christian voters actually end up voting against their values.

How? By voting for candidates who don't believe the Bible has anything useful or relevant to say about today's social issues.

Sometimes this happens because Christians don't know where candidates stand on certain issues.

Sometimes it happens because Christians don't care where the candidates stand on the issues – they just vote based on personality or looks, or they vote based on something the media reported that a candidate was saying or thinking.

Sometimes it's because they vote Democrat or Republican – because they have all their lives … or their parents did … or they are told to do so by a union or company.

In other cases, Christians may vote for a candidate and not care about what the candidate believes or where the candidate stands on issues because they are voting against the opposing candidate no matter what.

Or they may vote a certain way because of pressure from a union or an employer or from friends or family.

A variety of factors cause Christians to vote the way they do. But all Christians should cast their votes based on a biblical worldview.

The Bible speaks not only about faith in God and in Jesus Christ … but also about many other subjects and issues concerning life itself.

It also comprises God's literal message to mankind as we know from the original texts. The Holy Scriptures inscribed in the ancient manuscript present the truth about the world and universe that He created.

In short, the Bible presents a particular worldview – a view of reality … of what IS. We call belief in the Bible's teachings about reality a biblical worldview.

Those who believe the Old and New Testament scriptures to be the infallible word of God to mankind – and who are familiar with all that those scriptures teach – also believe the worldview presented in the Bible.

What's surprising, however, is how few people who say they are Christians agree with the worldview presented in the Bible.

So, what does the biblical worldview say about reality and about how the world works – and about how mankind should live in the God-created world? We will get to that a little later in this chapter.

Everyone Has a Worldview

For now, I want to make it clear that everyone has a worldview – or a combination of worldviews, whether they realize it or not – even if they don't understand what a worldview means.

Simply put, a worldview is a belief system of assumptions and presuppositions through which we:

- Form our self-image and our attitudes about ourselves;
- See and interact with the world around us; and
- Establish behavior patterns … make life decisions … and take actions.

A worldview is like a lens or a filter through which we view everything. It helps us make sense of the world around us and what we see and experience.

Worldviews have consequences.

For example, a person's worldview largely determines what ideas and beliefs he or she will consider to be:

- True versus false;
- Good versus bad;
- Righteous versus evil;
- Right versus wrong;
- Beautiful versus ugly; and
- Valuable versus worthless.

Since your worldview will have a great influence on what choices you make in life, and how you will behave in different situations and circumstances, important questions to ask and answer are:

- Which worldview do you embrace?
- On what is your worldview based?

Your worldview is critical, as is living it out on a daily basis.

When I speak to groups or in churches, I often describe what a biblical worldview consists of because it's important – and because there's such a huge disconnect with many people between what they think about social and economic issues or policies and their worldview.

Differing Worldviews

There are several contradictory and competing worldviews that vie for our attention and support. Each one has a different core principle – that is, a different central belief or a different concept of God, if you will.

Here is a brief summary of the major worldviews, the core central principle of each, and a quote from a well-known supporter of that worldview that summarizes it in a nutshell:

- Secular Humanism – Man-centered ("Man is the measure of all things." ~ Protagoras)
- Scientific Naturalism/Materialism – Things-centered ("The cosmos is all that is or was or ever will be." ~ Carl Sagan)
- Marxism-Socialism – Government-centered

("The voice of the people is the voice of God." ~ Hegel)

- Relativism/Post–Modernism – Nothing-centered ("There are no eternal facts, as there are no absolute truths." ~ Friedrich Nietzsche)
- Hedonism – Pleasure/Sex-centered ("The major civilizing force in the world is not religion, it is sex." ~ Hugh Hefner)
- Christianity – Christ-centered ("For by Him [Christ] all things were created, both in the heavens and on earth, visible and invisible… all things have been created through Him and for Him. He is before all things, and in Him all things hold together." ~ Colossians 1:16-17)

Key Characteristics of a Biblical Worldview

So, what exactly does the Christian or biblical worldview say about the world and about reality?

First, the Christian worldview contradicts Relativism and Post-Modernism by asserting that absolute truth exists – truth that is objectively true for everyone, whether anyone believes it or not.

The Christian worldview goes so far as to say that there is no area of neutrality in the universe – that is, no realm in which truth is relative[68].

Second, the Christian worldview asserts that all truth is God's truth[69] – created by Him for the governance of mankind and the universe. Man does not create objective, absolute truth. He either discovers God's truth or he creates his own relative "truth" in contradiction and rebellious opposition to God's truth.

Most people believe that objective, absolute truth exists in areas such as mathematics and the hard sciences; chemistry, physics, biology and astronomy. But the Christian worldview holds that objective truth – meaning truth that applies to everything in existence – can also be found in areas such as:

- Theology
- Philosophy
- Ethics
- Psychology
- Sociology
- Law
- Politics
- Economics
- History
- ... and more

Third, the Christian worldview asserts that the Bible contains all immutable truths about Reality, including:

- God
- Mankind
- Sin

- Jesus
- Redemption and Restoration
- Resurrection

Christianity is more than just another religious view. It's more than a source of moral teaching. It's a belief in the truth about Almighty God and all of His Creation. It's a personal relationship with the true and Living God, thanks to Christ's death and resurrection.

The Bible explains how God created the heavens and the earth, human beings and reality itself.

Beliefs vs. Actions

As I mentioned earlier in this chapter, few people who claim to be Christians fully understand the complete Christian worldview ... and even fewer agree with it and live it out in their daily lives.

George Barna – the well-known pollster – recently conducted three nationwide surveys of three different demographic groups.

His purpose was to determine how many adults in the United States actually have a biblical Christian worldview, compared with the 100+ million who *claim* to be Christians.

The surveys contained 20 questions assessing spiritual beliefs … and 20 questions examining actual behavior.

Here are the disturbing results:

1. How many *believe* they think biblically vs. how many *do* think biblically.

Barna's survey showed that 46% of adults – roughly 112 million people – claim to have a biblical worldview. Only 10%, about 24 million, actually behave in accordance with a biblical worldview.

2. The age gap.

Younger adults are much less likely to have a biblical worldview than older adults. Here's the breakdown by age group of those who have a biblical worldview:

- 18 to 29 – 4%
- 30 to 49 – 7%
- 50 to 64 – 15%
- 65 or older – 17%

Two takeaways from this research.

First, a Christian may say they have a biblical worldview in some areas – such as theology, philosophy, ethics or history – while having a conflicting secular or humanistic worldview in biology, psychology, politics or economics.

Second, if a Christian claims to believe according to a biblical worldview, but does not act or behave according to a biblical worldview, he or she doesn't really have a biblical worldview.

Beliefs are important. But if they don't lead to action, they aren't true beliefs. James makes this clear in his discussion of faith and works in James 2:14-26.

Here's a portion of the passage (NASB translation):

"What use is it, my brethren, if someone says he has faith but he has no works? Can that faith save him? If a brother or sister is without clothing and in need of daily food, and one of you says to them, 'Go in peace, be warmed and be filled,' and yet you do not give them what is necessary for their body, what use is that? Even so faith, if it has no works, is dead, being by itself.

But someone may well say, 'You have faith and I have works; show me your faith without the works, and I will show you my faith by my works.'...Was not Abraham our father justified by works when he offered up Isaac his son on the altar? You see that faith was working with his works, and as a result of the works, faith was perfected; and the Scripture was fulfilled which says, 'And Abraham believed God, and it was reckoned to him as righteousness,' and he was called the friend of God." (James 2:14-18, 21-23)

Notice from this passage that what we believe – that is, our faith, which includes our worldview – should affect the way we live our daily lives. Our faith should result in actions that are truly tangible works of faith.

Our worldview should also affect the way we vote. As a Christian, you want to vote according to a biblical worldview. And a biblical worldview has some key elements pertaining to social issues that align with what the Bible teaches.

These key elements we call "non-negotiable issues." No candidate should get our vote if their views and actions conflict with these non-negotiable biblical positions.

The following chapters describe those "non-negotiables."

CHAPTER 7

The War Against Christians in America: Trampling the U.S. Constitution

An all-out war is being waged against Christians. The evidence is so pervasive that few people are shocked by even the most outrageous stories they see and hear on social media, television, radio, podcasts, and in print publications.

Signs of the onslaught are obvious:

- Traditional marriage is under attack.
- The traditional family is under attack.
- The divorce rate among Christians now equals the divorce rate of non-Christians.
- Home Bible studies are under attack – banned and even outlawed in some cities and counties across America.

Church services were banned or even outlawed or restricted in attendance by state governors and mayors across the country during the Coronavirus pandemic. And most Christians obediently complied, behaving as if the government, not the Lord of hosts, was their shepherd.

Rarely has a pastor defied a government mandate to shut down his church by quoting Acts 5:29, *"We must obey God rather than men."*

How Did We Get Here?

How did we reach such a sad state of affairs in America, especially considering the Christian foundations of our Constitutional Republic?

For years, the war against Christianity in America was waged behind the scenes – in the halls of academia and in left-wing, Anti-Capitalist foundations, with trusted names like Ford, Rockefeller, and MacArthur. Marxist and Socialist college and university professors began teaching atheism, Socialism, and other anti-Christian ideas to their students.

The war began in the late 19th and early 20th centuries. It was introduced in America's public schools by the so-called "Progressive" education movement. But it didn't gain a dominant foothold in the public schools until the U.S. Supreme Court decisions in the early 1960s prohibiting organized prayer and Bible reading on school property.

In recent years, the war has focused on attacking the

free-exercise religion clause in the First Amendment of the U.S. Constitution.

Many voters – even Christians – are not fully aware of these attacks because the weapons being used by the anti-Christian forces are subtle:

- They use nice-sounding, anti-discrimination rhetoric.
- They pass laws and implement regulations designed to force Christians to compromise their religious convictions.
- They accuse Christians of bigotry if they resist so-called "anti-discrimination" laws that conflict with their biblical values.
- They are rarely willing to debate ideas and beliefs. Instead, they resort to name-calling, labeling Christians morons, haters, uneducated, or mentally ill.

Until recently, as long as Christians confined their beliefs and the exercise of their faith to the privacy of their homes, they were generally left alone. But a new, increasingly Radical movement has declared that "silence is violence" when Christians and others try to avoid confrontations. Now, the demand is for Christians to support Socialist/Marxist policies and actions in word and deed. Today's atheist, Christian-hating Radicals are targeting:

- Christian schools and Christian students;

- Christian teachers;
- Christian employees;
- Christian business owners;
- Christian pastors and churches;
- Christian nonprofits;
- Christian politicians and judges;
- ... and more

And the attacks are occurring at all levels of government:

- Federal
- State
- Local

The mainstream media have been complicit or even encourage the attacks, painting Christians as ignorant, uneducated, science-hating, irrational, fanatical freaks.

Here is just a sampling of the attacks that are happening with increasing frequency.

Name-Calling Attacks

Robert Jeffress – pastor of First Baptist Church, in Dallas – was asked by President Trump to offer a prayer at the opening of the new U.S. Embassy in Jerusalem.

Mitt Romney, blasted the choice and accused Pastor Jeffress of being "a religious bigot."

Here's what Romney said in a tweet:

> *Robert Jeffress says "You can't be saved by being a Jew," and "Mormonism is a heresy... He's said the same thing about Islam. Such a religious bigot should not be giving the prayer that opens the United States Embassy in Jerusalem.*

Jeffress responded to Romney's attack with a tweet of his own:

> *Historical Christianity has taught for 2,000 years that salvation is through faith in Christ alone. The fact that I, along with tens of millions of evangelical Christians around the world, continue to espouse that belief, is neither bigoted nor newsworthy.*

Notice that Robert Jeffress shares ideas and reasons to support the evangelical Christian doctrine that salvation for all of mankind – for Jews, Mormons, atheists, Muslims, Hindus, agnostics, etc. and others – comes by grace alone, through faith on the cross and His resurrection from the dead.

Mitt Romney, on the other hand, gave no ideas or arguments. He simply called Jeffress a name: "a religious bigot."

Does he mean he believes Jeffress holds views that differ from ***people*** who disagree with his religious beliefs? If so, he has a point ... but he gives no reasons or arguments to support the idea that Jeffress is a bigot.

Attacks on Christian Schools and Students

All across America, Christian schools, Christian parents who homeschool their kids, and Christian groups and individual students are enduring numbers of attacks because of their faith and values.

In January 2019, for example, River View Christian Academy, in rural Northern California, was raided by 16 armed law enforcement officials accompanied by two K-9 units and 17 social workers.[70]

The excuse? False accusations of illegal drugs and weapons on the campus. Of course, not one was found.

This fake raid would be appropriate for a terrorist group – NOT a Christian school were children were learning about God's commandments and principles for living.

Why were such draconian tactics used at a Christian school? Because California Protective Services (CPS) and the California state government want control over Christian education in the state.

Here are the deeper reasons for this and other assaults on Christianity and on the First Amendment guarantee of freedom of religious expression:

1. The biblical worldview is offensive to non-Christians.

This has been true ever since Satan tempted Eve in the Garden of Eden. Throughout the history of mankind, those who haven't wanted to follow God's rules for living have denied the truth of His Holy Word and dismissed it as foolishness.

The Apostle Paul in his first century letter to the church at Corinth:

*"For the word of the cross is foolishness to those who are perishing, but to us who are being saved it is the power of God. For it is written, **'I will destroy the wisdom of the wise, and the cleverness of the clever I will set aside.'** Where is the wise man? Where is the scribe? Where is the debater of this age? Has not God made foolish the wisdom of the world? For since in the wisdom of God the world through its wisdom did not come to know God, God was well-pleased through the foolishness of the message preached to save those who believe." (1 Corinthians 1:18-21)*

In his second letter to the Corinthian Church, Paul added that unbelievers are blinded:

"And even if our gospel is veiled, it is veiled to those who are perishing, in whose case the god of this world has blinded the minds of the unbelieving so that they might not see the light of the gospel of the glory of Christ, who is the image of God." (2 Corinthians 4:3-4)

Under so-called "separation of church and state," government officials in California and other states think they have a right to be hostile to all religions, especially Christianity.

Especially unacceptable to government bureaucrats are the biblical teachings regarding sex and marriage. The government education bureaucrats are demanding that River View Christian Academy change its teaching on sex to conform to the state's secular worldview.

2. River View Christian Academy is a boarding school run by a Christian group for the benefit of troubled teenagers.

The school is run by the Christian nonprofit Teen Rescue and assists troubled teens. The school receives no government assistance or support.

The state of California contends that River View Christian Academy is not a private Christian school, but is an "unlicensed community care facility," that requires additional oversight and regulation.

The state wants to bring the school under the supervision of the state's Department of Social Services. A new state law (SB524) gives the state added authority to regulate boarding schools.

3. Christian colleges, high schools and grade schools across America are being sued because of their biblical beliefs.

Parents, students and outside political groups have filed lawsuits against Christian schools' codes of conduct that uphold a biblical view of sexuality regarding things such as:

- Same-sex attraction;
- College students of the opposite sex living together in campus housing;
- Dress code requirements; and
- Transgender demands.

In a legislative attempt to prohibit Christian counseling and even the sale of certain Christian literature, the California State Assembly, in 2018, passed a bill making *"advertising, offering to engage in, or engaging in sexual orientation change efforts with an individual"* a fraudulent business practice subject to fines and other penalties.

The bill was withdrawn by its primary sponsor before coming up for a vote in the California Senate – only because of a massive phone-calling campaign and protests by Christians during the debate period leading up to the final vote.[71]

If the bill had passed, it would have resulted in a staggering censorship of free speech:

- A licensed counselor would have been prohibited from helping someone experiencing same-sex attraction or gender identity confusion to overcome those feelings.
- A church or other religious ministry would have been forbidden to conduct a conference on maintaining sexual purity, if the attendees were encouraged to avoid homosexual behavior.
- A bookstore – including online bookstores such as Amazon – would have been prohibited from selling any books that challenge same-sex marriage or gender-identity ideology.
- A pastor would not have been allowed to preach a sermon or speak at a paid event in which he tells attendees that they can prevail over same-sex desires or feelings that they were born with the wrong gender.

4. The California government wants to regulate Christian schools out of business.

Some proposed regulations would force Christian

schools to either give up their Christian beliefs and policies or close their doors.

It's another power grab by the Deep State bureaucracy, which always wants to expand its power and control.

Attacks on Christian Nonprofits and Employees

In 2015, California passed the Reproductive FACT Act – an abusive, anti-liberty, pro-abortion law that required crisis-pregnancy and health centers to inform their clients and patients how they could get an abortion. (FACT stands for Freedom, Accountability, Comprehensive Care and Transparency).

The crisis pregnancy centers had to provide such information even if abortion violated the consciences and religious beliefs of the institution and its employees!

In other words, businesses dedicated to promoting life had to also explain to clients how they could kill lives! The law was upheld by the U.S. Ninth Circuit Court of Appeals, in 2016.

In 2018, the U.S. Supreme Court – in a narrow 5-4 decision – struck down the FACT Act as a violation of the free-speech clause of the First Amendment.[72]

But attacks on the free-exercise clause of the First Amendment regarding the public practice of the Christian faith continue.

Military Personnel Discriminated Against

The U.S. military sometimes discriminates against Christians in subtle ways – some of which go unreported, or are swept under the rug, so to speak.

In some cases, even high-ranking officers have been relieved of their duty, reassigned or forced to retire for expressing their biblical opposition to transgenderism or same-sex marriage.

Jail for a Christian Elected Official

You may recall the case of Kim Davis, an elected county clerk in Rowan County, Kentucky, who went to prison in 2015, for refusing to issue marriage licenses to same-sex couples.

That's right. Her willingness to act in keeping with her religious beliefs landed her in prison – not in Cuba, but in America.

The crucial issue in Kim Davis' situation wasn't gay marriage – it was religious liberty. She refused to violate her conscience and her religious beliefs by signing a document validating same-sex marriage.

The thought that Christians in America would ever be imprisoned for refusing to endorse gay marriage has seemed impossible to many. But that reality has arrived.

The criminalization of Christianity has begun. Christians will have to choose either to worship our Lord and Savior Jesus Christ or bow to the false gods of secularism.

What happened in the Kim Davis case?

Kim Davis requested an accommodation in which the law would be changed so that she wouldn't be required to sign any marriage licenses.

She suggested that couples be permitted to obtain marriage licenses through another public official or online.

Any of these requests would have met the government's interest, while keeping First Amendment protection for free exercise of religion.

But instead of respecting First Amendment precedence and Kentucky law (the Religious Freedom

Restoration Act), federal judge David Bunning ordered Kim Davis to issue marriage licenses to same-sex couples – or else.

When Davis went back to work and still refused to issue these licenses, Judge Bunning ordered her to be imprisoned for "contempt of the court." After five days of incarceration, she was released when she promised not to stop her deputy clerks from giving marriage licenses to same-sex couples. And she was defeated later when she ran for re-election.

Kim Davis' stance

Many people disagreed with what Kim Davis did. Some said she was right in refusing to violate her conscience by authorizing something God condemns. Others said it was her job and she should have either issued those licenses or resigned, if she could not fulfill her duties.

But First Amendment protection is for everyone – government employees and private employees. And the free exercise of religion applies everywhere and at all times – at home, at church, in public and at work.

The belief that religion must be confined to one's own private life and home – that it has no place in the public arena – is utterly unconstitutional. Americans do not sign away their First Amendment rights when they become government employees.

In fact, there is a strong, well-established history of religious exemptions made for government employees and public officials regarding their job duties.

Regardless of whether you think Davis should have resigned, we should all agree that imprisoning Kim Davis for her conscience was an outrageous violation of her First Amendment religious liberty. Kim Davis was treated like a criminal. Jail is for criminals, not people of conscience.

Tactics of anti-Christian "civil rights" activists

The strategy is to make Christians look like insincere, bigoted hypocrites in order to discredit their beliefs and the significance of God's authority. These are some of the tactics these anti-Christian/pro-socialist activists use to undermine and uproot the constitutional right to freely exercise one's religion.

In Kim Davis' case, the media pointed out that she had been divorced three times and that she had a child out of wedlock. Then they pointed the finger and said "Hypocrite! Bigot!"

What they neglected to mention is that this part of Davis' story happened BEFORE she became a Christian. That omitted fact makes all the difference.

Many people writing about Kim Davis condemned her for thinking she could "choose not to obey the law" whenever "she feels like it." They reframed the controversy to entirely eliminate the relevance of the First Amendment.

The free exercise of religion principle protects people from being forced by the state to disobey a higher authority – God.

The First Amendment was added to the Constitution to guarantee that the government and man-made laws can never usurp God's authority in people's lives. When the government tries to claim this authority, it has overstepped its bounds.

The whole point is that God's authority trumps man's authority. The ability to obey God and follow one's conscience regarding divine authority is a basic right.

Framing Kim Davis' religious beliefs as arbitrary, biased feelings *of her own* made her case seem to be no longer a First Amendment issue. And that's what these activists want, because they want to ignore the First Amendment's protection of religious liberty.

Kim Davis said, "This has never been a gay or lesbian issue for me. This is about upholding the word of God."

The First Amendment protects the American people from being coerced by the government to violate their consciences *in regards to God's law*. It requires that government reasonably accommodate the rights of all citizens freely to exercise their religion beliefs.

Attacks on Christian Business Owners

Across America, Christian business owners have been harassed, attacked, boycotted, threatened with lawsuits, and more. Why? Because they dare to think they should be free to live out their Christian faith in the way they operate their businesses.

Take the famous ongoing case of specialty baker Jack Phillips. Jack loves Jesus – and his skill is baking and decorating amazing cakes. It's his ministry. It's his way of being an ambassador for Christ.

A Colorado native, Jack opened his Masterpiece Cakeshop in 1993. He has always wanted his business – and his daily life – to glorify God and to make Him known. He loves his customers and gladly sells his baked goods to anyone, regardless of their political or religious beliefs – or their sexual orientation.

In 2012, a gay couple filed an illegal discrimination complaint against Jack with the Colorado Civil Rights Commission because he declined to create a specialty same-sex wedding cake to their specifications. Instead, he offered – as an alternative – to sell them their choice of any standard cake from his display case – or to refer them to another baker down the street who wouldn't have a moral objection to fulfilling their special request.[73]

In ruling against Phillips, one of the commissioners demeaned his faith as "one of the most despicable pieces of rhetoric that people can use."[74]

The case dragged on for years in the Colorado courts– each time ruling against Phillips until his case was finally heard by the U.S. Supreme Court.

In 2018, in *Masterpiece Cakeshop v. Colorado Civil Rights Commission*, a 7-2 Supreme Court majority ruled:

"The government, consistent with the Constitution's guarantee of free exercise [of religion], cannot impose regulations that are hostile to the religious beliefs of affected citizens and cannot act in a manner that passes judgment upon or presupposes the illegitimacy of religious beliefs and practices."[75]

But that ruling didn't end the war on Jack Phillips' freedom to exercise his Christian faith in his business. Soon after his Supreme Court victory, a transgender woman filed a discrimination complaint against Phillips because he refused to design a cake celebrating her gender transition from male to female.

They are still going after him because he's an outspoken Christian who views his artistry in designing specialty cakes as an expression of his faith.

Here are five disturbing facts you should know about this trend:

1. Anti-Christian zealots and their supporters now view any outward public expression or exercise of Christian faith to be discriminatory.

It's a whole new definition of discrimination…

Here's why…

Phillips doesn't refuse business to anyone. He never has. He joyfully and lovingly sells products to all customers who come into his shop – without discrimination and without animus. He treats all customers with equal respect.

But as an artist, he will politely and respectfully decline to use his artistic talents to ***celebrate*** and ***endorse*** a lifestyle that contradicts and mocks his deeply held religious beliefs.

Toleration for peaceful coexistence with those that practice lifestyles you, as a Christian, find offensive are no longer sufficient.

Under the redefined definition of discrimination, if you don't **celebrate**, **endorse**, **embrace** and **support** the beliefs and practices of any "minority" or "protected" group, you are guilty of discriminating against them.

2. Christians are now expected to voluntarily violate their consciences and surrender their Christian rights.

If Christians won't do so voluntarily, they will be forced to obey by local and state civil rights commissions. These commissions are increasingly the number-one tool being used by governments to attack Christian rights and freedoms.

Civil rights commissions are not a part of the judicial branch of government, even though they often try to bully and intimidate citizens by acting with self-presumed judicial authority. They are legislatively-created administrative entities whose members are really just appointed bureaucrats. They are not elected officials and many of them are political activists with a socialist agenda.

This means several things:

- Commissioners don't have to be attorneys or have any previous experience in resolving disputes;
- Commissioners don't have to be fair and impartial arbiters of the discrimination complaints on which they rule;
- There is no requirement for diversity in the

backgrounds of commissioners; and
- A majority of commissioners must be members of an historically discriminated-against class.

These state commissions can levy fines and punish businesses by ordering "diversity training" and requiring other behaviors – but they have no accountability to the people they are harming.

In fact, in the Jack Phillips case which almost resembles conditions in Communist North Korea, he was "sentenced" to "re-education" counseling.

3. The U.S. Supreme Court hasn't yet ruled on whether state and local anti-discrimination laws and regulations violate the First Amendment.

But the Supreme Court ruled that Phillips' right to "a neutral and respectful consideration of his claims" was denied by the Civil Rights Commission's hostility toward his sincerely held religious beliefs that motivated his objection to designing a custom cake.

The Court made its decision on the basis of the Colorado Civil Rights Commission's hostility to Phillips' religious beliefs – not on the question of the free exercise of religion versus anti-discrimination law.

Thus, they failed to address his claim that he has

a First Amendment right to act according to his conscience in his business practices. This question is still open to debate and may eventually require another Supreme Court ruling.

But that's not all...

4. Those who accuse Christian artists of discrimination are unable to see the difference between the message and the person.

This is even difficult for some Christians to understand. An artist produces art for the purpose of conveying a message – whether it's a painting ... a photograph ... a sculpture ... or a cake.

It's certainly possible to discriminate against a message without discriminating negatively against a person.

Jesus did this all the time in the Gospel accounts – we are commanded in Scripture to do the same. It's called discernment.

"Beloved, do not believe every spirit, but test the spirits to see whether they are from God, because many false prophets have gone out into the world."
(1 John 4:1)

If the transgender woman had asked for a cake that expressed a message that didn't contradict and mock

Jack Phillips' Christian faith, he would have designed and made the cake.

Conversely, if a heterosexual Christian asked Phillips for a cake expressing support for same-sex marriage, he would refuse.

It's about the message, not the person!

5. The actions of the Colorado Civil Rights Commission highlight the importance of voting in every election – even in midterm elections.

The Colorado Civil Rights Commission is just one example of a developing trend across the nation.

State commissioners are appointed by state governors or by state legislatures.

Radical and corrupt anti-Christian, pro-socialist governors, legislators and politicians are weaponizing civil rights laws and commissions to attack Christians – and they are unwilling to protect free speech and the free exercise of religion for any American.

By electing pro-freedom governors, state legislators and local officials in every state, civil rights commissions will become more politically fair in their membership actions – or better yet, will be defunded and shut down altogether.

Attacks on Christian Pastors and Churches

Across America, hundreds of churches have faced frivolous lawsuits regarding zoning disputes, building expansions, use of public property for church-sponsored community charitable activities, and more.

Whenever I've been in Charlotte, North Carolina, I've loved attending Elevation Church. But some of the neighbors near the 1,600-seat Ballantyne campus (that opened in 2016) don't love that church.

They turned to local police – and to a local TV news station – to complain about the amount of joyful noise that was coming from the Southern Baptist megachurch.[76] They said the church was disturbing their right to peace and quiet.

"We can hear the music; we can hear the yelling and screaming going on when they are having outside activities," one neighbor said.

"It is a hard thing to have to do, to call 911 on a church," said another.

The local police captain responded to the complaining neighbors, telling them in an email that he had sent officers to the church to talk to the staff about the noise – and that he would ask his off-duty officers who attend the church to also monitor the noise.

Ballantyne campus pastor Jonathan Josephs said in an email that off-duty police officers regularly attend the church and that they help ensure that the noise from the worship music "is reasonable and within the limits of city ordinances."

He added: *"On the few occasions when we have received complaints, the police have assured us that we were not violating any noise ordinances. Our intent is to be good members of the communities we serve, and we will continue to cooperate with law enforcement should any issues arise."*[77]

As Christians, we must be sensitive and respectful to all; but we must also remember the command in Psalm 100:1-2 to *"Shout joyfully to the Lord, all the earth. Serve the Lord with gladness; come before Him with joyful singing."*

In any community there will always be a few people who will use any reason to stir up others to oppose and restrict a church – and to stop its expansion and growth.

Elevation Church was founded in 2006, and today it is one of the fastest-growing and largest megachurches in the United States. The church has 17 locations from Florida to Canada, and nine of those congregations are in the greater Charlotte area in North Carolina.

Attacks on Christian Judges and Other Government Officials

When the President nominates federal judges and other top government officials, they usually must be approved – that is, confirmed – by the U.S. Senate. If the nominee or appointee is an outspoken and committed Christian, some senators exhibit bias against that person because of his or her faith.

In 2017, Judge Amy Coney Barrett was nominated by President Trump to the U.S. Court of Appeals for the Seventh Circuit.

The anti-Christian, pro-socialist media and politicians attacked Barrett viciously and relentlessly for her Christian faith during her Senate confirmation hearing.

Her academic and professional credentials are extraordinary and impeccable:

- Graduate-*Summa Cum Laude* and first in her class from Notre Dame Law School
- U.S. Circuit Court of Appeals Judicial Clerkship to Judge Laurence Silberman of the U.S. Court of Appeals for the D.C. Circuit
- U.S. Supreme Court Judicial Clerk for Justice Antonin Scalia
- Professor at Notre Dame Law School

But there's just one problem in the minds of progressives. She's a devout Catholic Christian … and has been actively involved in an ecumenical Christian group called "People of Praise."

People of Praise teaches that husbands are the heads of their households … and that they are tasked with being the spiritual leaders of their families.

Progressives smear People of Praise as a "secretive religious cult."

So – in their minds – Judge Amy Coney Barrett is a member of a religious cult.

It's tragic that in America – the beacon of religious liberty – that the progressives have such dark hatred for all of those who hold deeply committed Christian beliefs.

A good example of this disturbing animosity is Senator Dianne Feinstein, who told Judge Barrett at her nomination hearing to serve on the U.S. 7th Circuit Court of Appeals: "Dogma and law are two different things. And I think whatever a religion is, it has its own dogma. The law is totally different…the dogma lives loudly within you, and that is a concern."[78]

Attacks on Christian Nonprofits – Hope Center, Anchorage, AK

The Downtown Soup Kitchen Hope Center in Anchorage, Alaska, is a Christian faith-based ministry to the homeless and working poor of Anchorage. The staff provides the following services:

- Daily meals;
- Laundry and clothing facilities;
- Bakery and Culinary job training program;
- Women's shower facilities; and
- Women's overnight shelter;

The first three services are available to both men and women. The last two – for obvious reasons – are offered to women only.

The Center consists of sleeping mats rolled out on the floor of a large room, where desperate, homeless women – some of whom have been victims of human trafficking and sexual assault – sleep next to each other on the floor.

One night, a transgender woman demanded entry at the Hope Center. The staff noticed she needed medical attention. So, as loving and concerned Christians, they gave her cab fare to get to the nearest emergency room. They also directed her to then go to another Anchorage shelter that houses both men and women.

But instead, she came back to the Hope Center the next day and again demanded admission to the shelter. She was turned away again – this time because the Center isn't open during the day.

The biological man claiming to be a woman then filed a complaint with the Anchorage Equal Rights Commission, claiming discrimination under the city's nondiscrimination law, which was expanded in 2015 to include sexual orientation and gender identity.[79]

The City of Anchorage also filed a complaint against the Hope Center, after an attorney for the facility told a local newspaper reporter that the shelter would never admit a "biological male" under any circumstances.

Attacks on Christian Nonprofits – Kingdom Center, Oxnard, CA

Let me tell you about my friend, Sam Galluci – a pastor in Oxnard, California.

His story illustrates how many government bureaucrats don't care about the poor, the hurting and the destitute. And they certainly don't want to empower Christians to help these people, nor allow them to be the loving hands of Jesus in a hurting and broken world.

Instead, they want to take away any sort of influence a Christian church might have and ensure their own control over every public charity and service. And they will go so far as to attempt to destroy any Christian service that doesn't go along with their political agenda, regardless of the cost to human lives and the suffering it might cause.

When Sam started his ministry, in 2007, there were hundreds of homeless people roaming the streets of Ventura. Sam and his church started taking them in.

Calling it "Operation Embrace," they offered their church as a sanctuary where people could get a hot meal and hear about and experience the love of Jesus.

With "Operation Embrace," the city of Ventura finally began to see a breakthrough with their homelessness problem:

- Families were being fed;
- Children were going to school again; and
- Single mothers were getting back on their feet.

The mayor of the city at the time – a Christian – was overjoyed with their progress. Here was a Christian Church making a massive difference and living out the call of Jesus described in Matthew 25:40:

'Truly I tell you, whatever you did for one of the least of

these brothers and sisters of mine, you did for me.'

In a short time, "Operation Embrace" was feeding 60 people every day. They were seeing dozens of people get off the street permanently. And they were working with kids who had been emancipated from their dysfunctional parents.

Eventually, "Operation Embrace" evolved into the "Kingdom Center" – a living center where homeless people could get back on their feet and reclaim their lives. Sam's ministry was transforming the city. And he continued to have favor with the city under a new mayor, who was Jewish.

But everything changed, in 2012, with the re-election of Barack Obama to a second term. There was a massive shift in the balance of power. Suddenly, there was a feeling that rights previously protected by the U.S. Constitution weren't really "rights" anymore.

Religious freedom came under unexpected and increasing attacks. And this didn't just happen on the national level. City governments also saw new, anti-religious-freedom leaders and bureaucrats come into power.

In Ventura County, California, a new progressive mayor was elected. In just 90 days, this new mayor transformed the city council into a group with a radically progressive, anti-Christian worldview.

Sam was told that the Kingdom Center needed to stop feeding people…stop reaching out to the poor…stop making a difference.

Why? Because they were deemed to be a "social service," a government responsibility.[80]

Sam's response to the city was, "This is our *faith* – not a 'social service.'"

The city then told Sam they couldn't serve people on Monday through Friday because those days were outside the bounds of "traditional" days of religious service.

This is where the city radically crossed the line. They decided it was their role to define a religious practice. For them, feeding people on a Monday or a Tuesday wasn't a religious act.

The local government wanted to destroy any sort of charitable giving. They didn't care that 300 to 400 hungry, destitute men, women and children were being fed every day by Sam's ministry. They didn't care that people's lives were being radically transformed and improved.

What they wanted was control. They wanted to institute a government-run, government-controlled system to solve the problem of homelessness and to keep anyone else from helping.

To prevent Sam from serving the homeless, the city council did what all bureaucrats do when they abuse their power to maintain control: they created endless rules and regulations.

First, they required Sam to obtain a permit that was nearly impossible for him to acquire.

Then, when Sam returned to the council and told them he was willing to move – but not shut down his organization – they created 68 new conditions for him to meet.

These conditions included ridiculous, Fascist-like rules, such as making every person he served wear a special badge that said, "I'm homeless."

In the end, 30 homeless people gave testimony in court to the transformational power of the "Kingdom Center." But the radically progressive, anti-Christian council still voted "no" on giving Sam a permit.

He was devastated. But the worst was still to come.

In April of 2014, the police showed up at the doors of "Kingdom Center" and forcibly shut it down. They turned away more than 120 homeless kids at the doors because Ventura's law enforcement officials decided that the children could no longer receive free care and aid from Sam's ministry.

With his free Christian ministry back down to 40 people – losing hundreds in the legal turmoil – Sam went to federal court with his case.

He appeared before a judicial activist – a judge who abused his power to legislate his own ideological agenda. This judge coldly asked Sam, "Where does the Bible say to care for the homeless?"

When Sam answered with Matthew 25:40,*'Truly I tell you, whatever you did for one of the least of these brothers and sisters of mine, you did for me',*" the judge told Sam, "'The least of these' doesn't mean the homeless."

This radical judicial activist decided that *he* had the power to interpret the Bible. In other words, now it was the responsibility of the city – not the Church – to decide what constitutes Christianity. And for this judge, Christianity did not include caring for the poor.

But Sam still didn't back down!

With the help of the Religious Liberty Council of Stanford and other churches, Sam won by appealing to the U.S. Court of Appeals for the Ninth Circuit.

Finally, the "Kingdom Center" won in court. The ruling against Sam's ministry was so outrageous that he received a unanimous decision in his favor.

Sam finally achieved a decisive victory, but the crisis had caused a lot of damage. He passed the ministry along to others … and now pastors a church in Oxnard that emulates the legacy of the "Kingdom Center."

Sam learned a powerful lesson from his battle with the city of Ventura. "When the U.S. Constitution is attacked, everyone is attacked," says Sam.

A few radically progressive city council members and judges decided that Sam's ministry could no longer exercise freedom of religion – the freedom to practice their faith in God by serving the poor.

In the end, the city of Ventura could have moved Sam's ministry for a quarter of the price it paid to fight the "Kingdom Center." In fact, the city council spent over $5 million to fight Sam's homeless ministry – $5 million torn from hard-working taxpayers' pockets and denied to the neediest and homeless in a contemptible lust for power.

By the grace of God, Sam emerged victorious. But the hypocrisy and absurdity of his story are disturbing indicators of an increase in religious persecution in this country.

It's also a powerful reminder of what happens when our Constitution is trampled on by radical, God-hating ideologues. Everyone loses. People are not cared for. The Church cannot do its job. Taxpayers lose. The poor lose. Society loses. America loses.

To prevent similar harassment and government shutdowns of Christian ministries that are giving love to hurting people, Christians need to vote for local city council members, mayors and other government officials who have voiced and proven their support for local churches and their community service ministries.

And our vote for Assembly, State Senate, Governor and State Offices, Congress and Senate all impact the growing war on Christianity.

CHAPTER 8

Non-Negotiable #1: Protection of Christian Liberty

Across America, Christian freedom is under attack.

That's why protecting Christian liberty is the number-one non-negotiable position that every candidate must support in order to get a Christian's vote.

We need candidates who will re-establish and hold firm on issues of defending the First Amendment rights of Christians to exercise their faith and consciences without interference from government.

In recent years, we have seen these disturbing trends in America:

- Churches shut down;
- Pastors told they cannot meet with their congregations;
- Doctors, nurses, and other medical professionals told they cannot express their viewpoint in the workplace;
- The teachers and students in public schools

discriminated against because of their Christian faith; and
- Christian florists, bakers, wedding photographers and many others told they will be fined or prosecuted for exercising their faith or for refusing to act in ways that violate their faith.

We need the protection of religious freedom. Although it's a basic right guaranteed by the First Amendment of the U.S. Constitution, it's under withering assault today – as is the Constitution itself.

Liberal activist judges – who "create" new laws from the bench – trample on religious freedom by forcing Christians to act in violation of their sincerely held biblical beliefs. The biased media mocks Christians who exercise their Faith, and many politicians want to limit or ignore the right to religious freedom.

The First Amendment states:

"Congress shall make no law respecting an establishment of religion, or prohibiting the free exercise thereof; or abridging the freedom of speech, or of the press; or the right of the people peaceably to assemble, and to petition the Government for a redress of grievances."

When James Madison introduced the Bill of Rights to the First Congress on June 8, 1789, *The Congressional*

Register recorded that in his speech, Madison moved that "the civil rights of none shall be abridged on account of religious belief or worship, nor shall any national religion be established, nor shall the full and equal rights of conscience be in any manner, or on any pretext infringed."[81]

This interpretation of the rights set forth in what is now the First Amendment of the U.S. Constitution is being continually challenged and reiterated by a steady stream of anti-Christian legislation and court rulings masquerading as anti-discrimination policy.

Christians should avoid supporting and voting for candidates for public office who advocate elevating anti-discrimination laws above the First Amendment guarantee of the free exercise of religion.

The Equality Act –10 Disturbing Facts

Cities, counties, states and even the federal government have all seen politicians and anti-Christian groups propose or establish laws and regulations that restrict Christian rights.

One of the most horrific and dangerous pieces of legislation ever devised to attack Christian liberty and the free exercise of religion is the so-called Equality Act.

This bill passed in the Democrat-controlled House of Representatives but has stalled in the Senate. As of this writing, it is still under consideration in the 116th Congress.[82]

If it should pass in the Senate, President Trump has promised to veto the legislation. Of course, the composition of the Senate and the occupant of the Oval Office could change very quickly.

Few people know about the Equality Act. Yet it will have a devastating impact on people of faith should it become federal law.

Here's what you need to know about this bill:

1. The Equality Act isn't about "equal justice under law."

This law will prohibit discrimination based on sex, sexual orientation and gender identity in areas such as:

- public accommodations and facilities;
- education;
- federal funding;
- employment;
- housing ;
- credit;
- the jury system;
- ... and more

The bill also will expand the definition of public accommodations to include all places or establishments that provide:

- Exhibitions;
- Recreation;
- Exercise;
- Amusement;
- gatherings or displays;
- anything that gives accommodations for goods, services or programs; And
- all forms of transportation.

2. The Equality Act defines Christians as "haters" subject to criminal prosecution in federal court.

Any recognition of the differences between the sexes – or any preference for traditional sexual morality – will be viewed as actionable "hate."

The result will be a proliferation of lawsuits claiming discrimination of all kinds.

The Equality Act will prohibit an individual from being denied access to shared facilities including restrooms, locker rooms and dressing rooms that are in accordance with the individual's gender identity.

The new standard of discrimination will be based on the concept that "gender identity" is in one's head ... and that it has nothing to do with biology.

The Equality Act says each individual must be treated according to the sex he or she *thinks or feels* he or she is at any moment … or face the full force of this retaliatory law.

The law will allow the Department of Justice to intervene in Fourteenth Amendment "equal protection" actions in federal court regarding alleged sexual orientation and gender identity discrimination.

3. The Equality Act puts lies into laws.

When lies are made into laws, people get hurt.

Here are some of the lies that are codified into the Equality Act:

- Biology is meaningless.
- The only thing that matters is what each person thinks or feels about their sexuality at any moment.
- If you believe biology determines gender identity, you're a bigot – tantamount to being a member of the Ku Klux Klan – who must be harassed and persecuted and shut out of society for your beliefs.
- Tolerance must be shown to everyone except Christians.

4. The Equality Act nullifies the Religious Freedom Restoration Act.

The Religious Freedom Restoration Act was created in 1993 in response to a Supreme Court ruling that makes it a requirement for government to prove a "compelling interest" before enacting any law or regulation that violates someone's sincerely-held religious beliefs or freedom of religious expression.[83]

The Equality Act ends freedom of religious expression in America.

Here's how:

- Christian doctors and hospitals will be forced to perform sex-change operations.
- Churches will be forced to host homosexual weddings and to hire and accommodate every possible gender identity.
- Christian schools will be forced to hire LGBTQ+ teachers ... and teach LGBTQ+ beliefs and values as normal and God-ordained.
- Christian businesses will be forced to create designs, artwork and symbols celebrating LGBTQ+ lifestyles and values.

The government will become the new "morality police," dictating to churches and other faith-based institutions who they can hire and how their facilities must be used.

And they will be prosecuted if they don't fall lock-step into a view of human sexuality that directly contradicts orthodox biblical teaching.

5. The Equality Act changes America for the worse.

As outlined above, this bill criminalizes the practice and beliefs of Christianity ... and those who try to live according to those beliefs and practices.

It also criminalizes parents who believe in and teach their children traditional values regarding sex and gender.

In addition, the Equality Act:

- Allows men to access women's bathrooms ... and women to use men's bathrooms.
- Allows children to choose their "gender identity" ... and even change their bodies without parental consent.
- Allows transgenders to compete in women's sports, ruining women's sports competition.

The bill will also require doctors to affirm a child's gender confusion. This means doctors could be forced to perform double mastectomies on healthy 13-year-old girls who feel like they are boys...

And pediatric endocrinologists will have to provide hormone blockers like Lupron to kids experiencing gender dysphoria … or be charged with discrimination.

Ten years ago, there were only two hospitals in the U.S. that performed sex-change surgery. Today there are 50 … and the backers of this bill want to see sex-change operations performed in every public and private hospital in America.

6. The Equality Act officially ends parental rights regarding rearing their own children.

The usurpation of parental authority has already begun.

Recently, when parents in Ohio declined to provide the risky hormone therapy their daughter requested to begin the process of transforming her into a boy, the child's doctors contacted the state's Child Protective Services.

Ultimately, the parents' rights were terminated.

Under the Equality Act, what happened to this couple in Ohio will happen nationwide.

7. The Equality Act outlaws disagreement on important matters such as marriage and sexual identity.

Disagreement on important moral and biological issues is not discrimination. But the Equality Act turns ideological, philosophical and moral disagreement with what the legislation defines as "equality" into "hate" punishable by both state and federal governments.

Kristen Waggoner, senior vice president of the U.S. legal division of Alliance Defending Freedom (ADF), said this:

"Our laws should respect the constitutionally-guaranteed freedoms of every citizen, but the so-called 'Equality Act' fails to meet this basic standard. It would undermine women's equality and force women and girls to share private, intimate spaces with men who identify as female… Like similar state and local laws, it would force Americans to participate in events and speak messages that violate their core beliefs… This bill – and similar proposals such as 'Fairness for All' – undermines human dignity by threatening the fundamental freedoms of speech, religion, and conscience that the First Amendment guarantees for every citizen. Americans simply deserve better than the profound inequality proposed by this intolerant, deceptively-titled legislation."[84]

8. The Equality Act is not just an attack on heterosexuality. It is also an attack on homosexuality.

Think about the ramifications of erasing all gender distinctions. If you erase gender:

- You erase women, because gender is important to the women's empowerment movement.
- You erase gays, because gender is important to gays.
- You erase lesbians, because gender is important to lesbians.
- You erase heterosexuals, because gender is important to relationships between people of opposite sexes

This is why many gay and lesbian activist groups are opposed to the bill. They see the ramifications of the legislation more fully and accurately than do most.

Martina Navratilova –the self-identified lesbian tennis pro who won nine Wimbledon championships between 1978 and 1990, and who is considered by many to be the greatest female tennis player of all time – is opposed to the Equality Act.[85]

9. Hollywood, the media and Silicon Valley companies are strongly pushing the Equality Act.

The bill has 161 corporate sponsors. Among them are:

- Apple
- Amazon

- Facebook
- Google
- IBM
- Levi Strauss
- Dow Chemical
- Twitter

Singer Taylor Swift has launched a petition drive to her 114 million social media followers to get them to join her in pushing the Equality Act through the Senate.

The pressure to pass this legislation is immense.

10. The Equality Act is the most dangerous assault on freedom of speech and freedom of religion ever proposed on a national level.

This law will effectively overturn and nullify the First Amendment.

The Equality Act is an all-out assault on parental rights, on the family, on the church, and on millions of Christians and people of faith all across America. It dictates that faith must be confined to the mind alone ... and not applied to actions or behaviors.

Note that there is no religious exemption in this bill.

Almost no institution or person of faith – Christian, Muslim, or otherwise – will escape the reach of this draconian law.

The Equality Act **must** be stopped. That's why elections are so critical – and why voting is so important for every position on the ballot:

- For President
- For Senators and Representatives
- For governor of your state
- For all other state government officials
- For county judges
- For local elected officials
- For propositions
- For state and local measures

Other Government Abuses of Christian Liberty

The Equality Act eliminates Christian liberty at the federal level. But the federal government isn't the only governing authority that's attacking Christians and their liberty.

State and local governments attempt to limit or eliminate Christian liberty within states and local communities. They do this in two ways:

- Through fiat decrees called executive orders
- Through land use zoning regulations

One clear example of state-level usurpation of

Christian liberty has been the use of executive orders by state governors to ban or restrict church services during the COVID-19 pandemic. These executive orders have been blatant violations of the free exercise of religion clause of the First Amendment.

In California, for example, Governor Gavin Newsom issued an unconstitutional mandate, restricting churches to operating with no more than one hundred worshippers or twenty-five percent of building capacity, whichever is less. He then had the audacity to decree a ban on singing in church, and to outlaw home fellowships and prayer meetings![86]

Another common practice of local city councils and zoning commissions is to revoke the zoning approval of churches after they have submitted plans for ministry expansions and have been given initial approval.

To prevent this abuse of power, Congress unanimously passed the Religious Land Use and Institutionalized Persons Act (RLUIPA) in 2000. It was specifically enacted in response to actions which were being taken by local governments to ban churches from residential neighborhoods.[87]

But the federal law hasn't prevented county and community government entities from harassing and attempting to shut down churches and church ministries.

Hundreds of churches have been denied the right to build or expand their ministries because of the arbitrary decisions of zoning commissions and city councils.

A case in point is Vision Warriors Church in Woodstock, Georgia. In 2017, the church wanted to purchase property to use for a ministry to men seeking to overcome long-term drug addiction.

Prior to the purchase, the church applied for and received zoning approval from the County Zoning Administrator – who issued a written determination of approval. Based on that written zoning approval, the church purchased the property and started the ministry.

After the ministry was up and running, the county changed its mind and revoked the previously granted zoning approval. The county also changed its zoning ordinance, requiring the church to follow a laborious process to reapply for zoning approval.

The church followed the new application process but was denied the zoning approval – a death sentence for the church's men's ministry. They presented a detailed appeal to the County Board of Commissioners to no avail.

As a last resort, Vision Warriors Church is now in federal district court, charging the county with violations of the Fourteenth Amendment to the U.S. Constitution, the Religious Land Use and Institutionalized Persons Act (RLUIPA), the Fair Housing Act (FHA) and the Americans With Disabilities Act (ADA).[88]

Conclusion

The specific legislation and cases mentioned in this chapter are merely the tip of the iceberg of the ongoing efforts to deny Christians, Christian churches and Christian ministries their First Amendment rights of the free exercise of their religious beliefs.

These efforts to limit and deny Christian liberty are spearheaded not only by government operatives at all levels of federal, state and local government, but also by anti-Christian individuals and by both public and private anti-Christian organizations.

As Christians, we need to do our homework and research the beliefs and political positions of all candidates who are running for any elected office – regardless of how mundane or unimportant the office may seem. We should avoid supporting and voting for any candidate who advocates elevating anti-discrimination laws or policies above the First Amendment guarantee of the free exercise of religion.

The people you vote for for city council, for school

board, for county and state offices, for congressional representatives and senators – and for President of the United States – must all stand firm as defenders of the First Amendment … and of the First Amendment rights of Christians.

This stance is non-negotiable.

It doesn't matter how pretty or good-looking a candidate is. It doesn't matter how intelligent or articulate a candidate is. It doesn't matter whether a candidate is a Republican or a Democrat.

It doesn't matter whether you like or dislike a candidate's supporters, and it doesn't matter whether you like or dislike a candidate's ads.

What's important is what each candidate will do for you.

If you're not sure about a candidate's stance on this issue, be sure to consult one of the voter guides mentioned in this book.

Be sure to consult our web site at electionforum.org for detailed information.

The candidates we recommend all have been clearly vetted.

We must understand – and seek to convey our

understanding to others in a gentle and respectful way – that disagreeing with others on moral beliefs and behaviors – and acting consistently with our moral beliefs – does not constitute personal discrimination against those with whom we disagree.

In other words, discriminating against ideas and beliefs is not the same as discriminating against people.

Here are our marching orders:

"And the Lord's bondservant must not be quarrelsome, but be kind to all, able to teach, patient when wronged, with gentleness correcting those who are in opposition, if perhaps God may grant them repentance leading to the knowledge of the truth, and they may come to their senses and escape from the snare of the devil, having been held captive by him to do his will."
(2 Timothy 2:24-26)

We would do well to learn and practice these tactics in our interactions with others – and in our voting.

CHAPTER 9

Non-Negotiable #2: Protection of Unborn Babies

Protecting the unborn is not always a popular political position. But for Christians, it is a non-negotiable issue.

Why?

Because God is the creator of all life. And God does not make mistakes in anything He does or creates.

Therefore, the protection and preservation of human life is of critical importance to anyone who believes in God.

The first chapter of the Bible – Genesis 1 – and our nation's founding document, the Declaration of Independence, proclaim that life is the first and foremost unalienable right given to all people by our Creator.

The United States of America was founded on the principle – the self-evident truth – that all human life is a gift from God.

Moreover, it is granted by God alone. Life is not a right granted by men and women. Endearing human life itself is not granted by mothers, nor by government, nor by any government agency or institution.

Those who support the willful and deliberate taking of an innocent human life are rebelling against and in opposition to the Bible, the Declaration of Independence – and God Almighty.

When I evaluate candidates for voter support – and rate them in voter guides – their position on protecting the unborn is critical.

Most politicians try to fudge on where they stand with respect to protecting the unborn. And that has been a big part of the problem.

Many candidates – even when they claim they are pro-life – fail to stand up and support the lives of the unborn when it comes down to a congressional vote on the issue.

That is why it's so important to vet each candidate – to make sure protecting the unborn is a non-negotiable position they will stand by in all circumstances.

Abortion is a deeply personal and controversial issue. When speaking at churches about abortion, I usually quote Psalm 139:13.

"For You formed my inward parts; you wove me in my mother's womb."

And while, standing for the protection of human life is vital, I also add that fighting for adoption is critical.

For me, this is personal.

Why?

Because I was adopted.

If abortion had been legal, when my birth mother was pregnant with me – as it now is under *Roe v. Wade* – I would not be writing this book. I would not have married my beautiful bride. I would not have had the privilege of raising five children. I would have potentially been killed.

When we talk about abortion – and when we talk about a partial-birth abortion – there is often silence in the church because many of the women have had an abortion.

I'm always quick to point out that God is a God of forgiveness and a God of love. He is a God of second chances.

I point out that God repairs broken hearts and restores people no matter what choices they have made in the past.

This being said, except under special circumstances, where wisdom and love suggest otherwise, we should never be silent about abortion. In fact, the most active pro-life leaders have been women who have had abortions themselves.

When Does Life Begin?

Christians are often accused of being anti-science – and therefore, by implication – "ignorant" and "backward" in their thinking. That charge is false and absurd.

It is actually the pro-socialist, secular politicians, the biased media talking heads and the so-called "pro-choice" advocates who are anti-science.

They are the ones, after all, who insist on identifying unborn babies in their mothers' wombs by non-human names such as "products of conception" and "fetal tissue."

They dismiss or ignore the scientific facts about the beginning of human life, including the following:

- The heart of a fetus begins beating at five weeks – even before the heart chambers have fully developed.[89]

- By six weeks, the heart has four hollow chambers – each with an entrance and exit to allow blood flow – and the heartbeat can be detected by an ultrasound.
- By week nine or ten, the mother can hear her baby's heartbeat through a Doppler ultrasound.
- Published scientific literature regarding neural development clearly shows that unborn babies can experience pain as early as 20 weeks or even earlier.[90]
- Fetal surgeons – when performing operations inside the womb – treat unborn babies as human patients and administer anesthesia if the baby is 15 weeks or older.[91]
- Sixty percent of babies born as early as 22 weeks will survive if they receive active medical treatment.[92] The survival rate increases to 81 percent at 24 weeks.

Despite these and other undisputed scientific facts, the pro-abortion extremists demand that women have the "right to choose" to end their pregnancies by killing their unborn children.

The fact that we are even having debates about abortion in the United States of America in the 21st century shows how far we've rebelled as a nation from the God we acknowledge on our currency, and from the Christian principles on which our country and our government are founded.

Most abortions are murder, pure and simple. It is the premeditated killing of another human being with "malice aforethought" – which is the definition of first-degree murder.

It is the reckless disregard for the life of the most innocent, the most vulnerable and the most helpless of all human beings: an unborn child.

The fact that our politicians, our courts and most U.S. citizens have been browbeaten and pressured into allowing and even supporting such barbarism is unconscionable.

What people are really saying and thinking when they repeat the pro-abortion slogan that women should have the "right to choose" is that women know better than God what is best for their lives.

How have we reached such a low point mentally, emotionally and psychologically – to where we summarily reject God's sovereignty over our bodies and over biological processes?

Historical Attitudes About the Unborn and the Newborn

Abortion and infanticide have occurred in various forms throughout history. Protecting life, on the other hand, has come about because of the Christian faith.

For example, Christians in ancient Rome routinely rescued babies that had been tossed on the sides of the roads or left under bridges to die. It was the Christians who adopted them and raised them as their own children.

The Romans were highly critical of the Christians for their obsession over the preservation of human life. They thought it was insane for anyone to value human life so much. They looked at anyone who would rescue and protect human life as an enemy of the state.

As science and medicine have developed and advanced, our understanding of the fetal heartbeat and of the viability of life has also advanced and become much clearer.

We now know, for certain, that life begins at conception. But far too many Christians in the church have kept quiet about this. Too many have ignored the science. Too many pastors have refused to talk about it because to do so might be considered controversial.

But none of this has stopped the politicians who

continue to advocate expanding the legalized murder of unborn children.

Planned Parenthood and the *Roe v. Wade* United States Supreme Court Decision

Margaret Sanger opened the first birth-control clinic in the United States in Brooklyn, New York, in 1916. She founded the American Birth Control League in 1921. Its name was changed to the Planned Parenthood Federation of America, in 1942.

Legal abortion, in the United States began in 1973.

In 1970, Hawaii became the first state to legalize abortion for residents of the state. In the same year, New York legalized abortion, but without a residency requirement. Alaska, California, Oregon and Washington State also subsequently legalized abortion before the famous *Roe v. Wade* lawsuit was filed.

In 1969, Norma McCorvey – a 21-year-old Texas woman – wanted to end her third pregnancy. She had already borne two children, which she had given up for adoption. At the time, Texas permitted abortion only for the purpose of saving a pregnant woman's life.

She sued the Dallas County District Attorney, in a case titled Jane Roe, et al v. Henry Wade, and cited that the Texas anti-abortion law was unconstitutionally vague and that by preventing women from purposely terminating their pregnancies by abortion, even when their lives and well-being were not threatened, the law violated the right to personal privacy implied by the First, Fourth, Fifth, Ninth and Fourteenth Amendments.

Roe v. Wade finally reached the U.S. Supreme Court, in late 1971, but the case was not decided until January 22, 1973.

The Court ruled that a woman's right to choose to have an abortion is implicit in a supposed right to privacy protected by the Fourteenth Amendment, and that the Texas anti-abortion law was unconstitutional because it violated that right.

This right, however, must be balanced, the justices ruled, against government's interests in protecting the health of women while also protecting "the potentiality of human life."[93]

The Court declared that the relative weight of these interests varies during the course of a pregnancy, and that the law must account for the variation.

Thus, the ruling divided pregnancy into three trimesters:

1. In the **first** trimester, a state may not regulate abortion. The choice to end a pregnancy during this period of pregnancy is entirely up to the woman;

2. In the **second** trimester, a state may regulate abortion – although not ban it – for the purpose of protecting the woman's life and health; and

3. In the **third** trimester, a state may regulate or prohibit abortion for the purpose of protecting an unborn child that could potentially survive and be "viable" on its own outside the womb. However, any regulation or prohibition must still allow abortion if it becomes necessary to save the life or health of the mother.[94]

Roe v. Wade radically altered the social and political landscape of America.

For the past 47 years, there have been numerous state expansions of the abortion rights granted by *Roe* – and some state restrictions of abortion rights. And the debate continues to rage today with misleading terms such as "pro-choice," "anti-choice" and "war on women" inflaming the rhetoric.

Abortion Statistics

According to the Guttmacher Institute – a division of Planned Parenthood Federation of America – almost **62 million** "surgical abortions" have been performed in the United States since the *Roe v. Wade* Supreme Court decision, in 1973.[95] Since 1980, more than **1.5 billion** abortions have been performed worldwide.

What's even more shocking is that the numbers above do not include chemically induced abortions.

Pharmacists for Life International – a pro-life organization that advocates for the rights of pharmacists who, because of their religious beliefs, refuse to fill or dispense prescriptions for abortion-causing drugs – estimates that, since 1973, there have been about **250 million** babies aborted chemically in the United States alone.[96]

Despite these horrific numbers, the abortion rate in the U.S. has been gradually declining since the peak year of 1990, when 1.6 million abortions were performed.[97] In 2017 – the latest year for which the Guttmacher Institute has reported complete statistics – the total number of United States abortions fell to about 1.2 million – 862,320 surgical abortions plus 339,640 chemically-induced abortions – representing 18 percent of all estimated pregnancies.[98]

Tragically, abortion remains the leading killer of

African American babies in the United States – claiming 259,366 lives every year.[99]

A startling 2016 study, in New York City, showed that more black babies are aborted than are born.[100]

While Planned Parenthood proclaims in their social media disinformation campaigns that "black lives matter," the organization is responsible for nearly 250 abortions of black babies per day – more than 90,000 per year.[101]

A 2010 census revealed that 79 percent of Planned Parenthood's surgical abortion facilities were located within walking distance of African American or Latino neighborhoods.[102]

Efforts to Expand Abortion Rights

Planned Parenthood is the nation's largest abortion provider. Its affiliates operate over 600 health clinics in the United States and kill more than 325,000 unborn babies every year – which amounts to about 900 murders per day. In fiscal year 2018, Planned Parenthood clinics performed 345,672 abortions – the most ever reported in a single year.[103]

Planned Parenthood has a vested financial interest in expanding abortion rights and abortion access, as abortions account for 95 percent of its "pregnancy services." In 2019, the organization received $616.8 million in taxpayer funding, $591.3 million in private donations, and nearly $400 million in fees for abortions. Their funding will be about the same in 2020.

A significant portion of Planned Parenthood's $1.6 billion in annual revenue is spent on:

- Advertising to increase donations:
- Indirect financial support of pro-abortion political candidates to buy votes and to keep taxpayer funding coming; and
- Advertising to defeat pro-life candidates.

I know first-hand about their use of funds to defeat pro-life candidates for elected offices. When I ran for a political office in 2014, they spent over half-a-million dollars trying to defeat me because I spoke the truth about them.

What truth did I reveal?

Planned Parenthood supplements their revenue stream by selling aborted baby organs to the highest bidder for "research" purposes and even cosmetic uses. The organs must be intact, so when a deal has been struck for specific organs, special abortion techniques are used to preserve them undamaged for illegal sale on the international black market.

In 2015, two associates from the Center for Medical Progress (CMP) secretly videotaped meetings with Planned Parenthood officials in which procedures and fees for selling aborted fetal organs were discussed.

After the videos were released to the public, both the National Abortion Federation and Kamala Harris, the Attorney General of the State of California, sued the two whistleblowers – David Daleiden, CEO of CMP, and his collaborator, Sandra Merritt – on a number of false charges related to their undercover video.

Following a September 2019 criminal hearing, Planned Parenthood filed a civil suit against Daleiden and Merritt in federal court, alleging that they engaged in fraud, breach of contract, unlawful recording of conversations, civil conspiracy and violation of the federal anti-racketeering law.[104]

This is how pro-abortion state attorneys general and Planned Parenthood react when anyone exposes the hidden and appalling actions of the baby-murdering abortion industry. The federal court ruled against David Daleiden, in November 2019, and ordered him to pay $870,000 in punitive damages to Planned Parenthood. The State of California court case in San Francisco is still pending as of this writing.

In 2018, Agenda Project Action Fund – a Planned Parenthood ally and front group tied to George Soros – created a 40-second TV ad in which a live baby girl is smiling and giggling while a lullaby is playing softly in the background. The baby's image is replaced three times during the ad by a black screen containing these lines of white text – one line at a time:

"She deserves to be … loved."

"She deserves to be … wanted."

"She deserves to be … a choice."

If you have the stomach to watch the ad, go to YouTube and enter the words "She Deserves to Be a Choice ad" in the search window.

Mainstream Pastors and Churches Also Support Abortion

As if it were not bad enough that the biased media and anti-Christian politicians and government officials support abortion, some pro-Marxist religious leaders openly support abortion also.

The Religious Coalition for Reproductive Choice (RCRC) – a national organization of pro-abortion "Christian" pastors, Jewish rabbis, Hindu priests and Muslim clerics – blesses abortion clinics and abortion doctors across the nation.

Legalization of Infanticide

Every year in the United States, there are babies who survive attempted abortions. Planned Parenthood and the rest of the abortion industry argue that these "extremely unlikely and highly unusual medical circumstances" rarely happen.[105] But they do.

According to the Centers for Disease Control and Prevention (CDC), 362 babies born alive following an attempted abortion died in the 10-year period between 2001 and 2010.[106]

We do not know how many of these babies could have survived and lived long, healthy lives if they had received proper medical care. But the fact is that many of these babies – because they were not wanted by their mothers – were not cared for after they were born. They were purposely left to die or murdered.

It's shocking and truly despicable that 19 states – as of 2019 – do not require that any medical care be provided for babies born alive after attempted abortions.[107] And an additional 16 states, plus the federal government, don't have adequate protections for babies who survive an attempted abortion.

Virginia Governor Ralph Northam, recently said that only a woman and her doctor should be able to decide whether her infant who survived abortion receives medical care or is left alone to die.[108]

New York recently passed a law called the Reproductive Health Act (RHA), which allows abortion up to the point of birth as a "fundamental right" in state law. The intent of the language in the bill is to keep abortion on demand legal in New York even if *Roe v. Wade* is overturned in the future by the U.S. Supreme Court.[109]

The RHA goes far beyond the ruling in *Roe* in that it eliminates legal protections and the right to immediate medical care for any baby born alive following an attempted abortion. Under the RHA, abortion survivors are literally left to die a slow, agonizing death and are then discarded as "medical waste."[110]

As of this writing, several other states are considering similar legislation. Among them are Vermont, New Mexico and Rhode Island. The Guttmacher Institute reported at the time the RHA was passed in New York that nine other states also had laws codifying *Roe* in state law in case the U.S. Supreme Court were to reverse and declare that *Roe v. Wade* is unconstitutional.[111]

Abortion Survivors – The Numbers Are Shocking

In spite of the states that allow abortion up to the moment of birth – and even allow for infanticide after birth – a surprising number of aborted babies survive, grow up and live full lives. No one knows exactly how many there are because the U.S. government does not keep detailed, or reliable statistics on these outrageous events.

At the beginning of this chapter, we noted that 60 percent of babies born as early as 22 weeks will survive if they receive emergency medical treatment. The Guttmacher Institute estimates that "only" about 14 out of 100 abortions occur at this stage of pregnancy or later.[112]

But if you multiply that percentage times 1.2 million abortions in 2017, times 60 percent that will survive with proper medical care, the result is an astounding 10,080 potential abortion survivors per year. Seven years ago, 44,000 abortion survivors were living in the United States[113] The number is undoubtedly higher today.

The Born-Alive Abortion Survivors Protection Act (S.311) was due to be voted on in the U.S. Senate in February 2019 at the request of Sen. Ben Sasse (R-NE). The purpose of the bill was "to prohibit healthcare practitioners from failing to exercise the proper degree of care in the case of a child who survives an abortion or attempted abortion."[114]

But the full vote by the Senate never happened. In fact, S.311 failed ***twice*** to reach the floor of the Senate due to the 60-vote requirement to invoke cloture – that is, to end debate on a measure. The votes were 53-44 on February 25, 2019 and 56-41 on February 25, 2020.

This is, yet another example of how important your vote is in electing senators and representatives in your state.

Proposed Senate bill S. 311 was a vital measure to protect babies born alive from being abandoned and left to die in closets or on operating tables. The intent of the bill is to stop the deliberate, horrific acts that are actually murder of babies who are born alive – taking place today.

You would think that at least 60 U.S. Senators and a majority of the members of the House of Representatives would be in favor of stopping the deliberate murder of babies. Americans of every background should be incensed that our elected leaders refuse to end a practice that mirrors Nazi Germany's contempt for innocent human life.

We must all work and pray that this will change after the 2020 election … and that we will still have a President who will sign the bill when it comes to his desk.

Efforts to Limit Abortion

Many states have recently enacted or have attempted to enact laws to protect the unborn:

- Mississippi passed a fetal-heartbeat law banning abortion after 15 weeks ... but the law was struck down as unconstitutional by judicial activists at the Fifth Circuit Court of Appeals;
- Missouri banned abortions beginning at eight weeks of pregnancy. At this writing, the law has been temporarily blocked by a federal judge;
- Georgia, Kentucky, Louisiana and Ohio have passed fetal-heartbeat laws that have been blocked by judges;
- Alabama passed a near-total ban on abortion. It was temporarily blocked by a judge in October 2019;
- Arkansas and Utah passed laws to allow abortion only up to the middle of the second trimester. The Utah law went into effect and the Arkansas law was temporarily blocked by a federal judge; and

Other states are at various stages of considering bills to restrict or ban abortion and protect the lives of unborn babies.

In some of these cases, judges are creating laws

governing abortion, instead of leaving lawmaking to the legislatures.

This is wrong. This is judicial activism. This is where a judge inappropriately legislates from the bench based on his or her own personal opinions and biases – not based on the law.

This is why Christians need to know the judicial philosophies and the worldviews of the judges they vote for and support.

People vote for local and county judges and, even in some states, Supreme Court Justices throughout the United States. And these are the judges who sometimes are promoted to federal district or even appeals court judges ... and even Supreme Court Justices.

They are nominated by the President and approved by the U.S. Senate. So, elected officials at all levels need to have a strong pro-life commitment.

Political Arguments For and Against Abortion

Political arguments in favor of or in opposition to abortion often consist of name calling rather than debate about rational points and counterpoints.

During the 2016 presidential campaign, Democrat candidate Hillary Clinton compared her Republican pro-life rival candidates to terrorists, when she said in a campaign speech in Cleveland, Ohio: "Extreme views about women – we expect that from some of the terrorist groups. We expect that from people who don't want to live in the modern world. But it's a little hard to take coming from Republicans who want to be the President of the United States. Yet they expose out of date and out of touch policies."[115]

Notice that Mrs. Clinton gave no rational reason or argument for why she believes all women should have a legal right – her campaign called it a "woman's reproductive health care choice" – to abort their babies.

Politicians rarely speak in rational, logical and principled terms. And if they do, it is not often reported in the news media. Such speech does not lend itself to attention-grabbing soundbite clipping and editing.

In a SiriusXM "Town Hall" discussion about the future of abortion rights in America, Chelsea Clinton gave three arguments for supporting *Roe v. Wade*:

1. Reversing Roe v. Wade would subject women to "unsafe abortion practices:"

2. Legalization of abortion has been a boon

to the U.S. economy; and

3. Returning to the "pre-Roe" era when abortion was illegal would be "unconscionable" and "un-Christian."

Let's consider and respond to each of these arguments.

1. Reversing *Roe v. Wade* would subject women to "unsafe abortion practices." By this logic, we should legalize dangerous and potentially deadly drugs and set up clinics where addicts can receive clean syringes to protect them from contaminated and "unsafe" needles.

Is an unborn child a human being? That is the question that needs to be asked and answered. Legalizing an immoral act to make it safer doesn't make the act moral or acceptable.

2. Legalization of abortion has been a boon to the U.S. economy. Chelsea Clinton argued in her radio interview that women "added three and a half trillion dollars to our economy" after abortion became legal because they could abort their babies and then enter the workforce – a truly depraved perspective.

But what about the economic impact of the millions of lives lost to abortion over the past five decades? By some estimates, the cost to America's GDP due to the loss of potential workers and taxpayers is $2.5 trillion per year.[116]

3. Returning to the "pre-Roe v. Wade" era when abortion was illegal, would be "unconscionable" and "un-Christian." During the radio interview, Clinton said, "When I think about all of the statistics that are painful of what women are confronting today in our country, and what even more women confronted pre-Roe v. Wade and how many women died and how any more women were maimed because of unsafe abortion practices, we just can't go back to that."

This argument is based on often-repeated "statistics" of more than a million illegal abortions and 5,000 deaths each year prior to *Roe v. Wade*.[117] But what are the actual numbers on abortion and abortion deaths prior to 1973?

Obviously, there was no official count of annual illegal abortions prior to the *Roe v. Wade* Supreme Court decision. However, *after* abortion was legalized, there were 744,600 abortions performed in 1973. The U.S. Department of Health and Human Services has estimated that the average number of abortions performed annually prior to 1973 was 615,831.[118] So, the pro-abortion public relations estimate of more than a million illegal abortions in 1972 and prior years seems highly exaggerated.

As for abortion-related deaths prior to 1973, these

are the numbers for ALL pregnancy-related deaths, according to the Vital Statistics of the United States, Volume II, Mortality, Part A, 1960-1977. Moreover, these include deaths from abortions as well as from childbirth and other complications during pregnancy:

- 1960 – 1,579 (289 from abortions)
- 1968 – 859 (133 from abortions)
- 1972 – 63 deaths from both legal and illegal abortions

The alternative to abortion is adoption.

For whatever reason, if a woman does not want to have her child, there are always many couples who will adopt that child.

And that is why we as Christians must step up and be people who are willing to adopt if possible … and who are excited about helping and loving children.

Scientific Arguments Against Abortion

Many women I speak with have had varying degrees of deep regret and emotional trauma if they've had an abortion.

Whether or not they've been conscious of it at the time, they've been permanently affected by the experience.

Scientists, doctors and other mental health professionals understand most women experience grief and suffer depression from aborting their unborn children.

In 2008, more than 100 scientists, doctors and mental health professionals released the following statement about the damage abortion does to women:

"As a scientist or medical or mental health professional, I agree with the following conclusions about abortion:

1. It is common for women to experience feelings of anger, fear, sadness, anxiety, grief or guilt after abortion. The United States Supreme Court is correct that some women come to regret their choice to abort the infant life they once created and sustained ... severe depression and loss of self-esteem can follow.

2. Women's reaction to these feelings vary considerably with their emotional coping abilities and preexisting functioning. It is undeniable that significant numbers of women are injured by abortion and should not be ignored by the medical profession and that significant numbers of women suffer serious physical, mental or psychological trauma as a result of abortion.

> 3. The conclusion that there is a causal connection between abortion and negative problems is supported by three independent lines of evidence: (a) the self-attribution of women themselves, (b) mental health professionals who have successfully diagnosed and treated post-abortion reactions, and (c) statistically validated studies controlling for a large number of confounding factors that have been published in peer-reviewed journals."[119]

The American Psychological Association (APA) denies that abortion causes mental-health problems for women.[120]

But, a New Zealand study suggests that women who have abortions significantly raise their risk of developing mental-health problems. According to the study:

- Forty-two percent of women who had abortions experienced major depression within four years – double the rate among women who never became pregnant;
- Women who have abortions are twice as likely to abuse alcohol to dangerous levels; and
- Women who have abortions are three times more likely to become addicted to illegal

drugs.[121]

Not all women who have had an abortion have had a strong emotional reaction to it, but some have. But we are blessed to know there is forgiveness, and that's why God wants us to forget those things which are behind and press forward to those things which are ahead (Philippians 3:13).

We have a God who forgives ALL sin … and a God who will use the evil experiences in our lives to bring about the good that is His perfect will. (Genesis 50:20)

Biblical Arguments For and Against Abortion

Alicia Baker, an ordained Free Methodist Church minister in Indianapolis, Indiana, argued for abortion using a Bible verse during the U.S. Senate confirmation hearings for Supreme Court nominee Brett Kavanaugh.

She said, "Jesus directs us to advocate for a just society that allows people to live their lives to the fullest. In John 10:10, Jesus says, 'I have come that you might have life, and have it to the full,' and this means supporting access to affordable birth control, because by permitting individuals to plan if, whether and when to become pregnant, birth control allows us to live our fullest lives."[122]

In John 10:10, Jesus isn't telling us to "advocate for a just society" at all. He is contrasting the goal of Satan's activity in our lives versus His goal for us – and His purpose for coming to earth. What He actually says is this: *"The thief comes only to steal and kill and destroy. I came that they might have life and might have it more abundantly."* (Some Bible versions translate "more abundantly" as "to the full.")

Ms. Baker's unbiblical argument was that women can experience a full life only if they have "the right to choose" to control their own bodies by either carrying their babies to birth or by aborting and killing them.

On the contrary, a full life is attainable only through Jesus. It's not something we can create on our own.

The context of John 10 is that Jesus is the Good Shepherd who cares for His sheep – His followers – and brings them into His sheepfold – His kingdom. The abundant life comes from knowing the Shepherd and following Him – not from going off alone and assuming it's okay to do whatever you want with your body.

Her interpretation of John 10:10 directly contradicts 2 Corinthians 3:16-17: *"Do you not know that your body is a temple of the Holy Spirit, which is in you, whom you have from God, and that* ***you are not your own?*** *For you have been bought with a price; therefore, glorify God in your body and in your spirit, which are God's."*

One of the most important truths all Christians must recognize when it comes to abortion or any other choice regarding our physical bodies is that our bodies do not belong to us – they belong to God.

God is the creator of all human life – not just the creator of the lives of the first two humans, Adam and Eve. He is also the creator of the human life in a mother's womb.

In Psalm 100:3 we read, *"Know that the Lord Himself is God; it is He who has made us, and not we ourselves; we are His people and the sheep of His pasture."*

This verse teaches us that God didn't just create us and then tell us to fend for ourselves throughout life, doing whatever we please with our own bodies. Rather, it teaches us that we belong to Him from the miracle of conception to death.

The psalmist also declares:

"For You formed my inward parts; You wove me in my mother's womb. I will give thanks to You, for I am fearfully and wonderfully made; wonderful are Your works, and my soul knows it very well.

My frame was not hidden from You, when I was made in secret, and skillfully wrought in the depths of the earth; Your eyes have seen my unformed substance; and in Your book were all written the days that were ordained for me, when as yet there was not one of them." (Psalm 139:13-16)

Based on these passages and others, we can use deductive reasoning to infer the following biblical principles:

- God is the creator of all human life.
- Because God creates all human life, all human life belongs to Him (Psalm 24:1).
- Because God creates all human life in His image (Genesis 1:26-27), all human life is sacred and infinitely valuable (Matthew 16:26).
- Because all human life belongs to God, He alone has the authority to end human life (Psalm 139:16).
- The sixth commandment prohibits murder (Exodus 20:1-17).
- Willful, deliberate, intentional abortion is murder in all cases except for one: when it is performed to prevent the imminent death of the mother. In this one instance, the death of the unborn baby would be classified as justifiable homicide rather than murder.
- God has a unique purpose in mind for each life He creates – and that purpose is determined while the baby is still in the womb. God reiterated this truth to Jeremiah the prophet when He said to him, *"Before I*

formed you in the womb, I knew you; before you were born, I set you apart; I appointed you as a prophet to the nations." (Jeremiah 1:5)
We also find the apostle Paul mentioning the same principle in his letter to the church in Galatia: *"But when God, who had set me apart even from my mother's womb and called me through His grace..." (Galatians 1:15)*

- In God's commands for the Israelites in the Old Testament, if people were fighting and injured a pregnant woman and she gave birth prematurely, if the baby died, the person who caused the premature delivery was treated as a murderer. (Exodus 21:22-24)
- God delegated to man the responsibility for implementing the death penalty – but only in very narrow and precisely defined circumstances; for example, for murder (Genesis 9:6).

Of course, most reporters in the American media do not want you to see or hear news about God's miraculous activities and love of God in the lives of people in such stressful circumstances.

A case in point: Faces of Choice – a pro-life organization created to bring awareness to the public and to give voice to those who have survived abortion – created an ad for the 2020 Super Bowl in which 14 abortion survivors ask in various ways the basic question, "Can you look me in the eye and say I don't have a right to exist?" Fox Sports – the media network broadcasting for the 2020 Super Bowl in Miami – rejected the ad and refused to air it.[123]

It's a sad commentary on the social, spiritual and moral condition of our society that we are prevented from engaging in a civil, rational discussion about the sanctity of life versus the sovereignty of God. "Choice" is not just a decision of the will devoid of morality and responsibility. "Choice" has a face. In the case of abortion, "Choice" is a person – a human life.

Conclusion

In the latest Pew Research Center poll, 70 percent of adults surveyed said they didn't want to see the Supreme Court completely overturn *Roe v. Wade*. That's up from 60 percent fifteen years ago.

When asked if abortion should be legal or illegal in all or most cases, the numbers are slightly different. Sixty-one percent are in favor of abortion being legal in all (27 percent) or most (34 percent) cases. This is just one percentage point higher than 15 years ago. Thirty-eight percent say abortion should be illegal in all (12 percent) or most (26 percent) cases – the same percentage as 15 years ago.[124]

Of course, Christians shouldn't base their opinions or their convictions on public polling information. We should base our thinking on God's Word in the Bible, the counsel of godly followers of Christ and on prayer and the leading of the Holy Spirit – all of which should align and agree with God's Holy Word.

The Declaration of Independence declares that all humans are "endowed by their Creator with certain unalienable rights," and that the first of these rights is the right to life.

Those who support abortion use the false argument that unborn babies are not human; therefore, killing them in the womb doesn't constitute murder.

We've shown that argument to be false in this chapter by demonstrating that human life begins at conception.

As Christians, we are compelled by God and by His Holy Word to protect human life at all stages of development.

Women have no more right to kill their babies in the womb because they don't want them than they have the right to kill their husbands because they don't want to be married any longer – or than they have the right to kill the father of their baby because they didn't want to get pregnant.

It's very unlikely in most elections to expect that any political candidate will have a totally biblical pro-life position in order to qualify for your vote.

But we must do our research and do our best to get specific answers about a candidate's position on when he or she would support abortion or would not support it.

This is why voter guides that vet candidates on the abortion issue are so important. And that's why web sites like electionforum.org and ivoterguide.com review and provide accurate information about judges nationwide. Many states also have their own Christian worldview-based voter guides.

One thing is clear: we should not support political candidates who defend Planned Parenthood nor allow public funding using millions of dollars from hard-working taxpayers for that baby-killing extermination empire.

Rev. Samuel Rodriguez, of the National Hispanic Christian Leadership Conference, has said, "Any Christian who would support a candidate who defends Planned Parenthood really needs to seek Scripture."[125] See the Chapter on Strategically Limiting Evil for more information.

When you vote, don't vote <u>against</u> your Christian values; vote **for** your values.

When you vote, make sure that the candidates you choose for every elected position support our non-negotiable value number two – protection of the unborn.

CHAPTER 10

Non-Negotiable #3: Constitutionalist Supreme Court Justices

The potential nomination of U.S. Supreme Court justices by a President during his or her term of office is an important consideration in nearly every presidential election. You may dislike both major political party candidates in an election – and if an Independent or third-party candidate is on the ballot, you may dislike that candidate as well.

But if you care about the U.S. Constitution and you want the Supreme Court to respect it and to render decisions based on its original meaning and intent, you need to vote for the presidential candidate who will nominate Supreme Court justices who will uphold the Constitution in their rulings and not act as if they are legislators.

The U.S. Constitution has been referred to throughout the history of the United States as "the supreme law of the land." This means several things:

- It is the founding document of our nation;
- It establishes the form, functions, and limits of the constitutional republic which the Founders chose to create, and which the states and the people agreed to;
- Its Articles and Amendments contain the fundamental laws and governing principles upon which all other federal laws should be based.

A major problem we have had as a nation for the past century is that our elected representatives and our appointed judges no longer agree on how to interpret and apply the Constitution to the legislative process. There are two opposing and competing schools of thought:

1. The U.S. Constitution should be understood to mean what the Founders and Framers intended it to mean. Judges who decide cases based on the original meaning and words of the Constitution are called "original constructionists," "strict constructionists" or "Textualists." They are also described as practicing "judicial restraint."

2. The second group believes the Constitution is a living, breathing document that must be continually reinterpreted as culture and societal norms and morals change. Judges who decide cases based on this view of the Constitution are called "judicial activists"

and are described as practicing "judicial activisms."

Strict Constructionist justices and judges view the role of the judiciary – the judicial branch of government – according to the words contained in the Constitution. They also frequently embrace the perspectives found in the Federalist Papers, a series of 85 articles and essays written by Alexander Hamilton, James Madison and John Jay, in 1787 and 1788, to explain the purpose, responsibilities and limitations of the proposed new federal government, and to convince the legislatures of the thirteen colonies to ratify the Constitution.

According to the Framers of the Constitution, the role of the judiciary and of the U.S. Supreme Court is to rule on the constitutionality of the laws by Congress and by state legislatures. It is not reserved to create new laws or exercise powers for the legislative branch of government.

By contrast, activist justices and judges, because they believe the Constitution must evolve according to changing cultural and societal norms, see their role as being interpreters. Therefore, they often overturn long-standing federal laws and "legislate from the bench:" in effect, they create new laws as part of their ruling in a case.

Judicial Activism on the U.S. Supreme Court

The terms “judicial activism” and “judicial restraint” were coined, in 1947, in a *Fortune* magazine article written by historian Arthur Schlesinger, Jr. He analyzed the viewpoints and opinions of the nine members of the Supreme Court at the time and divided them into two groups: those who favored judicial activism and those who favored judicial restraint.

The Warren Court – the Supreme Court presided over by Chief Justice Earl Warren between 1953 and 1969 – was the first Court to be labeled a judicial activist court. The Warren Court rendered several decisions during its tenure that had major effects on social policies in the country in the 1950s and 1960s.

The most well-known Warren Court decision was the landmark *Brown v. Board of Education* ruling, in 1954, which outlawed racial segregation in the nation’s public schools. Christians should be aware of a few important historical facts surrounding this case:

- *Brown V. Board of Education of Topeka* struck down a previous U.S. Supreme Court ruling – *Plessy v. Ferguson, rendered* in 1896 – which held that racially segregated public facilities were legal, if the separate facilities for blacks and whites were equal.[126]

- The *Brown* decision was labeled a judicial activist ruling because it overturned the precedent established by *Plessy*.

- In 1951, Oliver Brown had filed a class-action lawsuit against the Board of Education of Topeka, Kansas, after his daughter Linda Brown, was denied entrance to Topeka's all-white public elementary schools.

- Brown argued in his lawsuit that schools for black children were not equal to the schools for white children and that the segregation violated the equal-protection clause of the Fourteenth Amendment.

- The "separate but equal" doctrine of *Plessy v. Ferguson,* and the so-called "Jim Crow" laws that had resulted from that decision, were upheld in U.S. District Court in Kansas.

- When the case reached the Supreme Court, in 1952, the Court combined it with four other cases related to school segregation and created a single case, *Brown v. Board of Education of Topeka*.[127]

- The Chief Justice of the Supreme Court at the time, Fred M. Vinson, was of the opinion that the *Plessy* verdict would be upheld in the *Brown* case. But Vinson passed away before the case could be heard.[128]

- President Dwight D. Eisenhower nominated Earl Warren – then the Governor of California – to replace Vinson as Chief Justice.

- Warren – being much more liberal in his views on social policy than Vinson – engineered a unanimous decision in the *Brown* case on May 17, 1954.[129]

Sometimes the author of the majority opinion in a Supreme Court case recommends policies or regulations to replace the law that is being struck down. Those policies and regulations sometimes are accepted as new law, if Congress or the state legislatures don't enact new laws to replace the law being struck down as unconstitutional.

A good example of this was the famous *Roe v. Wade* Supreme Court case of 1973. The law being challenged in that case was a Texas state law that banned all surgical abortions in the state with one exception: If the pregnancy threatened the life of the mother, or if the mother was likely to die during childbirth.

The Court ruled that the Texas law was unconstitutional because it violated an implied "right to privacy" contained in the due-process clause of the Fourteenth Amendment. But the Court went far beyond merely striking down the Texas law.

The majority opinion, written by Justice Harry

Blackmun, established legislative guidelines for each of three trimesters of pregnancy. It also classified a woman's right to choose to kill her unborn child as "fundamental," which required lower courts to evaluate challenges to state abortion laws using the "strict scrutiny" standard – the highest level of judicial review possible in our legal system.[130]

In a further act of judicial activism, in 1992, the Supreme Court, in *Planned Parenthood v. Casey,* set aside the trimester regulatory framework established by *Roe v. Wade* and created a new regulatory framework based on fetal "viability." The Court also overruled the *Roe v. Wade* requirement that state regulations regarding abortion be subject to the "strict scrutiny" standard.[131]

As the above examples show, legislating from the bench has become so common that most people have come to expect it and accept it.

Two justices in the *Roe v. Wade* case dissented from the majority opinion – William Rehnquist and Bryon White. The legal reasons for their dissent are never acknowledged or broadcast in the media or by pro-life politicians. Rehnquist's dissenting opinion is worth reading.[132]

Justice Rehnquist basically had four reasons for his dissent:

- He believed the Court should not be legislating from the bench;
- He did not believe the Fourteenth Amendment granted a "right to privacy;"
- He believed that an abortion is not a "private" act; and
- He believed that "While a party may vindicate his own constitutional rights, he may not seek vindication for the rights of others."

He cited numerous previous court cases to support his position.

Judicial Activism in Federal District and Appeals Courts

Keep in mind that the President of the United States also nominates federal judges to District and Appeals courts. Typically, between 150 and 200 judges are nominated and confirmed by the U.S. Senate during a four-year presidential term.[133]

There are 856 Article III federal judges that are appointed by the President – 677 District Court judges and 179 judges on the Circuit Courts of Appeal. In addition, there are 350 U.S. bankruptcy court judges, which are appointed by Circuit Court judges, and 579 Federal magistrate judges, which are appointed by District Court judges.[134]

As you can see, a President's views on how the Constitution should be interpreted, his views on the proper constitutional role of the judiciary and his views on the separation of powers between the three branches of government are extremely important. Those views continue to have influence in American society and culture far beyond the length of a President's four or eight years in office. They live on in the decisions of the federal judges he nominates – and in the rulings of the lower-court judges they appoint.

If you've been closely following the news during the Trump administration, you've probably heard about the Ninth Circuit Court of Appeals – previously the most liberal and the most-overruled federal circuit court in the United States. It's also the largest federal appellate court in the Country with 29 judges.

The Ninth Circuit has appellate jurisdiction over Alaska, Hawaii, California, Oregon, Washington, Nevada, Idaho and Montana. Sixteen of its judges were appointed by either Bill Clinton (9) or Barack Obama (7). The remaining 13 Judges were appointed by George W. Bush (3) and President Donald Trump (10).[135]

If federal judges have an activist view of the

Constitution, the rights guaranteed to all citizens by the Bill of Rights will always be in danger of being eroded or stripped away. Not only that, but the sovereignty and territorial integrity of the United States of America will be threatened by judges who favor globalism over nationalism … and who want to free criminals from prison and obliterate our nation's borders.

On the other hand, if federal judges believe in preserving and strengthening the constitutional republic created by the Founders, if they believe in the original meaning and intent of the Constitution and are committed to practicing judicial restraint, and if every Justice remains faithful to their sworn oath, then they will preserve and defend religious freedom, freedom of speech, freedom of assembly, freedom from unlawful searches and seizures … and the other rights, responsibilities and freedoms enumerated in the Constitution and its Bill of Rights.

It's very important, therefore, to find out what each presidential candidate in an election believes and supports regarding the Constitution, the role of the judiciary, how the separation of powers should be preserved, how the protections of the Bill of Rights will be preserved by the courts, and what type of judges and Supreme Court justices he or she will nominate for senate confirmation.

Put simply, your presidential vote is critical!

CHAPTER 11

Non-Negotiable #4: Protection of Israel

For Christians, one of the key non-negotiable issues is support for Israel.

The nation of Israel has been under attack by its enemies worldwide – particularly by the Arab and Muslim countries in the region, who want to see it destroyed.

In many parts of Europe and in other countries around the globe, an anti-Semitic, anti-Israel hostility has also been growing at an alarming rate.

A large majority of the United Nations has been antagonistic toward Israel for decades.

Under the Obama-Biden administration, the United States for the first time exhibited an anti-Israel, pro-Palestinian attitude and promoted policies that undermined Israel's sovereignty, territorial integrity and national security.

Why was the Obama policy toward Israel so

worrisome for Christians? And why is support for the nation of Israel so important to Christians?

The short answer is in Genesis 12:3, Where God makes a covenant with Abram and his descendants – The Nation of Israel, *"I will bless those who bless you, and whoever curses you I will curse ... and, all the people on earth will be blessed through you."*

In a very real way, blessing the nation of Israel is key to the peace and well-being of every other nation.

Thus, if we want God to bless the United States of America, we must bless and protect the nation of Israel.

Over the years, I have organized petition drives against the United Nations because of its anti-Israel policies and actions.

Israel in Prophecy and in History

Christians who take the time to read, and study to understand the Bible, learn that the Jews are a people who were chosen by God to have a special relationship with Him. Here are some of the reasons why Christians should support and bless the Jews and the Nation of Israel:

1. Abraham, the father of both the Jews and the Arabs, was given a special calling and a special blessing by God.

In Genesis 11:10, we learn that Abram – which means "exalted father" in Hebrew – was a descendant of Shem, one of Noah's three sons.

Abram grew up in Ur of the Chaldeans – a city in present-day Iraq.[136]

God appeared to Abram and said:

"Go forth from your country and from your relatives and from your father's house, to the land which I will show you; and I will make you a great nation, and I will bless you, and make your name great; and so you shall be a blessing; and I will bless those who bless you, and the one who curses you I will curse. And in you all the families of the earth will be blessed." (Genesis 12:1-3)

God made five promises to Abram:

1. *I will make you a great nation;*
2. *I will bless you;*
3. *I will make your name great;*
4. *I will curse those who curse you; and*
5. *You shall be a blessing to all people.*

Notice what God said about how others will be blessed or cursed depending on how they treat Abram and his descendants: *"...and I will bless those who bless you, and the one who curses you I will curse. And in you all the families of the earth will be blessed."*

2. God also promised Abram land where he and his descendants would live for generations.

Then God led Abram to the land of Canaan, which is between the Jordan River and the Mediterranean Sea:

"Abram took Sarai his wife and Lot his nephew ... and they set out for the land of Canaan; ... The Lord appeared to Abram and said, 'To your descendants I will give this land.'" (Genesis 12:5-7)

And God spoke to Abram again:

"Now lift up your eyes and look from the place where you are, northward and southward and eastward and westward; for all the land which you see, I will give it to you and to your descendants forever..." (Genesis 13)

A Brief History of the Land of Israel

The small area of land in the Middle-East that is modern-day Israel has always been central to events in Bible history and prophecy – as have the Jewish people to whom God gave the land some 2,500 years before the birth of Christ.

The nation of Israel, however, kept falling away from trusting in God and repeatedly fell into idol worship and followed the gods of the pagan tribes that had not been driven out of the Promised Land.

As a result of the Jew's disobedience, the prophets of God told His chosen people that they would be driven out of their land into exile – not once, but twice.

The first exile began in 606 B.C., when King Nebuchadnezzar of Babylon laid siege to Jerusalem, plundered Solomon's temple, and took the Jews back to Babylon as captive slaves.

After 70 years of captivity in Babylon, the Jews were allowed to return to their land and rebuild their temple in Jerusalem.

In 70 A.D., Titus – commander of the Roman army and the son of Emperor Vespasian – conquered Jerusalem for the second time and destroyed the Jewish temple so thoroughly that not one stone was left standing upon another.

If you've ever been to Jerusalem and have seen the excavated temple foundation stones, you know that they are huge, weighing eighty tons each![137]

Shortly before His crucifixion, Jesus predicted the destruction of the magnificent temple in Jerusalem:

"Jesus came out from the temple and was going away when His disciples came up to point out the temple buildings to Him. And He said to them, "Do you not see all these things? Truly I say to you, not one stone here will be left upon another, which will not be torn down." (Matthew 24:1-2)

When Titus sacked and destroyed Jerusalem and the Jewish temple, the nation of Israel ceased to exist. The Jews fled and scattered throughout the world, never to see their God-given land become a nation again until May 14, 1948.

What About the Palestinians?

The original "Palestinians" were people who lived in Judea – mostly Jews – during the reign of the Roman Emperor Hadrian in the second century A.D.

Here are eight facts you should know about the people called Palestinians and "Palestinian Refugees:"

1. 132 – 135 A.D. – The first Palestinian refugees were Jews who fled – or were deported – from

Judea by the Roman Emperor, Hadrian, during and after the Bar Kokhba revolt.

The Emperor tried to destroy the Jews and Judaism after the Bar Kokhba revolt was crushed. He renamed Judea and called it Palaestinia – from the root word Philistia – a reference to the Philistines.

As Jews fled from Palestine to the Arabian Peninsula and to North Africa, they were replaced by Romans and the Philistines.

Palestine did not become predominately Arab until after the fall of the Roman Empire.

2. Jews began returning to Palestine after the Balfour Declaration, in 1917.

The **Balfour Declaration** was a public statement issued by the British government during World War I, which announced support for the establishment of a "national home for the Jewish people" in Palestine.

At the time, Palestine was part of the Ottoman Empire and was about 90 percent Arab and only about five percent Jewish.[138]

3. After World War I ended, the League of Nations divided the defeated Ottoman Empire into entities called mandates ... intended to lead to the creation of nation states.

Britain received the mandate for Palestine, in 1919. At the time, Jews and Arabs were living together there in peace.

4. In 1947, the United Nations General Assembly passed a resolution to divide Palestine into Jewish and Arab states.

The Jewish state was to receive 56.47 percent of the land and the Arab state 43.53 percent.

Jerusalem was to be an international city. The Jews accepted the partitioning of Palestine, but the Arabs did not.

5. The Jewish state declared its independence on May 14, 1948 – the same day the British Mandate ended.

Israel's founders urged the Arabs living in Palestine to remain in the new Jewish state. Instead, Egypt, Syria, Iraq, Lebanon, Jordan and Saudi Arabia declared war on Israel, seeking to destroy it. An estimated 650,000 Arabs living in Israeli territory fled to Jordan and Syria.

6. The Arabs don't want peace with Israel. In response to Gamal Abdel Nasser, president of Egypt, blocking the Straits of Tiran to Israeli ships, they want the Jews dead.

In 1967, Israel and its Arab neighbors again went to war.

In just six days, the Israeli army defeated the Arab armies and retook Jerusalem for the first time since Roman Legions conquered the city in 70 A.D. It was truly a miraculous intervention by God.

Israel took control of the following territory:

- East Jerusalem and the West Bank – from Jordan;
- The Sinai Peninsula – from Egypt; and
- The Golan Heights – from Syria

After the decisive victory, Israeli General Moshe Dayan issued a statement guaranteeing Muslims full freedom of worship on the Temple Mount.

He said, "We've not come to conquer the holy place of others but to live with others in harmony."

Instead of accepting Moshe Dayan's offer – or negotiating with the Israeli government, the defeated Arab leaders gathered in Khartoum, Sudan, and announced the following:

- No recognition of the state of Israel;
- No peace with Israel; and
- No negotiation with Israel.

The official motto of Hamas – the terrorist group

ruling Gaza ... and currently attacking Israel on a regular basis by crossing the border illegally – is "We love death as much as the Jews love life."

How do you reach a peace agreement with a terrorist group that has such hatred for Israel and the Jews?

7. There is no moral equivalence between Israel and Palestinian terrorists.

The global media and pro-socialist politicians accuse Israel of shooting "unarmed protestors." But a mob of 30,000 people pushing through barricades and crossing the Gaza border into Israel– is a dangerous force and a threat to Israel's National Security.

They are not peaceful protestors.

And the Palestinians use children as shields for their mass border crossings and the sites from which they launch rockets and explosives into Israeli territory.

They also send young men and women to blow themselves up in Jewish markets and on Jewish buses.

The Israelis don't do such things. Former Israeli Prime Minister Golda Meir once said:

"We can forgive the Arabs for killing our children. We cannot forgive them for forcing us to kill their children. We will only have peace with the Arabs when they love

their children more than they hate us."

8. There has never been a "Palestinian State" in the region of Palestine other than the state of Israel.

The Palestinians never spoke about a Palestinian state when the West Bank was under Jordanian rule.

They only began talking about wanting a Palestinian state when the area came under Israeli rule.

The Palestinians don't want a two-state solution to their conflict with Israel. They want Israel to cease to exist. Palestinian Authority President Mahmoud Abbas continues to reject the idea of conducting peace talks with Israel.

Why? Because they want to destroy Israel and drive all the Jews into the Mediterranean Sea.

Senior PLO (Palestine Liberation Organization) official Ahmad Majdalani announced a "Day of Rage" against the nation of Israel, on May 14, 2018 – the day the United States moved its embassy from Tel Aviv to Jerusalem.

And Hamas leader Yahya Sinwar – speaking about planned activities along the Gaza border with Israel – declared: *"We will take down the border and tear out their hearts from their bodies."*

These terrorist leaders are the very same people, politicians, anti-Semites and the world's media support and celebrate.

Various Degrees of U.S. Support of Israel

Relations between the U.S. government and Israel have always been complicated due to the desire of some government officials to maintain friendly relations with the Arab states in the Middle East, and with the Palestinians.

When Israel's first Prime Minister, David Ben-Gurion, declared Israeli independence on May 14, 1948, none of President Harry Truman's national security advisors was in favor of the United States recognizing the new nation.[139]

They believed that U.S. recognition of Israel "would destroy our relationship with the Arabs and our position in the Middle East."[140]

President Truman, however, officially recognized the Jewish state.

The fear of an Arab backlash in response to declaring support for Israel has existed in every administration from Truman to Trump.

The primary reason for this is the false view that sees Israel is a problem rather than a partner.

There are three errors that career State Department and national security bureaucrats routinely make:

1. Cooperating with Israel will adversely affect our relationship with the Arabs;

2. Distancing ourselves from Israel will benefit our relationship with the Arabs; and

3. The region will never change for the better, unless the Israeli-Palestinian conflict is resolved.[141]

These misguided views have held sway at the State Department, the Department of Defense and in the intelligence community.[142]

Summary

The Israeli-Palestinian conflict is a Jewish-Arab struggle that began in the time of Abraham.

He had his first son with Hagar, his wife, Sarai's, Egyptian maid. That son, Ishmael, became the father of the Arab nations.

Isaac, his son born to his wife, Sarah, fulfilled God's promise. Isaac became the father of the Jewish people.

The long-standing animosity between Arabs and Jews was revealed to Sarai by an angel of the Lord in Genesis 16:11-12 before either son was born. Those who do not believe in God, and do not believe in the accuracy and truth of that Bible passage, will never understand the Jewish-Arab problem.

The Jews have always wanted to live in peace with their Arab half-brothers. The Arabs' political leaders have refused to live in peace with the Jews. They have rejected every Israeli and U.S. offer of a two-state solution, and campaigned instead for the destruction of the Jewish state.

The Israel – United Arab Emirates Normalization Agreement

On August 13, 2020, Israel and the United Arab Emirates (UAE) signed an agreement to normalize relations between the two countries.

Israeli Prime Minister Benjamin Netanyahu agreed to cancel plans to annex parts of the West Bank territory in exchange for the UAE formally recognizing the existence of Israel.

The UAE was the third Arab country to officially recognize the existence of Israel, in addition to Egypt and Jordan.

So, what is behind this peace deal?

The answer seems to be survival and security in the face of Shiite Iran's continued threat.

Iran's expansionism and its drive to develop nuclear weapons represent a grave danger to neighboring Arab Sunni Muslims.

The Israel – Bahrain Normalization Agreement

On September 11, 2020, President Trump announced an historic agreement to establish full diplomatic relations between Israel and Bahrain – the second such agreement between Israel and an Arab nation in less than one month.

Israel and Bahrain have committed to exchange embassies and ambassadors, start direct flights between their countries, and launch cooperation initiatives across a broad range of sectors.

The agreement is a significant step forward for both countries. It further enhances their security, while creating opportunities for them to deepen their economic ties.

The announcement comes on the heels of the historic normalization agreement between Israel and the United Arab Emirates. The United Arab Emirates and Bahrain are the first Arab nations to normalize relations with Israel in more than 25 years.

Conclusions

U.S. government leaders need to become students of the Bible and educate themselves about the complete history of the Jewish-Arab conflict. Only in that way will they be able to better understand the motives behind the actions and rhetoric of Israel's friends and enemies.

The United States can be a force for good internationally. U.S. leadership is vital in the Middle East – and especially in working toward a Jewish-Arab solution.

As a nation and as Christians, we must always encourage and support good behavior between nations and groups – and oppose evil.

This is the most compelling reason why we must demand that our government leaders – both elected and appointed – support Israel unequivocally.

And Finally ...

In my travels to Israel, I've always seen the Bible come alive in powerful ways.

If you haven't been to Israel – and if you can possibly go ... you can walk the streets of Jerusalem. See the place where Jesus was crucified. Visit the empty tomb where He arose from the dead in Glory! And go to the places we read about in the Bible, such as:

- The Upper Room;
- The courtyard where Jesus was flogged and where the Roman soldiers bartered for his clothes;
- The house of Caiaphas, the acting High Priest who tried Jesus and turned him over to Pontius Pilate, the Roman governor of Judea;
- The synagogue in Capernaum where Jesus taught;
- The home of Simon Peter, in Capernaum;
- The dish-shaped grassy hill above the Sea of Galilee, where Jesus delivered His Sermon on the Mount;
- The Mount of Olives and the Garden of Gethsemane; and
- The descent from the Mount of Olives to the

gate where Jesus made his triumphal entry into Jerusalem.

This is the country that the Palestinians, the anti-Semitic Arabs, the Ayatollahs in Iran and other enemies of Israel want to wipe off the face of the earth.

On one trip to Israel, my wife Shelly and I were traveling near the Golan Heights area and we saw smoke and fires burning in various locations. As tourists, we thought we were just seeing fires.

But instead, what we were witnessing was Israel being attacked by rockets launched from Syria. The missiles were starting fires where they landed inside Israeli territory.

The Israelis live in constant danger of terrorist missile attacks.

The United States must stand by Israel. We must oppose the destruction of the Jewish nation.

We must pray for the peace of Jerusalem. And we must ensure that our politicians are providing moral, political, economic and military aid to Israel to help her defend herself from her many enemies.

The recent move of our embassy from Tel Aviv to Jerusalem was historic. This should have happened years ago, but the fear of offending the Arab world prevented previous U.S. Presidents from acting.

Support for Israel is vitally important to all Christians. Voting for candidates who unequivocally support Israel and who oppose the hostile words and actions of the United Nations and all those who seek Israel's destruction is absolutely essential!

CHAPTER 12

Non-Negotiable #5: Helping the Persecuted Church

Around the world, Christians and other religious groups are experiencing historic persecution. And the coronavirus pandemic of 2020 has made it even worse.

What American politicians do can either reduce the amount and severity of persecution around the world, or indirectly cause it to increase. This is why helping the persecuted church is such a non-negotiable issue for Christians.

Let me give you a few examples of what is going on ...

In central India, Hindu extremists raped the four-year-old daughter of a pastor who refused to stop sharing the Gospel.[143]

A school principal in Pakistan kidnapped a 15-year-old Christian student and took her to an Islamic madrasa to forcibly convert her to Islam.[144]

In Indonesia, a Christian pastor was fined $3,565 and sentenced to four years in prison for sharing his faith with a Muslim taxi driver.[145]

In Mosul, Iraq, anti-Christian militants shot each member of a family of eight in the face, while they were sitting on the living room couch in their home, because they refused to convert from Christianity to Islam.[146] The terrorists left their open, blood-stained Bible on the couch.

In Syria, terrorists cut off the fingertips of a twelve-year-old boy in front of his father because the father refused to reject Christianity and convert to Islam. The terrorists then executed the boy, his father and two other Christian ministry workers by crucifying them in front of their relatives.[147]

In Libya, 12 Ethiopian Christians were beheaded on a beach and 16 more were shot in the head in the desert – all executed for refusing to recant their faith in Christ and convert to Islam.[148]

These are just a few of the thousands of incidents of persecution, torture and death being inflicted upon Christians and Christian churches around the world.

These atrocities should horrify every Christian and every evangelical Christian church in America.

But because of mass media indifference that causes

most of the Christian persecution in the world to not be reported, most Christians aren't even aware of the suffering endured by their brothers and sisters in Christ.

The Most Dangerous Countries for Christians

Open Doors USA is a Christian nonprofit organization that tracks and reports on the persecution of Christians around the world. Each year, it publishes the Open Doors World Watch List – a report and ranking of the 50 countries in which Christians suffer the most severe persecution for practicing their faith.

The ranking is based on six spheres of persecution and social pressure – with physical violence, including torture and death, being just one of them. The other spheres of pressure and persecution are:

- National life
- Community life
- Church life
- Family life
- Individual life

Combining all six spheres of persecution together, the

20 most dangerous countries for Christians to live in during 2020 are:

1. North Korea
2. Afghanistan
3. Somalia
4. Libya
5. Pakistan
6. Eritrea
7. Sudan
8. Yemen
9. Iran
10. India
11. Syria
12. Nigeria
13. Saudi Arabia
14. Maldives
15. Iraq
16. Egypt
17. Algeria
18. Uzbekistan
19. Myanmar (Burma)
20. Laos

In some countries – even those not in this year's top 20 – the escalation of persecution has been more rapid than in others. For example, China – which is currently #23 – could well be in the top five by next year.

Open Doors USA estimates that 260 million Christians are experiencing severe persecution in 2020 in the 50 countries on its Watch List.[149] This is a six percent increase over 2019.

Open Doors USA also estimates that between 90,000 and 100,000 Christians are killed every year because of their faith.[150]

That amounts to one Christian killed every six minutes of every hour of every day of every year.

Let's look at a few of these countries…

North Korea - #1

North Korea has been the number-one worst country for Christian persecution for 18 consecutive years! The country is a totalitarian police state run by an iron-fisted Kim Jong-un – the sadistic North Korean dictator – who controls every aspect of life in the country and demands worship of his family.

Some outside groups claim there are about 300,000 Christians out of a total population of about 26 million. If Christians are discovered, they are put in prison or slave-labor camps – or shot to death on the spot. More than 50,000 are currently incarcerated in North Korea's vast network of slave-labor concentration camps.

China (#23)

China is rapidly turning into a high-tech, George Orwell *1984*-style surveillance state, with massive control of everyone and intense persecution of Christians and other religious minorities.

There are already more than 500 million surveillance cameras in China, with the number expected to grow dramatically in the coming years. There are cameras in every church; and during the past year, hundreds of churches have been completely demolished.

The country has also developed facial recognition software as part of its new Social Credit System (SCS) which rewards, "good citizenship" actions and punishes "bad citizenship" behavior that is deemed to be insufficiently "Chinese."[151] Bad behavior includes going to church and being a Christian.

A facial scan is now required before a cell phone and many other products can be purchased in China.

In 2019, there were 5,576 government-approved attacks against Christian churches in China – a huge increase from 171 the year before.[152] In addition to having crosses removed and church buildings destroyed, other forms of persecution include:

- Online sales of Bibles are banned.

- The Bible is rewritten to include communist propaganda.
- Worship and other church activities are only permitted in government-approved church facilities. No home Bible studies are allowed.
- Pastors are often jailed, sent to concentration camps or executed.
- Landlords are ordered by government officials to cancel rental contracts with churches.
- Christians and church leaders are monitored.
- Teachers and medical staff are forced to sign documents saying they have no religious faith.
- Elderly Christians are told their pensions will be cut if they don't renounce Christianity.
- Children under the age of 18 are forbidden from attending church.

The Three-Self Patriotic Movement

The Chinese Communist Party controls all churches and religious facilities in China through the Three-Self Patriotic Movement (TSPM) – a communist party and government controlled protestant organization designed to keep Chinese Christians patriotic, which means keeping them loyal to the Chinese Communist Party.

The three "Selfs" are self-governance, self-support and self-propagation. The TSPM rejects foreign influence on church leadership, foreign financing and foreign missionaries. Protestant churches in China must register with and be members of the TSPM to legally exist.[153] The 60,000 churches that belong to the TSPM are called Three-Self churches.

The Three-Self Patriotic Movement twists and stifles true Christianity by burying it under a myriad of social rules that serve the interests of the Communist Party. Three-Self churches face the following restrictions:[154]

- The Communist Party decides how many Christians can be baptized per year;
- The Communist Party has the final authority to decide who can preach and what can be preached;
- Preaching about the resurrection of Jesus is forbidden;
- Preaching about the second coming of Jesus is forbidden;
- Preaching against abortion is forbidden;

- Preaching against religions that deny the deity of Jesus is forbidden;
- Preaching cannot deny that all good communists go to heaven;
- Pastors can only preach at the Three-Self church to which they are assigned;
- Worshipping outside Three Self churches or other official "meeting points" is forbidden;
- Importing Bibles or printing Bibles is forbidden even if they are given away for free;
- Evangelizing or giving out tracts is forbidden;
- Government officials, police officers, soldiers and teachers cannot be Christians; and
- No one can become a Christian or be baptized until the age of 18.

Because of these restrictions on religious freedom, millions of Chinese Christians have gone "underground" and are meeting and worshipping in illegal house churches.

If a pastor or a congregation is found to be violating any of the TSPM rules for churches, the pastor is subject to arrest and severe punishment, and the church building is subject to destruction.

In October 2019, a 3,000 seat Three-Self church auditorium in Anhui province was demolished by a large excavator, while church members watched helplessly. Government officials detained the two church pastors for "gathering a crowd to disturb the social order."[155]

Summer Olympics Scare

Let me tell you about what my wife, Shelly, experienced when she went to Beijing to attend the 2008 Summer Olympics, and smuggled a suitcase full of Bibles into the country.

She knew she was risking possible arrest and detention. She knew the Chinese government could monitor who she talked to, and that every taxi driver she rode with could potentially turn her over to government agents for proselytizing. It was intense. It's a police state.

When she got to her hotel and opened her luggage, the suitcase of Bibles wasn't there! Instead, she had picked up the suitcase of a college student who had gone to the United States for school and was returning to Beijing. There was a church bulletin in the student's suitcase.

I received a call from her at 2:00 a.m. "What do I do?"

she asked with a panicked voice. I told her to go back to the airport and see if her suitcase was still there, and to check if she could exchange the student's suitcase for her own.

She got into a taxi and went back to the airport. Her suitcase – the one full of Bibles – was still there! She put down the student's suitcase, grabbed her suitcase and left. She was then able to distribute the Bibles to very grateful people during the Olympics, without further incident.

But there is no true religious freedom in China – only government controlling suppression and persecution.

India (#10)

With 1.3 billion people, India has been described as the largest democracy in the world. But the country is anything but a democracy, where religious liberty is concerned. Instead, it has become an oppressive regime that acts vigorously against freedom of conscience, religion and speech.

The government of India is also making plans to introduce a national facial-recognition system which could easily be used to target Christians.

In the 2020 Open Doors World Watch List reporting

period, there were at least 447 verified incidents of violence and hate crimes committed against Christians in India.[156]

The dominant political party in India is the Bharatiya Janata Party (BJP) – also called the Hindu Nationalist Party. Members of this group believe India should be united under:

- One religion – Hindu
- One language – Hindi
- One culture – Hinduism

Since Prime Minister Narendra Modi – a member of the BJP – took over the country, in 2014, thousands of non-governmental charitable organizations have been shut down – including World Vision and church ministries from the United States. Religious conversion activities have been banned. Christians and Muslims are treated as second-class citizens – and worse.

Hindu extremists committed acts of violence against more than 50,000 Christians in 2018.[157] The crimes included beatings, murders, assaults, rapes, detentions, harassments, hate crimes and social boycotts.

In one instance, Hindus in Bihar forced their way into

a Sunday church service and told worshippers, “We will not allow this foreign religion in our country, and if you continue we will kill you.”[158] When the police were called, they took the side of the Hindus and ransacked the pastor’s home.

In the Eastern region of Orissa, a Christian man who refused to deny Christ and become a Hindu was doused with gasoline, set on fire and burned alive.[159]

In March 2020, a pastor and a group of about 30 Christian youths from the Viluppuram Church of South India were helping the poor in a nearby village. After their presence was noticed, they were harassed and beaten by members of the Hindu Munnani extremist group. When the Christians called the police for help, the police took them into custody instead of their attackers.[160]

After verbally abusing the Christian group at the police station, the police commander released the detainees, and warned them never to return to that village again. The pastor of the church said his congregation had been providing grain, clothing and flashlights to the poor in that village for the past three years. But no more.

Some estimates report that churches are burned or pastors beaten 10 times per week in India. In spite of the ongoing persecution and hardship, the churches continue to grow. Pastor Samuel, a Christian worker in

India, gives this account:

"It's amazing. The Spirit of the Lord is working in the minds and hearts of the people ... When the church meets for prayer, worship and Bible study, miracles happen. People are receiving the Gospel of Christ and asking Christ to come into their lives. More and more people are coming every week. Even amid this difficult situation, Christians are sharing their faith with their neighbors."[161]

Myanmar (Burma) (#19)

Myanmar is a predominately Buddhist country of 53 million people in Southeast Asia. It is bordered by India and Bangladesh on the west, Laos and Thailand on the east, China on the north, and the Bay of Bengal and the Andaman Sea on the south. The country has both Christian and Muslim minority populations – both of which are heavily persecuted by the Burmese Army.

The Burmese government officially recognizes 135 distinct ethnic groups.[162] Most of the four million Christians in Mayanmar – or about eight percent of the population – belong to the Chin and the Kayin (also known as Karen) ethnic groups.

The Karen people have a long history of following

Christ and sharing the Gospel. Their story – along with the amazing tales of other cultures and ethnic groups – is told in the book, *Eternity in Their Hearts*.[163] This book shares the amazing accounts of how God, through His love, sovereignty and mercy, has enabled ethnic groups all over the world to understand the meaning of the Gospel, without it being available to them in written form.

One of several groups not recognized by the government is the Rohingya – a predominately Muslim population living in Rakhine State. The Rohingya have suffered devastating persecution and human rights violations at the hands of the Burmese Army – including summary executions, rape, arbitrary arrests and detention, torture and forced labor.

Since 2015, more than 900,000 of the approximately 1.3 million Rohingya have been driven out of Myanmar and into southeastern Bangladesh[164], with the remaining population subjected to, what has been described by the United Nations as, ethnic cleansing.[165]

Thousands of Christians have also fled the country to enter Thailand and China. More than 100,000 Christians and 100,000 Muslims live as refugees in Burmese Internal Displaced Persons (IDP) camps.

The major persecutors of Christians in Myanmar are Buddhist monks, working in cooperation with government officials and the Burmese Army. Since 2011, the military has burned more than 400 villages and 300 churches, and displaced more than 130,000 Christians in Kachin State – where the Karen people live.[166] Buddhist monks have invaded church properties and built shrines and temples next to church buildings.

Iraq (#15)

Before ISIS moved into Iraq and began murdering Christians, in 2014, there were about 1.5 million believers living in the country.[167] More than one million of them were either massacred or forced to flee for their lives.

Mosul, the third-largest city in Iraq and the capital of Nineveh province, saw its Christian population of 15,000 reduced to 40 people.[168]

ISIS militants marked Christian homes and businesses with the Arabic letter "N" - representing Nazarene or Nasrani, the Arabic word for Christian.

Christians were given four options: leave, convert to Islam, pay a "Jizya" tax or be killed. Thousands fled and had their possessions stolen or destroyed. Those who couldn't flee or who chose to stay were forced to convert, or were sexually abused, sold into slavery, tortured or beheaded.

One park in Mosul was filled with the heads of beheaded children that were impaled on stakes and driven into the ground.

A 14-year-old Yazidi girl who escaped after being taken captive by ISIS jihadists, said she had been raped every day and had attempted to kill herself. Another refugee told of his brother-in-law being crucified in front of the man's wife and children. His executioners told him that if he loved Jesus that much, he would die like Jesus.[169]

The city of Qaraqosh, once home to 60,000 people – many of them Chaldean or Syrian Christians – was turned into a mass grave.

Many Christian churches in Iraq were turned into mosques or warehouses.

An 1,800-year-old church in Mosul was torched, and other historic churches, landmarks and manuscripts were burned or bulldozed. Destroying evidence of Christian history is one of the tactics terrorists use to obliterate Christianity, to keep people of faith living in fear and to make them forget their Christian heritage.

The Gatestone Institute – a nonprofit, nonpartisan international policy council and think tank – wrote, "This cultural genocide, thanks to the indifference of Europeans and many Western Christians more worried about not appearing 'Islamophobic' than defending their own brothers, [has] sadly worked."[170]

There are 6 major radical Islamic groups according to Voice of the Martyrs. They include:

- Al Shabab
- Boko Haram
- al Qaeda
- Muslim Brotherhood
- ISIS
- Taliban

These groups have persecuted Christians from Afghanistan to Kenya to Libya.[171]

Europe

All across Europe there is a movement to permanently remove Christianity from public life. The Gatestone Institute International Policy reports that about 3,000 acts of violence, looting and property damage – largely unreported in the media – occurred across Europe in 2019.[172]

The spike in anti-Christian attacks in France and Germany corresponds to the recent open-borders mass immigration from Muslim countries. In Spain, the attacks are being spearheaded predominately by anarchists, radical feminists and other left-wing activists.

Documented acts of hostility include:

- vandalism
- arson
- defecation
- desecration
- looting and theft
- urination
- tagging using profanity and slogans representative of Satanism

In France, Christian churches, schools, cemeteries and monuments are being vandalized, desecrated and burned at the rate of three per day. In Germany, Christian churches are being attacked at the rate of two per day.

Jerome Fourquet – political analyst and author of *The French Archipelago* – noted that there is “a growing de-Christianization, which is leading to the 'terminal phase' of the Catholic religion ... For hundreds of years, the Catholic religion profoundly structured the collective conscience of French society. Today this society is the shadow of what it once was. A great civilizational change is underway."[173]

Why is Helping the Persecuted Church a Non-Negotiable Issue?

Religious freedom is the most basic and fundamental of the "unalienable rights" granted to us by God – next to the right to life itself.

It's why the early groups of settlers made the dangerous journey across the Atlantic Ocean: to escape from religious persecution in Europe. And it's why the United States of America was founded: to form a more perfect union and a nation where all people could speak freely and worship freely according to their beliefs and consciences. And, without fear of reprisals, punishment or persecution.

Because religious freedom is so important to all Americans – and because it's a right given to all by God and not by government – it should be a universal human right recognized by every country on the globe, not just by the United States of America. Religious persecution denies the God-given right to religious freedom.

Thus, our government should do everything in its power to foster religious freedom around the world and work to end religious persecution.

This is why helping the persecuted church – and helping all persecuted religious groups – is a non-negotiable issue for Christians. Every elected government official should be outspoken and active in supporting religious freedom and stopping all governments around the world from engaging in religious persecution.

What does this look like in terms of practical action by elected and appointed government leaders?

First, they should absolutely stand up for and support the human rights of all people and all groups of people. And they should speak out against ALL violations of human rights, regardless of whose human rights are being violated and regardless of who is violating those rights.

Political considerations should have nothing to do with our nation's protective actions in support of human rights. Nor should such things prevent our government from condemning violations of human rights – whether they are being conducted by a government, an agency of a government or by a rebel group or terrorist organization.

As Christians, we are commanded to love our neighbors as ourselves:

"You shall not hate your fellow countryman in your heart; you may surely reprove your neighbor, but shall not incur sin because of him. You shall not take vengeance, nor bear any grudge against the sons of your people, but you shall love your neighbor as yourself. I am the Lord. (Leviticus 19:17-18)

When one of the Pharisees – a lawyer – asked Jesus which was the greatest commandment in the Mosaic Law, he answered:

"You shall love the Lord your God with all your heart and with all your soul and with all your mind. This is the great and foremost commandment. And a second is like it, 'You shall love your neighbor as yourself.'" (Matthew 22:37-39)

Our neighbor may be a close friend, or it may be our worst enemy.[174]

Second, the reason our government leaders – and all Christians – should be especially supportive and helpful to persecuted Christians and to the persecuted Church is because of the doctrine of the Church as the body of Christ. The body of Christ concept is explained in 1 Corinthians 12:

"For even as the body is one and yet has many members,

and all the members of the body, though they are many, are one body, so also is Christ. For by one Spirit we were all baptized into one body, whether Jews or Greeks, whether slaves or free, and we were all made to drink of one Spirit. For the body is not one member, but many…

"But now God has placed the members, each one of them, in the body, just as He desired. And if they were all one member, where would the body be? But now there are many members, but one body. And the eye cannot say to the hand, 'I have no need of you;' or again the head to the feet, 'I have no need of you.' On the contrary, it is much truer that the members of the body which seem to be weaker are necessary; and those members of the body which we deem less honorable, on those we bestow more abundant honor… But God has so composed the body, giving more abundant honor to that member which lacked, that there should be no division in the body, ***but that the members should have the same care for one another.***

"And if one member suffers, all the members suffer with it; if one member is honored, all the members rejoice with it." *(1 Corinthians 12:12-14, 18-26 – emphasis added)*

The true church – the ekklesia, the "called out ones" – is comprised of believers in Christ from all over the world. How Christians are treated in other parts of the world actually affects the spiritual and emotional health of Christians here in the U.S.

How the U.S. is Helping Persecuted Christians

Article II Section 3 of the U.S. Constitution calls for the President of the United States to take the lead in establishing the foreign policy for the nation.

He can make treaties with foreign governments, with the approval of two-thirds of the Senate, and he can nominate and appoint ambassadors "by and with the advice and consent of the Senate."

In order to promote religious freedom around the world as a foreign policy objective, the International Religious Freedom Act of 1998 was created by Congress and signed into law by President Bill Clinton. The purposes of the legislation were:

- To promote religious freedom as an official foreign policy of the U.S. government;
- To promote greater religious freedom in countries which engage in or tolerate violations of religious freedom; and
- To advocate on behalf of individuals who are being persecuted for their religious beliefs.

Three government entities were created as a result of

the Act:

1. The Ambassador-at-Large for International Religious Freedom within the Department of State;

2. A bipartisan U.S. Commission on International Religious Freedom to provide policy, recommendations and independent fact-finding; and

3. A Special Advisor on International Religious Freedom within the National Security Council

On July 26, 2017, President Trump nominated Sam Brownback – Governor of Kansas at the time – as the fifth Ambassador-at-Large for International Religious Freedom.

For the first time since the passage of the International Religious Freedom Act of 1998, the U.S. government has both a Secretary of State – Mike Pompeo – and an Ambassador-at-Large for International Religious Freedom – Sam Brownback – who believe protecting religious freedom should be a top priority in U.S. foreign relations. And both President Trump and Vice President Pence agree.

On September 23, 2019, President Donald Trump gave a moving speech on religious freedom before the U.N. General Assembly. He said:

"The United States is founded on the principle that our rights do not come from government; they come from God. This immortal truth is proclaimed in our Declaration of Independence and enshrined in the First Amendment to our Constitution's Bill of rights. Our founders understood that no right is more fundamental to a peaceful, prosperous and virtuous society than the right to follow one's religious convictions."

"Regrettably, the religious freedom enjoyed by American citizens is rare in the world. Approximately 80 percent of the world's population lives in countries where *religious* liberty is threatened, restricted or even banned."

"Today with one clear voice, the United States of America calls upon the nations of the world to end religious persecution, to stop the crimes against people of faith, release prisoners of conscience, repeal laws restricting freedom of religion and belief, protect the vulnerable, the defenseless and the oppressed."[175]

Secretary of State Mike Pompeo believes religious freedom is "a right belonging to every individual on the globe."[176] He also says the United States is ready to stand with all those who yearn for religious liberty.

Moreover, he says, "Where fundamental freedoms of religion, expression, press, and peaceful assembly are under attack, we find conflict, instability, and terrorism. On the other hand, governments and societies that champion these freedoms are more secure, stable, and peaceful."[177]

In 2018, Secretary Pompeo initiated an annual event at the State Department called "Ministerial to Advance Religious Freedom." I was invited to attend this event in 2018 and again in 2019. It was historic.

More than 350 world leaders from over 80 countries gathered, in 2018, to hear about horrific examples of religious persecution that are affecting 5.5 billion people – 80 percent of the world's population. The 2019 event was attended by more than 1,000 delegates from 100 countries.[178]

The purpose of this annual event – largely ignored by the mainstream media – is to encourage all countries around the world to respect and honor religious freedom.

Andrew Brunson and the Pence Doctrine

Pastor Andrew Brunson is a missionary – originally from North Carolina – who spent 23 years pastoring a church in Izmir, Turkey. It was attended by both Turks and Kurds – who have been battling each other over Kurdish autonomy and statehood since 1978.[179]

But when people come to Christ, ethnic strife and

conflict disappears.

The combination of Turks and Kurds worshipping and fellowshipping together in the same evangelical congregation didn't sit well with the Turkish government.

Brunson was arrested, in October 2016, and was incarcerated in Turkish prisons for 18 months – without being interrogated, without being given a court hearing and without even being informed of the charges against him. He was held for months in solitary confinement and then transferred to an overcrowded cell with 20 inmates.

During this time, his wife wrote him letters every day, but he didn't receive them. He missed one daughter's wedding and another daughter's graduation. He was allowed no visitors, and only was permitted to speak to his wife by phone through a prison glass window for 35 minutes once per week.

When he was finally brought to court in April 2018, he learned that he had been accused of supporting and colluding with the Kurdistan Worker's Party – known as the PKK – a Kurdish terrorist group that the Turkish government blames for the attempted military coup against President Recep Erdogan in 2016 – it was a coup d'etat that some in the United States intelligence community think was staged by President Erdogan himself to expose his opponents in the Turkish government and military.

There is no evidence of any kind suggesting the charges against Brunson were justified.[180] Nevertheless, the prosecutors wanted him sentenced to 35 years in prison.

President Trump, Vice President Pence, Secretary of State Pompeo, and Ambassador Sam Brownback worked tirelessly to secure Pastor Brunson's release. The U.S. government leveraged its relations with a NATO ally to stand up for religious liberty – and for one persecuted and falsely imprisoned Christian pastor.

In a special State Department briefing, in July 2018, Vice President Pence announced what I call "The Pence Doctrine." He said that U.S. foreign and military aid would be withheld from any country that did not protect the religious freedom of minority religious groups.

When the Turkish president tried to turn negotiations for the release of Pastor Brunson into a hostage negotiation by demanding in exchange the extradition of U.S. Islamic cleric Fethullah Gulen – whom Turkey blames for the "coup attempt" against the Turkish government, in 2016 – President Trump refused.

Instead of agreeing to hostage diplomacy, he sanctioned Turkey's Minister of Justice and Minister of the Interior, freezing their U.S. assets.

Then he imposed economic sanctions and tariffs on Turkey and encouraged Americans to boycott Turkish Airlines and travel to Turkey until Pastor Brunson was freed.

The Turkish currency immediately fell by fourteen percent against the U.S. dollar, plunging the Turkish economy into chaos.

Pastor Brunson was suddenly and unexpectedly released on October 12, 2018, after being convicted and sentenced to three years in prison. He was brought back to the United States in a military aircraft and was welcomed home by President Trump in a special ceremony in the Oval Office.

How You Can Help Persecuted Christians

This brings us to the "bottom line" of how we can help the persecuted church and persecuted Christians. Help needs to be given to persecuted believers not only from the top echelons of our government, but also from all Christians in America.

One example of how government leaders and Christians can work together to help a persecuted Christian occurred, in 2014, in the case of Meriam

Ibrahim, a Christian mom in Sudan.

She was arrested when she was eight months pregnant with her second child and was accused of apostasy from Islam because she had married a Christian man – which is forbidden under Sharia law. When she refused to renounce her Christian faith, she was sentenced to death by hanging.[181]

While in prison, the Koran was read to her every day in an attempt to convert her to Islam. She was also forced to give birth to her baby girl while shackled to the floor.

President Obama and Secretary of State John Kerry did very little to try to help free her.

I started a petition drive with the subscribers of my online newsletter, *Reality Alert*. Many of my subscribers signed the petition and agreed to pray for Ibrahim's release.

Because of our petition, our actions with key members of Congress, and the prayers of many Christians, Ibrahim and her baby were finally freed after an 18-month ordeal.

Meriam Ibrahim, her husband Daniel Wani and their two children are now living in a Sudanese community in the U.S.[182]

President Trump and Vice President Pence have probably done more to promote religious liberty and to help persecuted Christians and churches in the United States and around the world than any President and Vice President since the early days of our republic. But they didn't appoint themselves to their high positions, or take over the U.S. government by force. They were elected by "we the people."

The President then appointed Mike Pompeo – a conservative Christian – as Secretary of State, and Sam Brownback – another conservative Christian – as Ambassador-at-Large for International Religious Freedom. And thankfully, the U.S. Senate confirmed those nominations.

But it all starts with us – with individual Christian citizens.

There are two practical things we as Christians can do to help the persecuted Christians and churches around the world:

1. Pray.

Pray for our leaders – for wisdom, integrity and discernment; that they will seek guidance from the Lord; And, that they will stand up for their convictions and not waver or cave in under pressure.

Pray also for our fellow believers who are suffering

physical, mental and emotional harassment, abuse, torture and even death for their faith in Christ.

"Remember the prisoners, as though in prison with them, and those who are ill-treated, since you yourselves also are in the body." (Hebrews 13:3)

2. Share.

Share what you've learned about the Christian worldview with your family and Christian friends. Share the non-negotiable issues for Christian voters. Give copies of this book to family members and friends, or pass your copy on to someone else.

Be a thermostat, not a thermometer! A thermostat controls and changes the temperature of the surrounding environment. A thermometer doesn't change or influence anything. It merely measures the environment and records the existing temperature.

Be an influencer in your world.

CHAPTER 13

Non-Negotiable #6: Protecting Tax Exemption for Churches

One of the key non-negotiable issues for Christians is protecting the tax exemption of churches.

A Christian should not vote for any candidate who will not support preserving the tax exemption for churches and church ministries.

Why?

Because removing the federal tax exemptions for churches would permanently damage thousands of churches in America. Some churches would close their doors and disappear. Most others would have to downsize their ministries due to the tax burden.

As Supreme Court Chief Justice John Marshall said in the famous McCulloch v. Maryland case, in 1819, "The power to tax involves the power to destroy."[183]

The Johnson Amendment

In 1954, Texas U.S. Senator Lyndon B. Johnson was running for re-election. He had won the Democrat primary for his first term, in 1948, in a run-off election by a razor-thin margin of 87 votes out of almost a million votes cast. Many historians believe his victory had been secured by at least two hundred fraudulent ballots that had been certified as valid by an election judge.[184]

During his re-election campaign, Senator Johnson found himself being heavily criticized by Christians, churches and other nonprofit organizations in Texas.

Some churches and Christian ministries were undermining his efforts to expand the power of the federal government. Johnson wanted to shut them down.

Almost secretly, he proposed an amendment to the final version of H.R. 8300 – a bill revising the Internal Revenue Code portion of the U.S. Code (U.S.C.). He also saw to it that the amendment was given no publicity, and there was no debate on the amendment in either the House of Representatives or the Senate.

The amendment revised paragraph (3) of subsection (c) in section 501 of Title 26 of the U.S.C. – which defines organizations that are exempt from federal income tax.

The amendment, which came to be known as the "Johnson Amendment," – effectively prohibits 501(c)(3) organizations – such as churches and Christian groups – from endorsing or opposing political candidates, and from participating in political campaign activities, including fundraising.

Ever since the Johnson Amendment became a part of the Internal Revenue Code, it has often been used by the IRS to silence pastors and churches from speaking out on the biblical principles that pertain to political issues.

Many pastors feared that if they said anything about where political candidates stand currently on issues that are clearly addressed in Scripture, their churches would have their tax-exempt status revoked by the IRS.

Churches have historically acted as the social conscience of the country. But for the past 55 years, they have been silent.

Every election cycle, secular and liberal Christian groups send letters – often registered letters – to evangelical pastors across the nation, warning them that if they voiced any endorsement or opposition to a political candidate or ideology, they would be reported to the IRS as having violated the Johnson Amendment.

Americans United for Separation of Church and State, the ACLU and other far-left organizations have acted as watchdogs over pastors and churches, using threatening letters and other intimidation tactics in their adamant insistence on silencing Christians and clergy in the political arena.

The stifling effect on culture and politics of trying to silence the most powerful voices for Christianity in the political arena recently started to boil over. Some bold evangelical pastors and ministry leaders decided they had had enough of the Johnson Amendment and began speaking out … ignoring the law and in effect daring the IRS to initiate enforcement action against them.

Unexpectedly, the IRS ignored purported violations of the Johnson Amendment when pastors and others raised serious questions about the constitutionally of the amendment itself.

In fact, the Johnson Amendment violates both the freedom of speech and the free exercise clauses of the First Amendment. Why Christian leaders and churches shirked their God-given responsibility to speak God's word concerning every area of life and thought – and failed to sue the IRS for violating the First Amendment – remains a mystery.

Donald Trump and the Johnson Amendment

Before the 2016 presidential election, my wife and I were invited to a special meeting of evangelical Christian leaders throughout the United States. At first it was supposed to be a small meeting of about 50 people. Then I was told it would be a hundred.

Eventually I got a call saying there would be 700 evangelical leaders in attendance. Among them were well-known leaders such as:

- James Dobson;
- Tony Perkins;
- Greg Laurie;
- David Jeremiah;
- Franklin Graham;
- Jack Graham

I was sitting at a table with the pastor of a mega-church in Florida – a famous Christian author, a nationwide radio minister and a televangelist.

In this special meeting, about one-third of the audience was against Donald Trump, about one-third was for him and about one-third was still undecided.

As we sat waiting for Donald Trump to appear, we had no idea what he was going to say or how he was going to try to encourage us to support him.

When he came out, Mr. Trump stunned the audience by saying that one of the first things he would do as President of the United States would be to abolish the Johnson Amendment.

For a moment, there was silence in the room. Everyone looked around at everyone else in shock.

And then, the entire audience stood up spontaneously and gave a thunderous standing ovation for about three minutes.

In his remarks, Mr. Trump said he would put an end to the censorship of pastors in America. Everyone could hardly believe what we were hearing.

No presidential candidate and no nationally influential politician had ever pledged to rescind the free speech restrictions of the Johnson Amendment. Donald Trump was the first.

He went on to talk about abortion, religious liberty, the persecuted church and much more. But his promise to stop the IRS from enforcing the Johnson Amendment against churches, Christians and religious organizations was one of the first pledges he fulfilled after he was inaugurated as President.

Because he didn't have the necessary congressional support to officially remove the Johnson Amendment restrictions from the IRS tax code, he wrote an executive order directing the IRS to cease any enforcement actions against churches or other nonprofits for violating those restrictions.

Churches are now free to talk about political and cultural issues. Pastors are free to say whom they endorse for different elected positions and why. Ministries are now free to inform their donors about their political positions on any issue.

Pro-socialist politicians and the mainstream media were enraged when President Trump issued his executive order. They attacked him and claimed it violated the separation of church and state. They called for the Johnson Amendment to be re-established and strictly enforced.

Tax Exemption and Compelling Governmental Interests

On May 24, 1983, the Supreme Court ruled 8-1 that the establishment and free exercise of religion clauses of the First Amendment do not prohibit the IRS from revoking the tax-exempt status of a religious organization whose practices are contrary to a "compelling governmental interest."

Do you see a potential problem here? As cultural and moral standards change, biblical teachings that are now acceptable under the free-exercise clause of the First Amendment may soon become unlawful due to a "compelling governmental interest" – which can be anything the Supreme Court says it is.

Christian nonprofits – including churches – are now on the slippery slope of being at the mercy of the next "compelling government interest" that conflicts with their sincerely held religious beliefs.

For example, now that the Supreme Court has ruled that same-sex couples have a constitutional "right" to marriage, one leader of a pro-traditional-family Christian organization says, "Already, some are calling for the ending of tax-exempt status for churches, religious-affiliated schools of all kinds, and nonprofits in general if they do not actively make accommodations for same-sex partners."[185]

Tax Exemptions for Churches Are Not Subsidies

Those who oppose church tax exemptions argue – among other things – they amount to government sponsorship of religion – or represent a government subsidy of religion.

The sponsorship argument was put to rest by the

1970 Supreme Court ruling in *Walz v. Tax Commission of the City of New York*. Chief Justice Warren Burger wrote for the majority that "the grant of a tax exemption is not sponsorship since the government does not transfer part of its revenue to churches but simply abstains from demanding that the church support the state."[186]

Walz was a pivotal case not only in establishing the precedent of tax exemption for churches, but also in preventing religious institutions from becoming entangled with the state.

In describing the importance of the ruling, Georgetown University's Berkeley Center for Religion, Peace, and World Affairs wrote:

"...the purpose of the exemptions was not to advance or inhibit religion; the exemptions were available to a broad class of institutions the state found desirable, including hospitals, libraries, playgrounds, scientific, professional, historical, and patriotic groups. After examining the long history in the United States of exempting religious institutions from taxation, the Court determined that the exemption has not resulted in the excessive entanglement of religion and the government. In fact, the Court found, taxing religious property could increase government entanglement by giving rise to tax valuation of church property, tax liens, and tax foreclosures. Further, demanding that religious

institutions support the government by paying taxes would also create entanglement."[187]

With respect to the subsidy argument, Richard Albert Mohler, Jr. – president of the Southern Baptist Theological Seminary in Louisville, Kentucky – says the *Walz* case determined that a "*subsidy would be the transfer of tax money to institutions. That's not what's going on here ... Rather, the tax exemption is granted with respect to institutions the government does not feel that it has the right to tax on the one hand and on the other hand, institutions that it believes are essential to the Commonwealth and to the commonweal, to the well-functioning of society.*"[188]

Taxation in the Bible

The Bible has much to say about taxation – the principles of taxation, the procedures of taxation and the purposes of taxation.

A detailed analysis of all three aspects of taxation is beyond the scope of this book. However some general principles will be of help in understanding the necessity of preserving tax exemption for the church.

The first truth every Christian should understand about taxation in general is that it represents a claim of both sovereignty and ownership over the entity being taxed. The easiest way to see this is to think about the consequences of not paying taxes.

If an individual or a business refuses to pay the taxes levied by the government, the government has the power to deny the individual or business the sovereign use of their property.

In extreme cases of tax evasion, individuals can be put in jail, which denies them sovereignty and control over their lives and their liberty.

Businesses can be shut down by the government, depriving them of sovereignty over their assets and operation.

Taxation is also a claim of ownership – it's the means by which government claims prior ownership over all that a person has.

For example, if a homeowner refuses to pay the property tax on his home, the state can confiscate it and sell it to others who are willing to pay the taxes demanded by the state. Likewise, if people refuse to pay their income taxes, the government can confiscate their wages or sell their property to pay their taxes.

Taxation in any society creates an absolute distinction between the Ruler of the society and the ruled within the society.[189]

In the Bible, the "Ruler" – the Sovereign, the Creator, the Lord – is God. The ruled, of course, are the human beings God has created. The Bible, therefore, treats every individual as a steward of his or her life and property, not the owner.

The Creator is the Owner and the Sovereign.
The individual merely takes care of the life and property with which he or she has been entrusted, and develops them according to the wishes and instructions of the sovereign.

This realization gives new meaning to this familiar passage from the Book of Psalms in the Old Testament:

"The earth is the Lord's and all it contains; the world, and those who dwell in it." (Psalm 24:1)

For this reason, even though the Levites collected the required taxes in Jewish society in the Old Testament, they were paid to God. Taxes were intended to be a reminder to the people that God had a prior claim on all that they were, all that they had and all that they did.

Reasons for Tax Exemptions for Churches

The taxation of churches in America would eventually

destroy the free exercise of religion and the First Amendment, which guarantees that freedom.

As we saw earlier in this chapter, in the famous 1819 *McCulloch v. Maryland* Supreme Court case, Chief Justice John Marshall wrote: "The power to tax involves the power to destroy."[190] Exempting churches from taxation protects churches from potential destruction by protecting them from government – the state.

On the other hand, giving government the authority to tax the church not only would breach the protective "wall of separation" that guards the church from government intrusion, it would tear down that wall.

Eliminating tax exemptions for churches would also amount to taxing free speech. The Congressional Joint Committee on Taxation has said:

"With respect to other nonprofit organizations, such as charities, tax-exempt status is not classified as a tax expenditure because the nonbusiness activities of such organizations generally must predominate and their unrelated business activities are subject to tax. As such, subjecting churches to taxation would be the opposite of a tax expenditure and would be, instead, a tax penalty for creating an organization to be a church. In other words, a tax on free assembly, free religion, and free speech. This would be, in essence, a 'Bill of Rights Tax.'"[191]

Tax exemptions for churches result in benefits to local communities – and to society at large – which are often overlooked or ignored.

Here are three ways churches provide social benefits to society:

1. Ministries to the broken and hurting.

Churches minister to the poor and needy in communities and provide numerous social services to the downtrodden – and they provide these services much more cheaply than the government ever could. Some of these services include:

- Mental health services;
- Substance abuse counseling;
- Health care;
- Auto replacement for needy families;
- "Clothes closets";
- English language classes;
- Assistance for military families;
- Sexual abuse counseling;
- Pregnancy care;

- Pornography addiction counseling;
- Personal and family counseling;
- Community recreational services;
- Premarital and Marriage counseling;
- Help for people with disabilities;
- Meals and food services;
- Employment workshops;
- Mentorship for students;
- Camps for inner-city youth;
- Disaster relief;
- Homeless shelters;
- Community clean-up services;
- Legal aid;
- Literacy programs;
- Care for seniors and shut-ins

2. Unseen but powerful benefits.

These are benefits that can't be measured in dollars,

such as:

- Reduced crime rates resulting from transformed lives;
- Suicides prevented when troubled people give their lives to Christ; and
- Destructive behavior patterns changed into productive behaviors that contribute to the well-being of the community.

3. Alternatives to wasteful, bureaucratic government programs.

The above-mentioned practical services provided by churches reduce overall government costs by relieving government of a portion of its taxpayer-financed programs.

Subjecting churches to taxation would cripple those services and increase the burden on government.

While some politicians favor a complete state-controlled takeover of all local social services, the results would not be pretty.

Rob Schwarzwalder, of Family Research Council, pulls no punches when he says, "State-run charity has been a colossal failure, increasing rates of poverty, corroding education, eviscerating families, encouraging massive intergenerational dependency."[192]

Conclusion

Everyone who is a Christian should take a stand to protect America's churches and our First Amendment rights of free speech and freedom of religious expression.

There are three ways Christians can do this:

1. Register to vote ... and vote!

2. Vote only for congressional candidates who agree that churches and religious ministries should not be subjected to taxation and control by the government.

In selecting among candidates who all support tax exemptions for churches and ministries, choose candidates who recognize the important roles churches play in being a positive influence on society.

Also choose candidates who understand that taxing churches in any way would create an entanglement between the state and the church that must never be tolerated.

3. Encourage pastors to understand that they can

preach about culture and politics without fear of losing their tax-exempt status.

Let them know that they ***can*** distribute a voter guide in church. They ***can*** mobilize their congregation. They ***can*** speak out on social issues from a biblical perspective.

They must not remain silent as they have in the past.

CHAPTER 14

Non-Negotiable #7: Protection of Homeschooling and Christian Schools

Another non-negotiable for Christians is the protection of homeschooling and Christian schools.

Across America, the education of children has never been more controversial.

Withering attacks are being launched constantly against:

- Home schools;
- Protestant, Catholic and other Christian schools; and
- Charter schools.

The opposition has been fierce.

Much of the controversy over privately funded education has been around for years. But it has sparked into a new battle because of the coronavirus pandemic.

The education bureaucrats, the politicians and the pro-socialist teachers' unions – including the National Education Association – have closed down the public schools and have used the pandemic as a means to try to stifle parents from turning to alternative forms of education.

Despite the opposition, the number of parents turning to home schooling has boomed, and the number of parents wanting to send their children to a private or Christian school has never been greater.

In addition, charter schools – another alternative to the government-controlled public school system – has never been more important.

This is why the protection of homeschooling and Christian schools is such an important and non-negotiable issue for Christians.

When we vote for candidates to serve on school boards, city councils, county and state and national offices – including representatives to both houses of Congress and President – we should ask ourselves, "where do these candidates stand on the protection of homeschools and Christian schools?"

Christians must be united in voting for candidates who will protect and expand choice and educational freedom for parents and children. Parents should have as many options as possible in choosing the best education for their children.

You'd think that everyone would be in favor of school choice, since children have different personalities and different learning styles. Unfortunately, this is almost never the case.

It turns out that many politicians, bureaucrats, education administrators and teachers' unions believe that all school age children should be required to attend government-funded, government-controlled schools, and that there should be no other education options available.

They are very adamant and passionate about this. They oppose homeschooling, they oppose Protestant and Catholic schools. They even oppose charter schools.

Why?

Because government bureaucracy is all about power, money and control.

Those who control the education bureaucracy wield the most power over education because they determine how much power is dispensed – by whom and to whom.

This means that whoever controls education controls America's youth and the future. And that's what those who oppose school choice want to maintain. They want power and control now – and they want more power and control in the future.

There hasn't always been a massive government education bureaucracy in America. It is a relatively new phenomenon that began growing in the late-19th century and has expanded steadily ever since. Each state now has its own department of education.

Federal involvement and control increased substantially when the cabinet-level Department of Education was created by President Jimmy Carter, in 1979.

The Pilgrims and the Puritans who came to America in the 1600s believed that education was a parental responsibility.

The parental responsibility for education comes across loud and clear in the Amplified Bible translation of Deuteronomy 6:4-7.

"Hear, O Israel: the Lord our God is one Lord – the only Lord. And you shall love the Lord your God with all your mind and heart, and with your entire being, and with all your might. And these words, which I am commanding you this day, shall be first in your own mind and heart. Then you shall whet and sharpen them, so as to make them penetrate, and teach and impress them diligently upon the minds and hearts of your

children, and shall talk of them when you sit in your house, and when you walk by the way, and when you lie down and when you rise up."

Now you may think that this command applies only to parents teaching their children about God and about spiritual truths. But remember the words of Proverbs 1:7.

"The reverent and worshipful fear of the Lord is the beginning and the principal and choice part of knowledge – that is, its starting point and its essence; but fools despise skillful and godly wisdom, instruction and discipline." (Amplified Bible)

We mentioned in an earlier chapter that ALL truth is God's truth. Students may be able to learn the process and mechanical operations of mathematics – and facts about science and the scientific method of analysis. But no one can fully understand or appreciate any subject area of knowledge apart from that which God reveals to mankind.

Another verse about parental training and education of their children is a little-understood verse in Proverbs:

"Train up a child in the way he should go [and in keeping with his individual gift or bent], and when he is old he will not depart from it."
(Proverbs 22:6, Amplified Bible)

Many Christians believe this verse is only talking about training children in the way they should go spiritually: to believe in and trust in the Lord and to follow His will for their lives. But as you can see from the Amplified translation, it's actually talking about training each child according to his natural "bent" – according to his individual learning patterns, his unique skills and interests, and his unique personality.

Every child is unique and different from other children. Children aren't all "wired" to learn from the same teaching methods or at the same rate.

Who, better than a child's parents, knows his or her unique and individual learning characteristics? It is probably not a public school teacher – who must cater to the needs of 30 different students, while trying to teach the same curriculum at the same speed to all of them at the same time!

There's no doubt that some public school teachers have amazing insights into the individual differences of their students, and many do a great job of adapting their teaching style to accommodate those differences.

But with rare exceptions, they are no match for the parents who have raised their children from birth and have seen them grow and develop in different ways with different personalities and learning capabilities.

Dads and moms are equally important in educating

children. King Solomon had much to say about their roles as teachers in the Book of Proverbs:

"My son observe the commandment of your father, and do not forsake the teaching of your mother. Bind them continually on your heart; tie them around your neck. When you walk about, they will guide you; when you sleep, they will watch over you; and when you awake, they will talk to you." (Proverbs 6:20-22)

Education in Colonial America

In the early days of the British colonies in America, the primary places where the education of children occurred were the home, the local church building or a community location.

In 1635, the town leaders of Boston saw the need to hire a schoolmaster "for the teaching and nurturing of children with us."[193] They were concerned that the religious fervor of the first generation of Pilgrims was waning.

Both the Boston Latin Grammar School and Harvard College opened the following year.

In 1647, Massachusetts mandated that towns of 50 or more families provide instruction in reading and writing, and that communities of more than 100 families provide grammar schools to prepare young boys for entry into Harvard College.[194] Other colonies adopted a more laissez-faire approach to education until after the American Revolution.

As early as the 1750s, the Deism and Agnosticism of the Enlightenment sweeping across Europe began to drift across the Atlantic and cause a gradual shift in thinking among social elites and educators in America.

Previously, the primary purpose of education had been the teaching of reading, writing and the spiritual development of the individual.

This primary goal of education began to subside, and it was replaced by an emphasis on more "practical" learning. Other deistic ideas also began to seep into educational philosophy and curriculum, such as:

- God is impersonal (Deism) rather than personal (Theism);
- God doesn't intervene in human affairs;
- Miracles and supernatural revelations don't happen;
- The Bible is not the infallible word of God to man; and
- At birth, every person's mind is like a blank slate (John Locke's philosophy). There is no human sin nature (Psalm 51:5, 58:3).[195]

Highlights of Public School Education in the United States

The public or common-school movement in the United States began in earnest, in 1837, when Horace Mann – a Massachusetts lawyer and state legislator – became the secretary of the newly formed State Board of Education for the Commonwealth of Massachusetts. Mann believed that:

- Education is the absolute right of every child;
- Political stability and social harmony are dependent on universal education;
- Schools should be nonsectarian and available to all children;
- The security and prosperity of property owners depended on having educated and law-abiding neighbors, who would respect the sanctity of private property because of their common-school education.

Mann believed in the moral teachings of Christianity, but not in the existence of miracles or the deity of Jesus Christ. He believed mankind is inherently good and that religious faith and values should be taught at home, not in school.

Mann's liberal views regarding educational philosophy, methodology and curriculum began spreading to other states. By about 1875, most education was under state control and most religious and private schools had gone out of business. Only the Mennonites and the Quakers (Religious Society of Friends) maintained their own private school systems.

Most of the teachers and administrators of the newly emerging public schools of the 19th century were still committed to Christianity.

However, a gradual but steady shift towards the tenets of Deism began to take place, and by the early 20th century, Humanism – with its emphasis on evolution – replaced Deism as the official "religion" of the public school system.

Humanism[196] has become more and more entrenched in the educational philosophy, the teaching methodology and in the curriculum of the public schools over the past century. Some of the factors and events that have contributed to and accelerated this trend have included:

- The shift from an emphasis on individual learning to group learning, introduced by John Dewey in the early 1900s.
- The Scopes Trial (*The State of Tennessee v. John Thomas Scopes*), in 1925, and the resulting influence of Charles Darwin's theory of evolution by natural selection on public school curriculum.

- The outlawing of public school prayer and Bible reading by the U.S. Supreme Court, in 1963.

Problems with the Government-Run School Monopoly

The government-controlled public school system in America today is rife with serious problems. We will cover several of them here:

1. Limited or no parental control

Sending your children to government-run public schools that are "free" means you have no control over their physical safety, let alone the ideologies and values they are taught.

I served on the Oversight Committee of my local school board. While the board gave the public appearance that we were to make independent decisions, it was clear that our activity and our decisions were guided by the school administrators, school district administration and the education bureaucracy.

Whenever I would object to different policies, my objections were usually overridden without consideration or debate.

The school board basically took orders from the school administrators – the so-called education experts.

Many public school teachers have the attitude that they need to protect themselves and their teacher colleagues from parental input –and from parental attempts to assert their lawful authority to have influence and control over the education of their own children.

2. Corrupted teaching focus.

The focus in public schools today is on TEACHING TO THE TEST. For years, public schools have engaged in widespread standardized testing. To make matters worse, in several states, teachers and administrators have unlawfully and corruptly manipulated scores to secure funding and future employment. Grace Chen, writing in Public School Review, said, "Educators feel that their school's reputation, their livelihoods, their psychic meaning in life is (sic) at stake."[197]

Why do teachers feel this pressure? Because test scores are often linked to career paths, bonuses and funding. Standardized tests have become less about checking student progress and more about funding schools. Do we ever ask ourselves why public schools test students two-thirds of the way through the year? If the tests show students are below grade level, that doesn't leave enough time to fix the problem.

3. Predatory teachers.

A shocking case study of five geographically and demographically diverse school districts across the United States estimated that 10 percent of K-12 public school students will be victims of sexual misconduct by a teacher or other school employee before they graduate from high school.[198]

When you consider that there were approximately 50 million students enrolled in elementary and secondary public schools in 2019,[199] that is a huge number of sexually abused students!

Sexual-predator teachers in the government-run public schools are often protected by tenure, which makes it almost impossible to fire them. And even if they could be fired, teachers' unions often ignore the complaints of sexual misconduct or defend the predators regardless of their behavior.[200]

4. Bloated budgets and bureaucracies.

Large public school districts have huge, bureaucratic administrative staffs. Instead of spending the lion's share of the district budget on the children and teachers, it goes toward a bloated administration and bureaucracy. This often causes shortages in supplies, furnishings and even basic maintenance of the school building and grounds.

5. Political indoctrination.

Many teachers use their classrooms to indoctrinate students in their political and social views – without giving any alternative or opposing views or encouraging children to think critically for themselves and develop their own beliefs.

Parents and grandparents are often completely shocked when they find out what their children are being taught about sex in school.

In some schools, children as young as kindergarteners are being told to think about whether they feel more like a girl or a boy.

Children are even being read and shown propaganda in elementary school claiming that homosexuality and lesbianism are natural and okay.

In 2018, at Rocklin Gateway Academy in California, Kaelin Swaney was named "Teacher of the Year" after she taught kindergarteners a story about a transgender child.[201]

Instead of being fired and prosecuted for child abuse, she was actually applauded for teaching inclusivity.

Another type of anti-Christian, brain-washing taking place across America is new teacher training in what is called Critical Race Theory.

This false, divisive, and dangerous "theory" is absolutely mind-boggling:

- Its central claim is that racism exists everywhere in white America. All whites are inherently racist. They are born racist; they will always be racist and there is nothing they can ever do to eradicate their racism.[202]
- Facts, logic, and the scientific method of acquiring knowledge are examples of white supremacy and racism and should not be taught in public schools.
  What this means is that facts are irrelevant and what matters is a person's group identity and level of victimhood. In other words, the greater number of oppressed groups a person belongs to, the more seriously that person's words and emotions must be taken.
- Knowledge is gained through storytelling and through one's personal experiences.
- Owning property is another sign of white supremacy. Children must be taught that individual property ownership is evil, and all property should be publicly owned.
- Capitalism is the evil basis of white supremacy and should be abolished and replaced with Marxist socialism – in other words, communism.

This could be the future of public, government-controlled and taxpayer-financed education in America.

When asked recently about "Critical Race Theory," U.S. Attorney General William Barr did not mince words:

"If you want to find systemic racism in America," he said, "then look no further than the public school system, which is maintained by the Democratic Party and the teachers' unions."

Barr slammed "the entire system (that) keeps inner-city kids in failing schools, instead of putting the resources in the hands of the parents to choose the schools to send their kids to."

"And people talk about implicit racism or systemic racism. That's empowering kids," he continued. "That's giving them a future."

"Now, a lot of the liberals will buy themselves out of that," he added. "They will go to resort towns and so forth, and they will escape the consequences of it. But the people in the inner cities won't. Their lives will be destroyed. They won't have the opportunity they otherwise would have. Their schools will be overrun by gangs," he concluded. "That's not caring about black lives."

6. Lack of conservative voices on school issues.

The collapse of cultural and moral standards has flooded our country with anti-Christian, anti-conservative attacks on America's traditional values.

- Anti-American, Anti-God and racist ideologies must be exposed as a pack of lies and stopped.

Today's government-controlled education monopoly has converted teachers into political partisans, intent on turning students into radical social activists.

This has been especially evident during the media hysteria over so-called climate change and the socialist Green New Deal. More and more students have been participating in marches and rallies – and shouting slogans and even giving speeches on issues about which they are completely ignorant.

Teachers and administrators have also encouraged students to engage in leftist radical activism on such issues as:

- Immigration;
- The COVID-19 pandemic;
- Welfare; and
- Income redistribution.

7. Intimidation and discrimination.

There is a concerted effort on the part of many public school teachers and administrators to silence Christians.

Christian students who are "outed" are mocked and ridiculed. Those who dare to speak up about their faith in Jesus Christ are sometimes punished by having their grades lowered.

It's a horrific and uncomfortable situation for Christian students in many of the public schools today.

8. Lack of Money is the Problem: Not! The Great Society in Action

National, state and local teachers unions, school administrators, a vast statewide education bureaucracy, other public-sector unions, office-holders beholden to teachers unions for heavy campaign contributions in the next election cycle, every Big Government, vote buying, special-interest group – and even most teachers themselves – will tell you with a straight face that the disasters that have been the government-run, public school monopolies in major cities have all failed because of insufficient funding and inadequate resources.

Yes. That's the story you will hear in almost every city and school district (large and small) in America.

It's all about the money. If only you stingy taxpayers would shell out a little bit more cash, the kids in our schools would be getting a great education and passing all those standardized achievements tests with flying colors.

There is only one problem with that compelling story: It's not true.

According to the National Center for Education Statistics, in 2016, the United States spent $13,600 per full-time student on elementary and secondary education, which was 39 percent higher than the average of OECD member countries (in constant 2018 U.S. dollars).

And at the post-secondary level, the United States spent $31,600 per student, which was 95 percent higher than the average of OECD countries – the nations with the world's largest economies.

The Baltimore, Maryland, Public School System is a striking example of the disconnect that exists between well-intentioned financial inputs and educational outputs in America's largest cities. Government-run schools have become a virtual pipeline to prison, poverty and despair for many in the African American population.

And here's the shocker.

According to the U.S. Census Bureau, Baltimore Public Schools were among the biggest spenders in the United States on a per-student basis, coming in third among the 100 largest school systems during fiscal year 2017.

In fact, Baltimore schools spent $16,184 per pupil, while national per-pupil spending for the rest of us stood at a paltry $12,201 for public elementary-secondary education.

And what did all that big spending in Baltimore's government-run education monopoly produce?

For that same fiscal year – 2017 – state testing showed that one-third of the 39 public high schools in Baltimore had zero students proficient in math. And in another six high schools, only one percent were proficient. In all, of the 3,804 Baltimore students who took Maryland's state test, 14 were proficient in math.

9. The Collapse of Traditional Families

Author and the William E. Simon fellow at the Manhattan Institute, Kay S. Hymowitz, argues that America's widely reported marriage crisis has been especially devastating to low-income and black Americans. Specifically, she says "entrenched, multigenerational poverty is largely black, and it is intricately intertwined with the collapse of the nuclear family in the inner city."

So, when did the traditional black family in America starts to disintegrate, what caused it and how has it led to a crisis of failure, resentment, and despair in inner city schools, neighborhoods, cultural institutions and even churches from Baltimore to Detroit and Miami to Los Angeles?

10. The War on Poverty Gone Wrong.

Many Christians, Libertarians and conservatives believe it began with President Johnson's ambitious, tax-and-big-spending program known as the Great Society. The stated goal of the Great Society was nothing less than the total elimination of poverty and racial injustice – a deeply ironic objective coming from Lyndon Johnson, a man who made no secret of his racist views to close friends and political allies in Texas and Washington, D.C.

In 1964, Johnson launched his "War on Poverty" – declaring the war would be waged "not only to relieve the symptom of poverty, but to cure it and, above all, to prevent it."

For some, the money pumped into the economy was a huge windfall. But for those at the bottom, the results were mixed. Especially hard-hit was the traditional black family, which had been remarkably stable for most of the preceding century. Less than a year into the War on Poverty, in 1965, for example, only 24 percent of black children were born to unwed mothers. By 2018, more than 70 percent of births among African Americans were to single mothers. Today, the percentage tops 85 percent in some of the most impoverished areas in the country.

Socialists have a well-earned reputation for caring about and focusing on having good intentions, and not so much about actual results.

Whatever good intentions that well-meaning people may have had for supporting Johnson's Great Society, which marked the beginning of " the welfare state" in capitalist America, few could have imagined the devastating effect it would have on the black family's unifying, stabilizing and positive contributions to American culture, scientific and educational advancement, economic prosperity, and religious heritage.

Perhaps more than any factor affecting a child's prospects for achieving educational success in America's black communities today – and for becoming a productive and successful citizen – is growing up in a loving, intact family with a mother and father who are caregivers, protectors and exemplary Christians.

We should all pray for revival in America, ask God to heal our land, bless and guide our mayors, school board members, principals, teachers, and school workers, strengthen our faith in His power to comfort those who are broken and open our hearts to helping students in need and ministering to them in word and deed.

The Politics of Public Education and the Coronavirus Pandemic

As of this writing, pro-socialist state governors, mayors, school district bureaucracies and teachers' unions across America are holding public education – and the children the system is supposed to serve – hostage to the COVID-19 pandemic.

Activist teachers say they are afraid to go back to the classroom because of the remote chance they might catch Covid-9 from an infected student.

Never mind that 99.8 percent of people who contract the virus in the United States recover fully from it. They say the risk is still too high.

School district administrators and bureaucrats are using the pandemic to make far-reaching financial and political demands on federal and state government agencies before they will agree to reopen the schools.

They are following the advice of President Obama's Chief of Staff Rahm Emanuel: "Never let a Serious Crisis Go to Waste."

In California, for example, the United Teachers' Los Angeles (UTLA) union released a document titled, "The Same Storm, but Different Boats: The Safe and Equitable Conditions for Starting LAUSD in 2020-2021."[203]

The list of non-educational demands in this so-called education document is breathtaking:

- They want the police defunded throughout the state of California;
- They are demanding single-payer, government-provided health care;
- They want full funding for housing California's homeless population;
- They want publicly funded, privately operated charter schools shut down; and
- They want a new set of programs to address "systemic racism."[204]

To pay for this outrageous laundry list of statewide demands, the union is demanding:

- A one percent wealth tax on California's billionaires;
- A 3.3 percent surtax on millionaires;
- Increased property taxes on businesses; and
- $250 million from the federal government.

The Big Labor Bosses and teachers unions don't care that keeping the schools closed and mandating that children take online classes at home is doing irreparable emotional and psychological damage, not only to the children, but also to their parents and entire families.

Online "classes" are a poor substitute for classrooms where students interact with teachers and other students.

Poor children, who are less likely to have educated parents and access to the internet, lag behind their better-off peers.

Children who can't go to school are more likely to suffer abuse at home. And those who depend on the school nutrition program to provide their breakfast and lunch are in danger of suffering malnutrition and mental health challenges.[205]

Child abuse has also surged since most child abuse is discovered and reported in schools.

Advantages of Christian and Home Schools

Because of the extended public school closures caused by the COVID-19 pandemic, homeschooling and startups of small, private Christian schools have skyrocketed.

Here are some of the advantages Christian schools

and homeschools have over government-controlled schools:

1. Children can be kept safer in a Christian school or a home-based school.

Social distancing and other health and safety precautions are much easier to implement in a home than in a large classroom.

2. Subject matter is determined by parents, not by state or district education bureaucrats.

Parents should be able to decide at what age it's appropriate to introduce their children to complex and controversial social issues.

As their children's primary teachers, parents have the right and the responsibility to protect them from exposure to social issues, ideologies, social apps, television, radio and other media that promote things that the parents believe is not appropriate.

Christianity teaches us to love all people, and that all people are created in the image of God.

However, this does not mean we have to agree with transgenderism or other radical cultural changes that conflict with our religious or philosophical views. Nor does it mean we want others to discuss these controversial issues with our children.

As Christians, we have the constitutional right to decide what our children are exposed to and when. Parents – not government - must direct the upbringing of our children, including education and religious beliefs.[206]

3. Parents and Christian schools have a wide range of outstanding curriculum choices.

Parents who are homeschooling – and Christian schools – have an opportunity to use a God-centered curriculum rather than one that is centered on humanism and secular ideologies.

Parents have the right to choose how their children are educated and what they are taught. This is true for Christians, Buddhists, Jews, Muslims, and other faiths.

The data for structured homeschooling support using a published, professionally organized curriculum. According to a study conducted by Martin-Chang & Gould, *The Impact of Schooling on Academic Achievement, 2011*:

*"When the homeschooled group was divided into those who were taught from organized lesson plans (structured homeschoolers) and those who were not (unstructured homeschoolers), the data showed **structured homeschooled children achieved higher standardized scores compared with children attending public school.**"*[207]

4. Christian schools and homeschools are much more likely to have Christian teachers who teach a biblical worldview.

While there are Christian teachers in public schools across the United States, they are not permitted to teach a biblical worldview to their students.

By contrast, in Christian schools and homeschools, children can be taught that God is the source of all truth.

They can teach that God created everything that exists, and that all things have a purpose in God's universe.

They can teach that God created language and that He created math and science. And they can teach that history is His story.

I was in the district that probably has some of the best public schools in Tennessee. But even there – in a conservative state – the public school teachers are not conservative.

Even though Christian culture still dominates much of the politics and society in Tennessee, many of the public school teachers are not Christians.

5. Homeschool associations and conventions help parents and provide socialization for students.

When parents decide to homeschool their children, they aren't "left out in the cold" to fend for themselves.

Lots of help is available.[208] Homeschool associations in all states provide a substantial body of printed and online education resources for parent-teachers – and group activities for students, such as physical education and sports programs, science fairs, music camps and other activities.

I spoke with to one mother in Tennessee who told me that, since the public schools were closed and possibly not going to reopen in the fall, she and her husband began praying about what to do for their school-age children.

As they were praying, they both began to feel that God wanted them to send their kids to a Christian school.

They were hesitant, because they weren't sure they could afford to do it. But they both believed that God wanted them to send their children to a Christian school.

As she was telling me her story, she said the Lord revealed to her that the Christian school He wanted for their children was a homeschool.

She told me she was afraid because she had never thought about homeschooling before. But she was determined to do it.

The good news for her – and for other parents like her – is that with the abundance of high-quality homeschool curricula available, and with the local homeschool associations in every state and in many counties within each state, there are lots of resources, help and support available.

Why Do Some People Want to Ban Christian and Homeschools?

Some politicians, judges and other people want to ban homeschooling at the state level and the support for public education.

In many states – such as California – socialist politicians run on a platform of getting rid of homeschools. To achieve that objective, powerful groups and individuals pour millions of dollars into statewide and local elections.

Originally, the fight against homeschooling was based on the mistaken view that a child wouldn't develop properly either socially or academically if they were taught without being in the presence of other children.

No evidence has ever been produced to support that. In fact, the opposite is true.

In 2016, Brian Ray – a researcher from the National Home Education Research Institute (NHERI) – evaluated SAT test scores from students who were taught in different settings and found the following:

"The SAT 2014 test scores of college-bound homeschool students were higher than the national average of all college-bound seniors that same year. Some 13,549 homeschool seniors had the following mean scores: 567 in critical reading, 521 in mathematics, and 535 in writing (College Board, 2014a). The mean SAT scores for all college-bound seniors in 2014 were 497 in critical reading, 513 in mathematics, and 487 in writing (College Board, 2014b). The homeschool students' SAT scores were 0.61 standard deviation *higher in reading, 0.26 standard deviation higher in mathematics, and 0.42 standard deviation higher in writing than those of all college-bound seniors taking the SAT, and these are notably large differences ...* **Test scores of homeschool students are higher than the national average for all students."**[209]

Another objection to Christian education has been the focus on whether in a Christian school or homeschool teaching creation science rather than Darwinian evolution.

Perhaps the strongest and most descriptive example of the religious fervor of Humanism was an article that appeared in the Jan/Feb 1983 issue of *Humanist*

Magazine. Humanist author and "evangelist" John Dunphy said this:

"I am convinced that the battle for humankind's future must be waged and won in the public school classroom by teachers who correctly perceive their role as the proselytizers of a new faith: a religion of humanity that recognizes and respects the spark of what theologians call divinity in every human being. These teachers must embody the same selfless dedication as the most rabid fundamentalist preachers, for they will be ministers of another sort, utilizing a classroom instead of a pulpit to convey humanist values in whatever subject they teach, regardless of the educational level . . . . The classroom must and will become an arena of conflict between the old and the new ... the rotting corpse of Christianity, together with all its adjacent evils and misery, and the new faith of humanism..."[210]

This was a declaration of war. Our children are under attack in their public school classrooms day in and day out, yet many parents do not even know that a war is under way! When parents do show concern about this danger, what they usually hear from educators is denial and ridicule. Despite the denials, consider the evidence that humanism is indeed the predominant philosophy of modern public education.

Another disturbing perception about homeschooling comes from a Harvard Law professor, Elizabeth

Bartholet, who states, "…many homeschooling parents are extreme ideologues, committed to raising their children in evangelical Christian 'belief systems'." She goes on to say it's dangerous, "because society may not have the chance to teach them values important to the larger community, such as tolerance of other people's views and values."[211]

By making this statement, Bartholet is revealing her intolerance for Christians. Would she express the same hostility to a Muslim or Jewish parent choosing curriculum based on their faith? Who defines what an "extreme religious ideologue" is? Is it someone who doesn't agree with her views and values regarding the teachings of Christianity?

What is truly dangerous is for Ms. Bartholet's to be making such hateful statements dressed up as facts. As a Harvard lawyer, she is using her status to bully those with steadfast Christian beliefs.

Sound morals, values and beliefs are usually instilled in young people by their parents. We cannot allow anti-Christian intellectuals to trample on our First Amendment Rights.

Principles for Success
Educational Achievement, Religious Liberty and Wisdom from God

- Loving parents or guardians are a child's first

and most important caregiver, teacher, protector and counselor – and they have the lead role and responsibility for their education.

- Competition among schools or other settings to encourage and reward outstanding teachers and student performance is essential to driving innovation, progress and superior results.
- State funding for education should go to the parent(s) or guardian(s) of each student for use at the learning environment of their choice, including homeschooling, career and technical education, private or parochial schools, magnet schools, charter schools, online learning and other options at their discretion.
- Education is the process by which parents, families and communities give to the next generation knowledge, skills, ethical, behavioral and spiritual values, norms, codes of conduct and traditions.
- Every child's ability to succeed in school should be based on his or her God-given talent, motivation and perseverance - not an address, zip code or economic status.
- Archaic tenure practices should be replaced with a merit-based system that will attract and retain the best, most talented and exemplary teachers to the school.
- Everyone who interacts with school children must pass rigorous background checks and be held to the highest standards of integrity and

personal conduct.

- Every student who attends a school or interacts with teachers, administrators or other students must enjoy all rights to which he or she is entitled as set forth in the U.S. Constitution and Bill of Rights.
- No child or parent should be deprived of any right guaranteed by the U.S. Constitution, including the right to the free exercise of religion, except by due process of law.

So, What Should We Do?

How do we provide the best education for our children?

Above all, parents must be given the freedom to choose the type of education that is the best "fit" for each of their children.

This means that we must:

1. Support and fight for school-choice laws at the federal, state and local levels; the children – not the school – should get the education money and they can decide which school choice is best for their family;

2. Only vote for candidates, including judges, who support school choices;

3. Only vote for candidates, including judges, who will protect and vote for homeschools, private schools, Christian schools and charter schools; and

4. Work within your local community to bring about school choice initiatives.

We must fight for Christian homeschooling and private Christian schools, if we are to protect the future for our children and our young people. On her blog page – Why on Earth Homeschool? – Rebecca Devitt sums up our responsibility:

"Homeschooling is important when we want to move beyond damage control of bullying and sexual harassment to developing sound moral principles and talents in our children. Homeschooling allows children to develop their own creativity and not be stifled by mass education." [212]

If we want to preserve the future and growth of Christianity in America, those of us who are parents must commit ourselves to instilling biblical Christian values the lives of our children and grandchildren. This is a call to Christian parents and grandparents.

We should also demand that families that choose homeschooling or private schools to educate their children receive the same per-child funding and constitutional protections provided to their public school peers by the United States Constitution.

CHAPTER 15

It's Time for Pastors to Take Action

Up to this point in the book, we have laid out the case for Christians to be active participants in the civic life of the local communities where they live and work.

We've given a brief overview of the history of the interconnection between Christian revival and political activism in America.

And we have explained what a biblical worldview comprises. We have also shown why Christians should judge political candidates on seven key non-negotiable issues when determining whom to vote for in local and national elections.

We come now to the application – the translation into concrete actions – of everything we've talked about up to this point. It's important that we think about – and come up with action items – for each of the following questions:

- How can we be salt and light in an increasingly hostile post-Christian culture?

- How can we apply biblical principles and biblical truths to every area of thought and life – including government and politics?
- How can we influence and help bring about positive change in our culture and politics that reflect only the best qualities and principles that prevail at our nation's founding?

In the final three chapters of this book, we will address what pastors can do, what churches can do and what individual Christians can do.

Equipping the Saints for the Work of Service

Pastors have a daunting task: equipping Christians for the work of service, for the purpose of building up the body of Christ (Ephesians 4:12). They cannot do this without the supernatural power and grace given to them by the Holy Spirit.

If you are a pastor reading this book, I take my hat off to you. I appreciate the work you do and the services you perform – which are basically around-the-clock, 24/7, without a break.

You should serve and teach and mentor and minister to a wide variety of personalities from all walks of life and from every possible family background and personal situation. And you must do your all to bring them together in Christian love and fellowship.

Jesus faced similar challenges with His disciples. He had to forge unity and a spirit of acceptance and teamwork out of:

- The brashness and assertiveness of Peter;
- The competitiveness and the bickering of James and John, the sons of Zebedee;
- The reputation of Matthew – a hated tax collector for the Roman government;
- The whining and complaining of Judas and his "non-essential" and wasteful spending on goods; and
- The skepticism of Thomas.

And Jesus only had 12 in his "congregation." Most pastors in today's churches have a variety of personality-types and backgrounds in their congregations.

Pastoral Concerns

It's natural for pastors to be wary of speaking out

from the pulpit about controversial social issues because even Christians often hold opposing views.

It's also natural for pastors to avoid alienating church members and regular attenders, which might cause a decline in tithes and offerings.

Today's pastors ask questions, such as: "How can I maintain unity in my congregation and ensure that the church doesn't split apart, if I talk about public policies on social issues such as abortion, the United States Supreme Court, support for Israel versus the Palestinians or support for Christian schools and homeschooling versus public schools?"

These are complex issues often that require thoughtful analysis, careful study and examination of biblical principles … and prayerful guidance from the Holy Spirit.

But if we believe God is the sovereign Creator and Ruler of the world and universe, and if we believe His Word applies to every area of life and thought, how can pastors NOT teach the biblical principles that apply to controversial social and political issues?

The apostle Paul gave some explicit instructions to Timothy, a pastor in Ephesus in the first century. In 1 Timothy 1:5-7, he reminds Timothy:

"But the goal of our instruction is love from a pure

heart and a good conscience and a sincere faith. For some men, straying from these things, have turned aside to fruitless discussion, wanting to be teachers of the Law, even though they do not understand either what they are saying or the matters about which they make confident assertions."

Regarding the importance of studying and applying God's word to every area of life, Paul says:

"Be diligent to present yourself approved to God as a workman who does not need to be ashamed, handling accurately the word of truth." (2 Timothy 2:15)

"All Scripture is inspired by God [literally "God-breathed"] and profitable for teaching, for reproof, for correction, for training in righteousness, that the man of God may be adequate, equipped for every good work." (2 Timothy 3:16-17)

Regarding preaching boldly, Paul exhorts:

"...preach the word; be ready in season and out of season; reprove, rebuke, exhort with great patience and instruction." (2 Timothy 4:2)

"For God has not given us a spirit of timidity, but of power and love and discipline. (2 Timothy 1:7)

Whose Ministry?

If a pastor boldly proclaims the whole counsel of God, will some members or regular attenders be offended and leave the church? Perhaps.

"For the time will come when they will not endure sound doctrine, but wanting to have their ears tickled, they will accumulate for themselves teachers in accordance to their own desires; and will turn away their ears from the truth, and will turn aside to myths." (2 Timothy 4:3-4)

But whose ministry is it? Whose church is it?

Is it the pastor's church or is it God's church?

Is it the pastor's congregation or is it God's ekklesia – His "called out ones?"

Is it the pastor's ministry, or is he simply overseeing the ministry that God gave him?

Remember what Paul said to the believers in Corinth, some of whom claimed allegiance to him and some of whom claimed that Apollos was superior:

"What then is Apollos? And what is Paul? Servants through whom you believed, even as the Lord gave opportunity to each one. I planted, Apollos watered, but God was causing the growth. So then neither the one

who plants nor the one who waters is anything, but God who causes the growth." (1 Corinthians 3:5-7)

When Jesus began calling Himself the "bread of life" and "the bread which came down from heaven," many of his disciples walked away and stopped following Him. (See John 6:35-66.)

Sound doctrine separates the wheat from the chaff – the truly committed believers from the curiosity seekers and the nominal believers who think they can earn their way to heaven by attending church.

It's important for pastors to focus on quality, not quantity, on voluntary sacrifice, not greediness.

It's also important for pastors to not identify with one political party or another.

Pastors should never be Republicans or Democrats or even Independents.

Instead, pastors must be ***for*** the non-negotiable biblical principles and values described in these pages.

These are not political issues or positions. They are biblical issues and positions.

The apostle Peter exhorts church elders, which would also include pastors:

"...shepherd the flock of God among you, not under compulsion, but voluntarily, according to the will of God; and not for sordid gain, but with eagerness; nor yet as lording it over those allotted to your charge, but proving to be examples to the flock. (1 Peter 5:2-3)

And again, Paul urges Timothy:

"But you, be sober in all things, endure hardship, do the work of an evangelist, fulfill your ministry." (2 Timothy 4:5)

Casualties in Spiritual Battle

Pastors must remember that they are not only humble shepherds leading a flock of wandering sheep, but they are also fierce warriors who are boldly leading an army of soldiers into battle in a life-or-death spiritual war:

"For our struggle is not against flesh and blood, but against the rulers, against the powers, against the world forces of this darkness, against the spiritual forces of wickedness in the heavenly places." (Ephesians 6:12)

And there are only two offensive weapons available for them – and for all of us – to use in this ongoing battle: the Word of God and the ideas it proclaims:

"For though we walk in the flesh, we do not war according to the flesh, for the weapons of our warfare are not of the flesh, but divinely powerful for the destruction of fortresses. We are destroying speculations and every lofty thing raised up against the knowledge of God, and we are taking every thought captive to the obedience of Christ..."
(2 Corinthians 10:3-5)

Battle Plans

How can pastors tear down and destroy "speculations and every lofty thing raised up against the knowledge of God," and help their congregations take every thought captive to the obedience of Christ?

Here are some possible ideas.

1. Teach your congregation what constitutes a biblical worldview.

The percentage of evangelical Christians who understand and embrace a biblical worldview is shockingly low.

A study by the Cultural Research Center (CRC) at Arizona Christian University – conducted under the guidance of Dr. George Barna of the renowned Barna Group – found that the number of Americans holding to a biblical worldview has declined by 50 percent over the past 25 years and is at an all-time low.[213]

The survey also found that a biblical worldview is held by only:

- 21% of Americans who attend evangelical Protestant churches;
- 16% of those attending charismatic or Pentecostal churches;
- 8% of mainline Protestants;
- 2% of Americans between 18 - 29 years of age; and
- 1% of Catholics.

Only one out of every five evangelical Christians believes in the worldview proclaimed in God's word.

Evangelical pastors can and must take responsibility for doing all they can to increase this percentage.

You might consider beginning by preaching a series of messages on the biblical concept of truth versus the relativism of post-modernism and identity politics.

If you are an expositional speaker or teacher, you can easily integrate this into your studies.

2. Preach and teach the important responsibilities of Christian citizenship.

The material in chapters one through five of this book can be used for this purpose.

It is sobering, but 30 – 40% of your church will not register to vote and of those who are registered, 40 – 50% will not vote. As a pastor, you must be the shepherd of your flock. The sheep are lost and wandering.

3. Preach a series of sermons or teach a series of lessons on the biblical view of the non-negotiable issues covered in this book.

- The biblical view of abortion;
- The biblical view of religious liberty;
- The biblical view of the requirements for judges;
- The biblical view of support for Israel;
- The biblical view of the persecution of all those who believe in God;
- The biblical view of taxation; and
- The biblical view of education.

For pastors who are expository teachers, rather than topical preachers, try to weave some of these biblical worldview principles into the texts you are teaching in your Sunday messages.

Also consider bringing in guest speakers to cover some of the worldview principles, if you feel uncomfortable speaking about them yourself.

4. Encourage your congregation to vote for candidates who share their Christian values.

Use the strategy covered in chapter three, "Strategically Limiting Evil While Voting For – Not Against – Your Christian Values."

If you live in California or Tennessee, you can find out which local and state candidates best adhere to Christian values – including judges – by going to electionforum.org and accessing our voter guide.

If you live in other states, go to ivoterguide.com for non-judicial elected officials ... and judgevoterguide.com for judges.

5. Conduct voter registration at your church before and after your Sunday morning services.

By some estimates, more than 15 million evangelical Christians across the country are not even registered to vote![214] How can we possibly expect for the best people to be elected, who meet the biblical qualifications of leaders and representatives of the people, if Christians don't even vote?

In Exodus 18:21, Moses was instructed to appoint "able men who fear God, men of truth, those who hate dishonest gain" to be civic leaders and representatives of the people.

The pastor who takes the lead can boost Christian voter registration – and increase the Christian vote.

6. Schedule a special "Day of Prayer" or "Night of Prayer" service.

Bring your congregation together to pray for our nation, for our national government leaders (by name), for your state and local leaders (by name) and for the 2020 election and the future of our country.

7. If "ballot harvesting" is legal in your state, offer a ballot collection service at your church.

Designate a special time for your church members to bring their ballots to the church so they can be filled out together, signed and sealed, collected and then taken to your county voter registrar's office by you or one of your trusted staff members.

Advertise this service as a convenience to your people – so they don't have to physically go to the polls or put their ballots in the mail themselves ... and so they don't accidentally forget to vote.

You can schedule this activity for the Sunday before Election Day, or if you prefer, you can schedule it for your mid-week service during the week before Election Day. Call it "Voter Appreciation Sunday" or "Voter Appreciation Night" or something similar.

Be sure to set aside enough time to go down the ballot and share the biblical worldview recommendations so all those who haven't yet filled out their ballots can fill them out together and vote according to their Christian values.

Make sure all ballots are signed and sealed before they are collected. Unsigned ballots will be void and will NOT be counted.

And finally, be sure to identify all church members who are shut-ins or live in nursing homes or long-term healthcare facilities. Arrange to help them cast their vote – and do whatever is necessary to help them do so.

The next chapter explains why church voter registration and church ballot harvesting are now critical to every U.S. election going forward.

Salt and Light Ministry

Even after reading or hearing everything that's been said in this chapter, some pastors may still feel uncomfortable speaking from the pulpit about political issues that have the potential of being "controversial." A possible creative solution for such a situation is to set up a "Salt & Light" ministry at your church.

In the Sermon on the Mount, Jesus described His followers as "the salt of the earth" and as "the light of the world." (Matthew 5:13-14)

Salt is not only a flavor enhancer; it's also a preservative. Jesus was saying that His followers were to live and interact in society in such a way as to enhance and preserve it. He never advocated that we withdraw from it.

In Jesus' day, if salt was removed, or if it had lost its preservative properties, two things would happen:

> 1. The process of decay would begin because there was nothing else available that could prevent it.
>
> 2. Contaminated or otherwise ineffective salt was spread along the pathways to fill in holes.

Therefore, Jesus said that salt that had lost its savor was *"good for nothing any more except to be thrown out and trampled underfoot by men."*

Consider also some of the functions of light:

> 1. It exposes darkness, evil, and everything that was previously hidden; and
>
> 2. It provides guidance.

As followers of Jesus, we have a responsibility to

expose evil in the world and to provide guidance not only to those who are lost, but also to those who are on the right path, but who cannot see well enough to stay on it.

Jesus emphasized this responsibility when He said:

"Nor do men light a lamp and put it under the peck-measure, but on the lampstand; and it gives light to all who are in the house. Let your light shine before men in such a way that they may see your good works, and glorify your Father who is in heaven."
(Matthew 5:15-16)

Good Leaders Delegate

Pastors don't need to work in every ministry in the church. Some ministries – even teaching ministries – can be delegated to other church members who have the knowledge, the temperament, the spiritual maturity and the passion to lead a ministry.

If you are a pastor who lacks the time or the energy and passion to lead a ballot-harvesting effort, or to carry out the other activities recommended in this chapter, do this instead:

1. Pray for guidance, discernment and wisdom to find someone on your staff or in

your congregation to conduct a "Salt & Light" ministry.

2. Make sure the person or persons you select meets the qualifications of a leader in Exodus 18:21 and in 1Timothy 3:1-13.

3. Meet with this person – or these people – to strategize, plan and pray together regularly. Remember Proverbs 16:3 – *"Commit your works to the Lord, and your plans will be established."*

4. Commit to supporting that ministry and the people you've appointed to lead it.

I don't need to tell you that everything you do and say as a pastor is crucially important in the crumbling society in which we are living.

Our Christian heritage CAN be rescued from obliteration. Our culture and our politics CAN be transformed and turned back toward what our Founders envisioned and created.

But it will take every evangelical pastor, and congregation and individual Christian working together as the Body of Christ to accomplish it. And be assured that with God, all things are possible.

May the Lord give you success in your ministry.

CHAPTER 16

Maximizing the Christian Vote: Church Ballot Harvesting

The upcoming 2020 election is one of the most critical in America's history. Will conservative, libertarian and Christian candidates be wiped out like they were in the 2018 midterms, or will they achieve a stunning victory?

Will we see even more growth of job-killing regulations ... a bigger "Nanny State" ... failing schools ... social engineering ... and crackdowns on free speech and freedom of religion?

Today's elections are no longer about who smiles the most, who gives the best speeches, or who looks the best on TV. Today's elections are about who can mobilize volunteers and voters better than their opponent.

To turn things around – to win – candidates must utilize a key tactic that's already been used effectively by the Democrat socialists: "ballot harvesting."

What is ballot harvesting?

It is the process of collecting ballots from registered voters, who for any reason desire to have someone else deliver their ballots to their local polling place, election office or county registrar of voters. It's a convenience for legal voters.

Ballot harvesting is now legal in 27 states and is banned in 18 states. Some states that allow ballot harvesting have restrictions on who can collect ballots and/or how many ballots they can legally collect and deliver.

The remaining states have yet to rule one way or the other on ballot harvesting as of this writing.

Since the legality of ballot harvesting can change from state to state – and even from county to county – you should check with your county registrar of voters if you are unsure as to what laws pertain to ballot harvesting in your location.

In 2018, Democrat ballot harvesters collected ballots from hundreds of thousands of vote-by-mail voters and delivered them to the office of the registrar of voters or to local polling places. Some picked up and delivered more than 100 ballots each.

As a result of ballot harvesting in 2018, a Republican U.S. Senate seat was lost in Arizona for the first time in thirty years.

Sen. Ted Cruz of Texas nearly lost his re-election race because of Democrat ballot harvesting.

In Virginia, a conservative congressman lost because of ballot harvesting. The same thing happened in Colorado and Florida. It even happened in Tennessee.

Ballot harvesting transforms elections. And even if it's illegal, people do it anyway.

In 2020, Christian conservatives need to do the same thing – but in a larger, more expanded effort.

How? I call it "church ballot harvesting."

By helping churches to conduct a targeted, organized effort of ballot harvesting within their congregations and within their local communities, we can mobilize millions of evangelical Christians to vote according to their values who would not otherwise bother to vote.

In this chapter we will reveal eight principles and strategies you can use to help candidates at every level to win in 2020 – and help turn around your city, your state – and the nation.

Principle #1: Ballot harvesting produces higher voter turnout – and leads to victory.

Ballot harvesting is a highly strategic method of what

is called "Get Out the Vote" (GOTV). It allows paid or volunteer workers to collect and drop off hundreds of ballots at a local polling station – without any sort of filtering process.

In some locales, no records are kept of who delivers the ballots. No audit "trail" exists.

Church ballot harvesting works best with evangelical, born-again-oriented churches. It produces an estimated six percent to 12% higher voter turnout for a candidate – even more if an evangelical pastor is leading the effort. This is enough to win most elections.

It was also a strategy used widely by Democrats to win the midterm elections in California and other states.

Tactical Outreach

In 2018, Democrat socialists outmaneuvered and overwhelmed their opposition in the following ways:

- They held potlucks and other events to collect ballots;

- They visited low-income housing projects and went door-to-door in massive organized efforts;

- They engaged in a manipulative activity called "granny farming" – going to nursing homes and collecting ballots from the elderly; and

- They used volunteer and paid workers to register and identify key potential voters.

Then they tied these events to a data-driven, door-to-door, Get Out the Vote (GOTV) campaign.

Winning Unwinnable Seats

In the midterm elections of 2018, ballot harvesting helped socialist Democrats win previously "unwinnable" seats in Republican-controlled congressional districts. How did they do it? They employed a multi-pronged strategy that included:

1. Registering potential voters;

2. Using advanced digital and targeted marketing to identify likely voters – creating a database;

3. Organizing paid staff and volunteers to go door to door in a highly-targeted, data-driven GOTV campaign;

4. Picking up the ballots; and

5. Helping voters with voter guides which impacted races in the lower offices.

These ballots were brought in to the voter registration office by ballot "harvesters" who had used strategy number three above to gather data on voters in order to collect only identifiably "friendly" votes.

Here's what one ballot harvester, caught on camera, said at the door of a potential voter. She had gone to this house multiple times. She did not want to talk to the conservative parents of this target – an independent millennial.

So, if the person wanted to vote for a Republican candidate, this ballot harvester wouldn't take the ballot. She even volunteered to show "how to fill out her ballot."

Ballot harvesting strategies were tremendously successful in areas where votes were critical in election outcomes. They helped activist judges and socialist candidates for Senate, Congress, Governor, statewide and city offices, and socialist propositions to win.

In Orange County, California, with a population of 3.2 million people – higher than many states – more than 250,000 absentee ballots were harvested by the

Democrat Socialists in 2018.

The voter registrar in Orange County reported that people were routinely coming in with 100 or 200 ballots they had collected.

Those additional Democrat votes were enough to defeat four members of Congress, a state Senator and Assembly members, state and county office holders and local elected officials – including pastors running for office who should have won.

The result was that districts which typically elect conservative candidates went blue.

Ballot harvesting was the explanation for many late Democrat victories in which Republicans initially won – but lost after the vote-by-mail ballots turned in by ballot harvesters were counted.

Here are some examples from California:

- Republican Mimi Walters was up 51.7-48% on Election Day. She lost by 12,523 votes after Election Day.

- Republican Jeff Denham was up 50.6-49.4% on Election Day. He lost by 9,990 votes after Election Day.

- Republican Steve Knight was up 48–43%

on Election Day. He lost by 21,396 votes after Election Day.

- Republican David Valadao was up 50–39% on Election Day. He lost by 862 votes after Election Day.

Over and over, Republicans who were ahead on Election Day lost post-election.

Assembly races in California had the same results:

- In the 38th district, Democrat Socialist Christy Smith was behind by one percentage point, but late vote-by-mail ballots helped her win by nearly two percentage points.

- In the 74th district, Democrat Socialist Cottie Petrie-Norris beat incumbent Matthew Harper by four points, even though she was down by one point on election night.

Down-Ballot Ticket Wins Also

The California Superintendent of Instruction race was won by Tony Thurmond – even though Thurmond was outspent by former charter school executive Marshall Tuck by $2 million. Thurmond won because of ballot harvesting and the Democrat GOTV effort.

One volunteer said, "We were not wasting time talking to people who weren't going to vote for Democrat candidates."

Voter Fraud?

Ballot harvesting is not voter fraud. It's a clever and well-organized ground game, devised to increase voter turnout among voters who may otherwise not show up to the polls.

However, even though ballot harvesting isn't voter fraud, it does open the door for voter fraud.

When anyone can turn in anyone else's ballot, people can manipulate ballots, toss out "bad" ballots, and lie and cheat the system.

Vote buying, in which a ballot harvester pays a voter for their ballot and then fills it out, is responsible for some of the high numbers of votes for a candidate.

Voter coercion is also used by some Democrat socialist-leaning unions to control and manipulate the vote. People are bullied into voting a certain way, or their ballots are collected and then tossed if they don't agree with the leader's opinion.

Illegal votes are also harvested – caused by the motor voter registration system, which allows noncitizens to illegally register to vote when they obtain a driver's license.

It's easy for illegal immigrants to register to vote, since there is no verification of citizenship at the time they get their driver's licenses – at least not in California and some other states.

Poorly managed voter rules, and other factors that vary from one state to another, also affect each election.

Principle #2: Church ballot harvesting is the key to ensuring conservatives, libertarians and Christians win in 2020.

To win in 2020, conservatives, libertarians and Christians need to utilize the same powerful strategy that Democrats did in 2018 – but do it even better.

Church ballot harvesting takes ballot harvesting to the next level by mobilizing pastors to educate evangelicals and born-again Christians, help them fill out their ballots and then turn those ballots in to the proper election officials.

It is the key to victory even when a district is lopsided in favor of the wrong choices.

Why?

Because church ballot harvesting is a secret weapon that only evangelicals and born-again Christians can do. The Democrat socialists don't have church congregations that they can mobilize.

What's the difference between evangelical Christians and born-again Christians?

Pollster George Barna has defined the differences very well.

Born Again vs. Evangelical

Born-again Christians are defined as people who say they have made a personal commitment to Jesus, and who believe that Jesus Christ died on the cross and rose again for the forgiveness of their sins.

They believe Jesus took on their sin and they took on His righteousness only because of His death and resurrection.

Because they have accepted Jesus as their Savior, they believe they will go to heaven. They have been "born again" – spiritually – by the power of the Holy Spirit.

Evangelicals meet all of the above conditions, plus have the following characteristics:

1. Evangelicals say their faith is very

important in their daily lives;

2. Evangelicals say they have a personal responsibility to share their faith with non-Christians;

3. Evangelicals believe Satan exists; and

4. Evangelicals believe salvation is possible only through grace, not works;

5. Evangelicals believe Jesus lived a sinless life on earth;

6. Evangelicals believe the Bible is fully accurate;

7. Evangelicals believe God is the all-knowing, all-powerful deity who created the universe and still rules it today.

Evangelicals are the more important target group for church ballot harvesting because they will vote more according to the non-negotiable issues we've covered in this book. They will vote for the candidate who takes a biblical stand for these non-negotiable positions, regardless of their party affiliation.

A born-again Christian may not necessarily have a strong Scriptural viewpoint on the non-negotiable issues and may not vote in line with all of them. But most of them agree with the non-negotiable positions in principle.

A Giant Voting Block

There are 60 million potential evangelical voters in the United States. But 35-46 percent of them are not registered to vote. And 45-55 percent of them are not voting at all. That means up to 33 million evangelicals are not voting!

In 2018, only 26 percent of evangelicals actually voted.

About 74 percent – a full 44.4 million Bible-believing voters – did not vote their values. The result? The "Socialist Tsunami" wiped out even traditionally conservative districts.

This was especially true in California, where out of 14 million evangelicals, only 6.72 million voted. This resulted in major "socialist wipeouts," such as those described earlier in this chapter.

But Arizona, Nevada, Texas, South Carolina and Tennessee also saw surprise results. Socialist Democrat candidates won their races in typically conservative areas.

Church ballot harvesting could have completely turned around election results across the nation. But Republicans kept campaigning like it was 2008!

Transforming the Election

It's not too late for 2020. We can still win. But we need to use this tactic.

Imagine mobilizing 15, 20, or even 25 churches, with tens of thousands of members, to vote in just one congressional district.

The impact could change the election outcome and help transform your district with quality leadership and sound values.

Principle #3: The Pastor and churches do not need to fear losing their tax-exempt status.

Game-changing free speech is now available for pastors, due to the suspension of the Johnson Amendment penalties.

The Johnson Amendment – named for its sole sponsor, Texas U.S. Senator Lyndon B. Johnson – was added to the U.S. Tax Code in 1954. Since then, pastors have been prohibited from supporting or opposing political candidates from the pulpit. They have also been barred from engaging in political campaign activities within their pastoral role as leaders of a church congregation.

Some fear ballot harvesting activities could cause churches to lose their tax exempt status. But that's not true.

In 2017, shortly after his inauguration, President Trump took a stand for religious liberty and suspended the enforcement of the Johnson Amendment restrictions, giving pastors back their freedom of speech to express their views about political issues and candidates.

Church ballot harvesting is now legal for pastors, giving us a massive opportunity to mobilize the evangelical vote.

Principle #4: Mobilize pastors to educate their congregations, gather ballots and turn them in at the polls.

Pastors are the key to helping make this happen. In order to mobilize the vote at churches, pastors must:

1. Educate their congregations about voting from a biblical viewpoint (You'll learn more about that in Principle #6);

2. Ask church members to bring their ballots to church, and help them fill them out on a special Sunday – “Ballot Sunday”; and

3. Take the ballots to the polls.

These three steps are critical to church ballot harvesting. They could have a dramatic effect on an election outcome, especially in districts with large churches.

If churches do not do harvest ballots and the secular world does the wrong side could win every election.

Why?

Because the socialist Democrats of the secular world are organized, they’re disciplined, they have valuable and detailed data about their constituents and they have already demonstrated that they have the ability to get out the vote.

Principle #5: Encourage church members to give their ballots to a pastor.

One of the challenges in ballot harvesting is that many conservatives – especially those over the age of 50 – may be hesitant to give their ballots to someone else to take to the polls.

But giving them to their pastor, whom they trust, will

succeed if the pastor assures his congregation that their support is vital and explains exactly how and when and where the ballots will be delivered.

The pastor needs to expect some resistance to ballot harvesting and explain the process in detail. This will also encourage others who might not otherwise go to the polls, to take part in the process.

Principle #6: Educate evangelicals about how to vote their values.

In chapters 7 and 8, we talked about the war that has been waged against Christianity in this country – against individual Christians, against Christian values, against homeschooling, churches, Christian businesses and more.

More than ever, evangelicals need pastors and church leaders who will stand for Christian values and beliefs, and for our First Amendment rights.

Evangelicals will respond to a pro-faith, pro-family and pro-freedom message – but they need to be educated about how to vote from a biblical worldview on non-negotiable issues like abortion, the sanctity of life, support for Israel, helping the persecuted church and Christian civil liberties.

Regardless of their opinions on the economy or other issues, 81 percent of evangelicals will vote Republican, if motivated and educated about how to vote.

The problem is, many of them aren't sure about how to vote their Christian values, and don't realize what kind of an impact they can have on their city, state and the nation.

Before every election, I publish a special voter guide that educates voters about how to vote their values on the local, state and federal level. I perform in-depth research on candidates to determine where they stand on key issues ... and then award them a star rating based on their alignment with biblical values.

The result is an easy-to-use guide that shows voters how to vote from a biblical viewpoint, and how to see their core values adopted and defended by their leaders.

You can find this Voter Guide at electionforum.org. It covers local, state and federal elected positions in all of California and Tennessee. We also recommend that all Christian voters carefully review the national voter guide for judges in all other states at judgevoterguide.com.

For state and local elected officials in other states, go to ivoter.com.

Voter guides are essential to helping people vote for the best candidates.

Principle #7: Use strategic targeting and digital marketing.

The Democrat socialists were strategic and brilliant in their campaigning for the 2018 midterm elections. And they received millions of dollars from Pro-Socialist billionaires like George Soros, Michael Bloomberg, and others. In California alone, they raised an army of 1,700 volunteers, knocked on 580,000 doors, made 190,000 calls, and reached more than 350,000 voters – all in select districts. The result was a 10 percent increase in voter turnout.

The Democrat socialist movement has an organized, strategic approach to resisting President Trump, all consolidated into their action guide – their "bible" – a pamphlet called *Indivisible*.

They distributed this guide online to inform and educate tens of thousands of volunteers across America to help them spread progressive and Socialist propaganda in their local communities.

Indivisible is a brilliant manual regarding ground-game operations. And it works.

Left Behind

Sadly, most conservative, libertarian, and Christian candidates still ran their campaigns like it was 10 years ago – with antiquated and anemic efforts.

To win in 2020, we need to use church ballot harvesting and this formula:

Money + Data Collection + Message + Advanced Digital & Traditional Targeting + GOTV = Victory

Democrat organizations do a great job of this. They go door-to-door in some neighborhoods, contact people on the phone, hold potlucks and community forums – and even sign people up for Obamacare and other social services to collect data.

Then they find out who isn't registered to vote, or who is an infrequent voter. Then they make sure everyone is registered to vote – and actually does vote on election day. They make sure people get vote-by-mail ballots and know how to fill them out with their voter guide.

We need to do the same thing – and more – at our churches by helping people register to vote, educating them about the importance of voting and then helping them turn in their ballots.

Doing it Right – Even with Less Money

We also need to outdo the Democrat socialists in their branding and positioning, in their outreach and in their marketing efforts.

In 2016, Donald Trump's team outperformed Hillary Clinton's team – a team that was four years behind all the great new advances. And he did it with less money.

Trump spent $957.6 million and Hillary spent $1.4 billion. He should have lost the election, if money was the only thing that counted. And yet, he won. How did he do it?

Powerful Messaging and Marketing

Trump had a brilliant marketing strategy. He had powerful messaging that spoke to core issues concerning evangelicals – such as support for Israel, protection of the unborn and support for the persecuted Church around the world.

In the 2020 election, we need to follow Trump's lead and do it again. We need to use the most advanced marketing strategies to create a massive GOTV effort.

I run a 97-award-winning marketing agency, where we use the most cutting-edge strategies to help expand businesses, raise funding – and help political candidates win campaigns.

Our tactics include:

- Facebook advertising "on steroids";
- Advanced data modeling to identify the perfect voters and donors;
- Email follow-up and targeting;
- Targeted direct mail using Transactional Data Modeling (TDM);
- Pre-roll videos on YouTube and cable to boost response;
- Programmable TV to select audiences;
- Direct mail and digital retargeting;
- A cutting-edge, laser sharp strategy called "geo-fencing" (I'll explain that in Principle #8);
- ...and more.

In 2020, we need to train consultants and candidates to use these tactics and strategies to create powerful messaging, target voters in their districts and GOTV (Get Out the Vote). The result will be a massive increase in voter turnout … and election results that will surprise the Democrats.

Note: For details on these powerful tactics, read my article: "29 Surprising Marketing Trends for Political Campaigns" at https://cdmginc.com/2019/10/01/29 14 -surprising-marketing-trends-forpolitical-campaigns-update/.

Principle #8: Use geo-fencing to do church ballot harvesting when pastors say "no."

In the event a pastor says "no" to church ballot harvesting, we can implement an advanced tactic called "geo-fencing" that educates and mobilizes evangelical voters in their church.

Geo-fencing sends targeted videos by Facebook, pre-roll and Google to the cell phones of people who have visited certain locations or events – such as churches. This powerful digital strategy reaches voters with a targeted, relevant and critical message they need to hear about specific candidates.

You can identify any church. Market to anyone who has attended … last Sunday or even everyone in the last year. This can also be done for Christian concerts and crusades.

Geo-Fencing Produces Powerful Results

I ran a marketing campaign for a Christian candidate in California who had zero name recognition and less than $100,000 to spend. He was running against three well-known candidates and the Republican establishment with budgets of more than $1 million.

And yet, he nearly made it to the top two in a field of 17 candidates – which in California is a nearly impossible achievement. How did we do it?

Data Is Key

First, I tied his campaign to a petition against California's horrific "Ban the Bible" bill.

Then, I geo-fenced residents of the district he was running in who had gone to Greg Laurie's Harvest Crusade and Franklin Graham's crusade. I also geo-fenced more than 50 churches in the same area, targeting people who had gone to church in the past six months.

We reached 95,000 people with Facebook ads, pre-rolls ads and Google ads for this candidate's campaign. The results were amazing: 942,000 impressions of the campaign and 288,000 video views. With a couple more weeks, (the candidate only gave us 60 days) and an extra $25,000, we would have won.

By using targeted petitions, a digital GOTV campaign and geo-targeting in combination with church ballot harvesting to a GOTV campaign to evangelical voters before the 2020 election, the results can be tremendous!

We can obliterate the "Socialist Tsunami" the Democrats are already planning. And we can see Christian values upheld, not squashed.

Be Proactive and Make a Difference

In 1964, Republicans were down to 127 members of Congress. Many thought that there was no return and that the Party would die. It was supposed to be the death of the GOP.

But then, in 1966, Ronald Reagan appeared and turned California away from the edge of destruction. And again, in 1980, he led Americans to a cruising victory over Democrat Jimmy Carter's doomed campaign, restored hope and the American dream to millions.

We can win in 2020. We can win the "culture war" that's attacking our churches, our schools and any other pro-freedom, pro-faith, pro-family, institution.

We can obliterate the Socialist Tsunami … and see conservatives, libertarians and Christians elected – even in states like California.

Remember, it's not about who is the most well-spoken or has the best appearance. Candidates who mobilize voters better than their opponents will win the election.

But we must be strategic, thorough and disciplined in our approach.

And that means we have to use church ballot harvesting to generate massive increases in the numbers of Christian conservatives voting in the next election.

We have to educate voters by using voter guides, advanced digital marketing and targeting and high-tech targeting to reach evangelicals, and we must also use geo-fencing to reach potential voters with powerful messaging.

The Socialist Tsunami can be stopped. But we need your help and your partnership.

You are the answer. Your actions can and will change election outcomes.

Here are eight things you can do starting today to transform our culture and politics … and to help stop the coming attacks, cheating and dirty tricks of Democrat Socialist politics.

1. Sponsor a ballot harvesting event or campaign at your church.

Ask your pastor about hosting a "Ballot Sunday" at your church … including voter registration.

2. Be informed and tell your friends and neighbors about community ballot harvesting.

Socialists and community organizers use this as one of their main tactics. They have coffee, they hold events, they use their email and texting to market to their candidates.

They act as if we are at war – and we are. Use your own contacts. Use your contact list to educate and get out the vote.

3. Read my newsletters and books to be better informed.

I publish three weekly newsletters to keep you updated and informed about the latest political news, current events for Christians and cutting-edge marketing tools and tactics.

Reality Alert keeps you updated on everything you need to know as an active, involved Christian who wants to see political and cultural transformation. To subscribe, go to electionforum.org.

The Huey Report provides the latest news and current events. To subscribe, go to craighuey.com.

Direct Marketing Update gives you tools and tactics for cutting-edge marketing. To subscribe, go to cdmginc.com.

Also, read my book, *The Deep State: 15 Surprising Dangers You Should Know*.

You'll be shocked and disturbed to discover how pervasive and widespread the Deep State really is. You'll learn how it operates and controls dark forces from strategic strongholds of power throughout our government, the media and culture. Buy it at deepstatebook.com/.

You'll also want to take a look at my new book, *The New Multichannel, Integrated Marketing: 28 Trends for Creating a Multichannel, Integrated Campaign to Boost Your Profits Now*. This comprehensive guide is packed with insider strategies – based on more than 40 years of direct-response marketing – you can use to get powerful results and GOTV. To order *The New Multichannel, Integrated Marketing: 28 Trends for Creating a Multichannel, Integrated Campaign to Boost Your Profits Now* – and get a signed copy for 20% off – go to multichannelintegratedmarketingbook.com.

4. Volunteer for a political or social action group.

Your presence, input and activity will help a group make a big difference. Maybe you could even lead one.

5. Volunteer for a candidate.

Helping a candidate will make a great difference. With your help and the added energy of many other hard-working volunteers – our candidates will win!

The greatest needs are for GOTV volunteers to go door to door. The next greatest need is for phone volunteers. There are many other activities where your time and talents will make a big difference in electing outstanding candidates.

6. Help register voters.

Since up to 46 percent of evangelicals are not ready to vote, a church that is prepared and committed ready to do ballot harvesting can register nonregistered voters. This is especially effective if it is led by pastors.

7. Reach out to the Hispanic community.

I've spoken to more than 2,000 Hispanic pastors, who all want to vote conservatively and from a biblical worldview.

For many of these pastors, their congregations only speak Spanish. Many of their church members and neighbors can't vote legally, but the pastors want those who can vote, to vote properly.

That's why it's so critical to help us reach out to Hispanics through Election Forum. We are now running the Voter Guide with recommendations for President and other campaigns in Spanish. There's a link at electionforum.org/president/.

8. Run, or help someone else run for office.

Consider running for office yourself ... yes, you! If you're running for office or know somebody who is running for office, give me a call at (615) 814-6633 and I can help you or another candidate win.

Over the past couple of years, I've spoken to close to 3,500 pastors about motivating and activating their congregations. I have spoken at over 50 churches, hosting Election Forums where I go straight down the ballot, evaluating the positions of candidates and the pros and cons of propositions.

Here's the one thing I've learned from this experience. The time is now. The church is ready. And it's time to do church ballot harvesting.

It's time to transform our culture and our politics by electing candidates and judges who share our biblical Christian values.

CHAPTER 17

Winning the Culture War

In the first two chapters of this book we talked about:

- Why it's critically important for Christians to fulfill their responsibility as citizens and vote in every election (Chapter 1), and

- How Christians have the power to transform culture and politics if a higher percentage of them would simply vote. (Chapter 2).

In the middle chapters we described and explained the rationale of seven non-negotiable positions on which Christians who share a biblical worldview agree. In most cases, these positions determine which candidates we will choose to vote for.

We have now come full circle: we are back to the question of what Christians can do to help transform American culture and politics, returning both our culture and our politics to at least a semblance of the bedrock values that inspired our nation's original Christian foundations and influence.

What practical steps can Christians take other than voting for candidates who agree with our non-negotiable positions?

Understanding the Times

First of all, we need to have a thorough and accurate understanding of the post-Christian culture and times in which we live in the 21st century. We need to realize that our country is in the throes of a culture war, not merely a political battle between the members of two opposed political parties.

The recent riots, destruction of historical monuments and physical assaults and attacks against the law enforcement institutions of our society have not been about racial inequality – although racial tensions have provided a convenient smokescreen for the political groups and organizations that hate America and want to see the country torn apart and destroyed.

The real conflict we are facing is a cultural conflict between two opposing world views. At its root, it's a spiritual war raging in the hearts and minds of men and women who reject God and who are living in rebellion against Him. And ultimately, its only solution is a spiritual solution, not a political one.

The apostle Paul describes this spiritual war in

Ephesians 6:

"Put on the full armor of God, that you may be able to stand firm against the schemes of the devil. For our struggle is not against flesh and blood, but against the rulers, against the powers, against the world forces of this darkness, against the spiritual forces of wickedness in the heavenly places." (Ephesians 6:11-12)

1 Chronicles 12 in the Old Testament records the names of some of the noteworthy men who helped David become king over Israel after the death of King Saul in battle. In this chapter we find these words:

"Now these are the numbers of the divisions equipped for war, who came to David at Hebron, to turn the kingdom of Saul to him, according to the word of the Lord... Of the sons of Issachar, men who understood the times, with knowledge of what Israel should do..." (1Chronicles 12:23, 32)

Our nation desperately needs Christian men and women who "understand the times," and who have knowledge of what America needs to do to deal with complex and controversial issues such as:

- Human trafficking
- Health care
- Business, corporate and personal taxation

- Government regulation vs. business independence and individual freedom
- Prison reform
- Police reform
- Abortion
- Marriage
- Gender identity
- Religious liberty
- … and much more.

Dealing with issues such as these shouldn't be left to those who don't have a biblical worldview and who don't ask and trust God for wisdom and discernment.

As Christians, we can and should provide counsel and advice to our elected leaders. Remember the extent of the resources we have at our disposal:

- **Wisdom** – *"But if any of you lacks wisdom, let him ask of God who gives to all men generously and without reproach, and it will be given to him." (James 1:5)*
- **Knowledge** – *"And concerning you, my brethren, I myself also am convinced that you yourselves are*

full of goodness, filled with all knowledge, and able also to admonish one another." (Romans 15:14)

- **Discernment** – *" For if you cry for discernment, lift your voice for understanding; if you seek her as silver and search for her as for hidden treasure; then you will discern the fear of the Lord and discover the knowledge of God." (Proverbs 2:3-5)*

- **The mind of Christ** – *"Now we have received, not the spirit of the world, but the Spirit who is from God, that we might know the things freely given to us by God, which things we also speak... For who has known the mind of the Lord, that he should instruct Him? But we have the mind of Christ." (1 Corinthians 2:12, 13a, 16)*

Also don't forget the power your input can have:

"Where no wise guidance is, the people fall; but in the multitude of counselors there is safety."

(Proverbs 11:14, Amplified Bible)

Here are four things we should understand about the segment of our society which is waging ideological warfare against those of us who believe we live in a God-created universe.

1. Right and wrong are turned upside down.

What used to be right and good is now wrong and evil ... and what used to be considered wrong and evil is now praised as right and good. God warns against turning morality upside down:

"Woe to those who call evil good, and good evil; who substitute darkness for light, and light for darkness; who substitute bitter for sweet and sweet for bitter!.... who justify the wicked for a bribe, and take away the rights of the ones who are in the right!"
(Isaiah 5:20, 23)

2. People mock the idea of a future judgement.

"Know this first of all, that in the last days mockers will come with their mocking, following after their own lusts and saying, 'Where is the promise of His coming? For ever since the fathers fell asleep, all continues just as it was from the beginning of creation." (2 Peter 3:3-4)

3. Most people no longer believe absolute truth exists.

The philosophy of relativism – called post-modernism – is being taught exclusively on most college campuses in the U.S. today. Many professors believe and teach that objective truth – truth that is true for everyone whether they believe it or not – doesn't exist. Instead, they claim that all "truth" is relative to one's identity group – or groups. And the more identity groups one belongs to, the more validity one's "truth" has.

The problem with this muddled and destructive thinking should be obvious to Christians: it's self-refuting. These college professors – and their "progressive" students – believe that their assertion that all truth is relative is in fact objective – meaning it is true for everyone. But you can't have it both ways. You cannot say that ALL truth is relative and then turn around and assert an absolute truth!

This is why no one can live in a completely relative, post-modern world. No one can live and function in a world where nothing is true objectively for everyone. Such a world would quickly turn into utter chaos and anarchy. Believe it or not, this is exactly what some radical political groups want to have happen in the U.S.

4. People deny the existence of God while asserting that they themselves are gods.

This was the crux of the Serpent's temptation of Eve in the Garden of Eden. After denying God's warning that if she ate the forbidden fruit, she would die, the Serpent said, *"For God knows that in the day you eat from it your eyes will be opened, and you will be like God, knowing [literally, 'determining for yourself'] good and evil." (Genesis 3:5)*

This is what mankind in rebellion against God always longs for: to be his own god – to be autonomous from his Creator – and to live by his own rules, made up by himself for his own convenience.

Listen to how Isaiah the prophet describes those who rebel against their Creator:

"Oh, your perversity! You turn things upside down! Shall the potter be considered of no more account than the clay? Shall the thing that is made say of its Maker, 'He did not make me,' or the thing that is formed say of Him who formed it, 'He has no understanding'?"
(Isaiah 29:16, Amplified Bible)

This, in a nutshell, is the mindset we are facing today in our culture, in our government and in our politics. This is what we are up against. And as Christians, we need to be up to the task of combating and defeating it.

We need to be able to form good, logical arguments against these four man-made, Serpent-inspired attitudes of atheism. Since you are reading this book, you are well on your way to being a spokesperson for the kingdom of God in this battle. It's a battle of ideas.

And it's a battle against the spiritual forces of darkness and evil.

"For though we walk in the flesh, we do not war

according to the flesh, for the weapons of our warfare are not of the flesh, but divinely powerful for the destruction of fortresses. We are destroying speculations and every lofty thing raised up against the knowledge of God, and we are taking every thought captive to the obedience of Christ."
(2 Corinthians 10:3-5)

Christian Battle Plan – Step One: Repentance

At the end of Chapter 2, we laid out an action plan for Christians to implement to enable them to increase their transformative power and influence leading up to the 2020 election. We are repeating some of these actions here, along with additional steps and information.

It all needs to begin with self-examination and repentance. Scripture commands us to correct *"in a spirit of gentleness"* those who are in error, *"looking to yourself, lest you too be tempted." (Galatians 6:1)*

Towards the end of the Sermon on the Mount, Jesus gave some practical advice to His disciples on the topic of judging and criticizing others. He said:

"For in the way you judge, you will be judged; and by your standard of measure, it will be measured to you. And why do you look at the speck in your brother's eye,

but do not notice the log that is in your own eye? Or how can you say to your brother, 'Let me take the speck out of your eye,' and behold, the log is in your own eye? You hypocrite, first take the log out of your own eye; and then you will see clearly enough to take the speck out of your brother's eye." (Matthew 7:2-5)

In addition to individual repentance, there is also a need for group repentance. A church-wide prayer meeting or special service – as suggested in Chapter Fifteen – provides a good opportunity for church-wide repentance and renewal.

In 2 Chronicles 7— after King Solomon had finished building the Jewish temple in Jerusalem – God gave him a promise which is often quoted out of context and misapplied to the church today. The promise is not for us today – it was for the Jews and for their God-given land. But the principle of repentance still applies to us today. Here's the familiar passage – in bold text – with the context included:

"Thus Solomon finished the house of the Lord and the king's palace, and successfully completed all that he had planned on doing… Then the Lord appeared to Solomon at night and said to him, 'I have heard your prayer and have chosen this place for Myself as a house of sacrifice. If I shut up the heavens so that there is no rain, or if I command the locust to devour the land, or if I send pestilence among My people, ***and My people who are***

called by My name humble themselves and pray and seek My face and turn from their wicked ways, then I will hear from heaven, will forgive their sin and will heal their land.'" *(2 Chronicles 7:11-14)*

We know without a doubt that God will preserve a city or even a country on behalf of a few Christians who live there and who are close to God in their personal relationships with Him. He did it for Nineveh during the life of Jonah, and He was willing to do it for Sodom if there had been any followers of God in that wicked city other than Lot and his family (see Genesis 18:16-33).

Other Cultural Battle Plan Action Steps

Here are some other action steps for Christians to take after repentance is completed:

2. Pray for broad revival among Christians.

Why a revival among Christians? Because when non-Christians start seeing Christians loving each other – and the world – instead of fighting with each other and complaining about all that's wrong with the world, they will become attracted to Christianity. When **that** begins to happen, revival will spread. But revival has to start among Christians.

Jesus said to His disciples the night before His crucifixion, *"A new commandment I give to you, that you love one another, even as I have loved you... By this all men will know that you are My disciples, if you have love for one another." (John 13:34-35)*

3. Be a part of the Christian revival yourself.

How? Begin to serve the hungry and satisfy the desires of the afflicted by joining a group of like-minded Christians through your church or through another voluntary nonprofit organization.

Begin serving and loving the poor ... the downtrodden ... the strangers and the aliens living in your own community ... or in nearby communities.

4. Pray for revival and changed hearts among non-Christians. Remember that we are called as Christians to pray for all, regardless of nationality, race, ethnicity, religion, color or gender.

"First of all, then, I urge that entreaties and prayers, petitions and thanksgivings, be made on behalf of all men [and women], for kings and all who are in authority, in order that we may lead a tranquil and quiet life in all godliness and dignity."
(1 Timothy 2:1-2)

Pray for your local and state government leaders – even the ones you want to see defeated in the next election! And pray for our national government leaders as well. God works miracles. He can guide and direct the actions of all leaders and save the most rebellious and godless soul.

If you doubt this, read the incredible story of King Nebuchadnezzar of Babylon – which is in modern-day Iraq – in Daniel chapters 2, 3 and 4. Especially notice the amazing, miraculous conclusion of the story:

"Now I, Nebuchadnezzar, praise, exalt and honor the King of heaven, for all His works are true and His ways just, and He is able to humble those who walk in pride." (Daniel 4:37)

Notice also that God's perfect will is for all people to come to repentance and to be saved:

"The Lord is not slow about His promise, as some count slowness, but is patient toward you, not wishing for any to perish, but for all to come to repentance."
(2 Peter 3:9)

5. Educate yourself prior to every election.
Research the positions of the candidates who are running for every office. Research the pros and cons of every proposition and local measure on the ballot.

Plan to attend one of my Election Forums if there is one scheduled in your area. Check my Election Forum speaking schedule here: https://www.electionforum.

org/biblical-world-view

Also review Step 3 and Step 9 of the list of action steps at the end of the previous chapter of this book for other educational opportunities.

6. Plan to vote in every local, state and national election from now on. Don't let anything stop you from letting your voice be heard at the ballot box!

7. Help educate other Christians and encourage them to vote also. Encourage your family and friends to attend an Election Forum and consult our voter guides. Perhaps you can help babysit children while their parents go to the polls, or collect and turn in the ballots of the shut-ins from your church who aren't able to go to the polls.

8. Volunteer to help in an election campaign. There are many ways Christians can help support a local or national candidate. For example, you may have a few hours available on a weekend to:

- Work at a phone bank making phone calls to voters.
- Work at a literature table on a college campus or in a mall answering questions and engaging people in conversations about candidates and issues.

- Work in a local campaign headquarters designing or producing or distributing lawn signs, banners, rally signs, etc.

- Volunteer to address or stuff envelopes for direct mail projects.

- Volunteer to distribute flyers or campaign information in neighborhoods, working in groups with others.

9. Encourage your pastor. Many pastors refrain from speaking out during election cycles because of unfounded concerns about IRS rules, regulations and sanctions.

Even if the so-called "Johnson Amendment" of the IRS Revenue Code were being enforced – which it isn't during the Trump administration – there is still much that a pastor can do legally to help influence the voters in his congregation. Encourage him to:

- Preach a series of sermons on the biblical principles that apply to complex social issues without endorsing or disparaging any political candidate.

- Preach sermons on the biblical principles at stake in the various propositions that will be on a ballot.

- Schedule me to give an Election Forum at the church.
- Schedule a church-wide prayer meeting specifically regarding the 2020 national election.

Conclusion

Christians can and must work to restore and rebuild the foundations of our Republic. In fact, we are commanded to do so:

"And if you give yourself to the hungry and satisfy the desire of the afflicted, then your light will rise in darkness and your gloom will become like midday. And the Lord will continually guide you, and satisfy your desire in scorched places, and give strength to your bones; and you will be like a watered garden, and like a spring of water whose waters do not fail. Those from among you will rebuild the ancient ruins; ***you will raise up the age-old foundations; and you will be called the repairer of the breach, the restorer of the streets in which to dwell.****" (Isaiah 58:10-12)*

Endnotes

Chapter 1:

[1] Quoted in "Politics, Government, and Worldview." *the Journal*, March 2012, Volume 12 Issue 3.

[2] Rushdoony, R.J., "The Myth of Neutrality," February 1, 2004. https://chalcedon.edu/magazine/the-myth-of-neutrality, Accessed May 20, 2020.

[3] Whitehead, John W. *The Separation Illusion: A lawyer examines the first amendment*, Mott Media, 1977.

Chapter 2:

[4] Schaeffer, Francis A. *A Christian Manifesto*, Crossway Books, 1981.

[5] "First Continental Congress Meets 1774." History Central. https://www.historycentral.com/Revolt/Cont.html, Accessed June 17, 2020.

[6] Ibid.

[7] Ibid.

[8] Barton, David. "America's Godly Heritage"(CD). Wallbuilders. https://www.historycentral.com/Revolt/Cont.html, Accessed June 17, 2020.

[9] "Continental Congress." History.com, February 4,2010. https://www.history.com/topics/american-revolution/the-continental-congress, Accessed June 17, 2020.

[10] Ibid.

[11] Barton, David, Op.Cit.

[12] Barton, David, Op. Cit.

[13] The first three bullets are from Barton, David, Op. Cit.

[14] "Andrew Jackson Quotes." https://www.brainyquote.com/authors/andrew-jackson-quotes, Accessed June 18, 2020.

[15] "George Washington Quotes About Morality." AZ Quotes. https://www.azquotes.com/author/15324-George_Washington/tag/morality, Accessed June 18, 2020.

[16] Barton, David, Op. Cit.

[17] Barton, David. "Is America a Christian Nation?"(CD). Wallbuilders. https://shop.wallbuilders.com/is-america-a-christian-nation-cd, Accessed June 18, 2020.

[18] Barton, David. "Is America a Christian Nation?"(CD), Op. Cit.

[19] Ibid.

[20] Ibid.

[21] Ibid.

[22] Ibid.

[23] Eleftheriou-Smith, Louella-Mae. "America, New Zealand and Canada top list of world's most generous nations." Independent, February 2, 2016. https://www.independent.co.uk/news/world/americas/america-new-zealand-and-canada-top-list-of-world-s-most-generous-nations-a6849221.html, Accessed June 19, 2020.

[24] "11 Facts About the 2004 Indian Ocean Tsunami." DoSomething.org. https://www.dosomething.org/us/facts/11-facts-about-2004-indian-ocean-tsunami, Accessed June 20, 2020.

[25] "Humanitarian response to the 2004 Indian Ocean earthquake." Wikipedia. https://en.wikipedia.org/wiki/Humanitarian_response_to_the_2004_Indian_Ocean_earthquake, Accessed June 20, 2020.

[26] "Fact Sheet: Continuing Support for Tsunami Relief." The White House: Office of the Press Secretary, February 9, 2005. https://georgewbush-whitehouse.archives.gov/news/releases/2005/02/20050209-20.html, Accessed June 20, 2020.

[27] "History of Pennsylvania Hospital: In the Beginning." Penn Medicine. http://www.uphs.upenn.edu/paharc/features/creation.html, Accessed June 20, 2020.

[28] See chapter 3 of my book, *The Deep State: 15 Surprising Dangers You Should Know*. Media Specialists, Torrance, California, 2018.

[29] Sohn, Paul. "Reclaiming the Seven Mountains of Culture." February 21, 2013. http://paulsohn.org/reclaiming-the-7-mountains-of-culture/, Accessed June 21, 2020.

[30] Ibid.

[31] "Incarceration in the United States." Wikipedia. https://en.wikipedia.org/wiki/Incarceration_in_the_United_States#Security_levels, Accessed June 21, 2020.

[32] Barton, David. "Is America a Christian Nation?"(CD), Op. Cit.

[33] Riley, Jennifer. "Christian Charities Rank High in Top 100 U.S. Nonprofits." The Christian Post, December 10, 2007. https://www.christianpost.com/news/christian-charities-rank-high-in-top-100-u-s-nonprofits.html,

Accessed June 21, 2020.

34 Eleftheriou-Smith, Louella-Mae, Op. Cit.

35 Hall, Holly. "Americans Rank 13th in Charitable Giving Among Countries Around the World." The Chronicle of Philanthropy, December 3, 2013. https://www.philanthropy.com/article/Americans-Rank-13th-in/153965, Accessed June 21, 2020.

Chapter 3:

36 "James A. Garfield Quotes. AZ Quotes. https://www.azquotes.com/author/5343-James_A_Garfield, Accessed June 21, 2020.

Chapter 4:

37 "Lyndon B. Johnson." Wikipedia. https://en.wikipedia.org/wiki/Lyndon_B._Johnson, Accessed July 9, 2020.

38 Ibid.

39 Ibid.

40 Ibid.

41 Heyrman, Christine Leigh. "Religion and the American Revolution." Divining America, TeacherServe©. National Humanities Center. April 6, 2020.

42 "The Church and the Revolutionary War," https://www.pbs.org/opb/historydetectives/feature/the-church-and-the-revolutionary-war/ Accessed April 3, 2020.

43 Ibid.

44 "Brigadier General John Peter Gabriel Muhlenberg." National Park Service: Yorktown Battlefield, February 26, 2015. https://www.nps.gov/york/learn/historyculture/muhlenbergbio.htm, Accessed August 18, 2020.

45 "Did the Bible Play a Role in Shaping the U.S. Constitution?" Dr. Jerry Newcombe, *Truth in Action Ministries*, April 18, 2018.

46 Ibid.

47 Ibid.

48 Ibid.

49 *Annals of Congress*, 1789, pp. 440ff. https://memory.loc.gov/ammem/amlaw/lwaclink.html

50 "Christianity in the Constitution," Dave Miller, Apologetics Press, 2008.

51 Rowland, Kate, The Life of George Mason (New York: G.P. Putnam's Sons, 1892), Vol. 1:244.

52 James Madison, *Federalist Papers, #51* (New York: New American Library, 1961), 322.

53 "The Federalist Papers," Kerby Anderson, Probe Ministries, 2015.

54 For reader reviews of this book, click here: https://www.goodreads.com/book/show/682253.Christianity_and_the_Constitution. For additional information about the author and the book, go here: https://search.myway.com/search/GGmain.jhtml?p2=%5EBZA%5Exdm101%5ES17547%5EUS&ptb=3C4F299F-4BAA-4CB4-9A0F-9E5FF4106A8F&n=782b8def&ln=en&si=1566-CuTM4u1NlDu1y1wNlDCu&tpr=hpsb&trs=wtt&brwsid=ACDFA569-E0F0-4448-BE5E-6EC344C21D2E&searchfor=John+Eidsmoe+Christianity+and+the+Constitution&st=tab

55 Charles Grandison Finney, *Lectures on Revivals of Religion*, ed. William G. McLoughlin (Cambridge: Belknap Press of Harvard University Press, 1960), 16.

56 Thomas, T. (2016). "Engines of Abolition: The Second Great Awakening, Higher Education, and Slavery in the American Northwest." Retrieved from http://krex.ksu.edu, April 9, 2020.

57 Berry, Daina Ramey. "American slavery: Separating fact from myth." The Conversation, June 19, 2017. https://theconversation.com/american-slavery-separating-fact-from-myth-79620, Accessed July 11, 2020.

58 Guasco, Michael. "The Misguided Focus on 1619 as the Beginning of Slavery in the U.S. Damages Our Understanding of American History." Smithsonian Magazine, September 13, 2017. https://www.smithsonianmag.com/history/misguided-focus-1619-beginning-slavery-us-damages-our-understanding-american-history-180964873/, Accessed July 11, 2020.

59 Retrieved from https://en.wikipedia.org/w/index.php?title=Christian_abolitionism&oldid=946417157, April 10, 2020.

60 Retrieved from https://en.wikipedia.org/wiki/An_Act_for_the_Gradual_Abolition_of_Slavery, April 10, 2020.

61 Wyatt-Brown, Bertram. "American Abolitionism and Religion." Divining America, TeacherServ®. National Humanities Center. April 10, 2020. <http://nationalhumanitiescenter.org/tserv/nineteen/nkeyinfo/amabrel.htm>

62 Ibid.

63 "Christian Abolitionism," op. cit.

64 Ibid.

65 Thomas, T., op. cit.

66 Retrieved from https://en.wikipedia.org/wiki/Christian_views_on_slavery, April 10, 2020.

Chapter 5:

67 *Elane Photography v. Willock*, April 7, 2014, Alliance Defending Freedom. http://www.adfmedia.org/News/PRDetail/5537, Accessed May 26, 2020.

Chapter 6:

68 See The Roots of Christian Reconstruction, R.J. Rushdoony [Vallecito, CA: Ross House Books, 1991], 1112-1114.

69 See The Pattern of God's Truth: The Integration of Faith and Learning, Frank E. Gaebelein [New York: Oxford University Press, 1954]

Chapter 7:

70 Morris, Andrea. "Christian School Hit with SWAT-Style Raid, CA Demands They Allow Sexual Exploitation or Be Shut Down." CBN News, June 7, 2019. https://www1.cbn.com/cbnnews/us/2019/june/christian-school-hit-with-swat-style-raid-ca-demands-they-allow-sexual-exploration-or-be-shut-down&p=5&pos=5, Accessed July 2, 2020.

71 "California Assemblyman Drops So-Called' Gay Conversion Therapy Ban' Bill." CBN News, August 31, 2018. Accessed July 2, 2020.

72 Wetterhahn, Madeline and Boumil, Marcia. "U.S. Supreme Court Strikes Down California FACT Act." Health Affairs, June 29, 2018. https://www.healthaffairs.org/do/10.1377/hblog20180628.429780/full/, Accessed July 2, 2020.

73 "Client Story Jack Phillips." Alliance Defending Freedom. https://adflegal.org/client-story/jack-phillips, Accessed July 3, 2020.

74 "First Amendment Protection of Religious Freedom and Christianity Won this Week in the Supreme Court." The Blog, Election Forum, June 8, 2018. https://www.electionforum.org/first-amendment/first-amendment-protection-of-religious-freedom-and-christianity-won-this-week-in-the-supreme-court/?highlight=Colorado%20Civil%20Rights%20Commis-

sion, Accessed July 3, 2020.

75 Ibid.

76 McGinty, Bill. "Neighbors Making Noise Complaints About a Church." WFMY News2, May 5, 2018. https://www.wfmynews2.com/article/news/weird/neighbors-making-noise-complaints-about-a-church/83-549119563, Accessed July 3, 2020.

77 Ibid.

78 Editorial, "JFK, Amy Coney Barrett and Anti-Catholicism." National Catholic Register, September 22, 2017. https://www.ncregister.com/daily-news/jfk-amy-coney-barrett-and-anti-catholicism, Accessed July 5, 2020.

79 Gryboski, Michael, "Christian women's shelter sues city over complaint saying it must admit transgender females." The Christian Post, November 16, 2018. https://www.christianpost.com/news/christian-womens-shelter-sues-alaska-city-ordering-admit-transgender-females.html&p=2&pos=2, Accessed July 5, 2020.

80 "Religious Freedom Violated, the Destitute Abandoned and Children Sent to the Streets: How Deep State Government Bureaucrats Shut Down a Ministry to the Homeless." The Blog, Election Forum, September 13, 2018. https://www.electionforum.org/uncategorized/religious-freedom-violated-the-destitute-abandoned-and-children-sent-to-the-streets-how-deep-state-government-bureaucrats-shut-down-a-ministry-to-the-homeless/?highlight=Operation%20Embrace, Accessed July 5, 2020.

Chapter 8:

81 Read, James H. "James Madison." The First Amendment Encyclopedia. https://mtsu.edu/first-amendment/article/1220/james-madison&p=1&pos=1, Accessed July 6, 2020.

82 H.R.5. – Equality Act. Congress.gov. https://www.congress.gov/bill/116th-congress/house-bill/5, Accessed July 6, 2020.

83 Groppe, Maureen. "As Trump prepares to sign executive order, here's a history of 'religious freedom' laws." USA Today, May 3, 2017. https://www.usatoday.com/story/news/politics/2017/05/03/trump-prepares-sign-executive-order-heres-history-religious-freedom-laws/101250064/, Accessed July 7, 2020.

84 "ADF: 'Equality Act' profoundly intolerant, deceptively named." News and Media, Alliance Defending Freedom. March 13, 2019. https://www.adflegal.org/press-release/adf-equality-act-profoundly-intolerant-

deceptively-named, Accessed July 7, 2020.

85 Chart, Natasha and Nance, Penny. "Feminists, Conservatives Join Forces to Oppose 'Equality Act.'" RealClear Politics, May 6, 2019. https://www.realclearpolitics.com/articles/2019/05/06/feminists_conservatives_join_forces_to_oppose_equality_act_140261.html#!&p=3&pos=3, Accessed July 7, 2020.

86 Krayden, David. "California Gov. Newsom Bans Singing in Churches." Daily Caller, July 3, 2020. https://dailycaller.com/2020/07/03/california-gov-gavin-newsom-singing-churches-coronavirus-covid-19-lockdown/, Accessed July 8, 2020.

87 Dalton, Daniel P. "What Is the Religious Land Use and Institutionalized Persons Act ("RLUIPA")?" Dalton Tomich, February 11, 2010. https://www.attorneysforlanduse.com/what_is_the_religious_land_use_and_institutionalized_persons_act_rluipa/, Accessed July 8, 2020.

88 Southerland, Abigail A. "ACLJ Files New Lawsuit to Defend Religious Organization." https://aclj.org/religious-liberty/aclj-files-new-lawsuit-to-defend-religious-organization-against-discrimination, Accessed July 8, 2020.

Chapter 9:

89 "Fetal Heartbeat: The Development of Baby's Circulatory System." https://www.whattoexpect.com/pregnancy/fetal-development/fetal-heart-heartbeat-circulatory-system/, Accessed April 15, 2020.

90 Fact Sheet: Science of Fetal Pain. Charlotte Lozier Institute, February 19, 2020.

91 Ibid.

92 Ibid.

93 "Roe v. Wade." *Oyez*, www.oyez.org/cases/1971/70-18. Accessed April 17, 2020.

94 These specific rules about what is legal and illegal during each trimester of a woman's pregnancy is a classic example of legislating from the bench. The Supreme Court's role is to rule on the constitutionality of laws created by the legislative branch; its role is not to create legislation, which is exactly what the Court did in this case.

95 "Number of Abortions – Abortion Counters." http://www.numberofabortions.com/, Accessed April 21, 2020.

96 Ibid.

97 "Number of abortions in U.S. falls to lowest since 1973." Denver Post, September 18, 2019.

98 "Induced Abortion in the United States." Guttmacher Institute, September 2019. https://www.guttmacher.org/fact-sheet/induced-abortion-united-states, Accessed April 21, 2020.

99 "Planned Parenthood Claims 'Black Lives Matter," But Kills 247 Black Babies in Abortion Every Day." Opinion, LifeNews.com, June 4, 2020. https://www.lifenews.com/category/editorials/, Accessed September 3, 2020.

100 Ibid.

101 Ibid.

102 Ibid.

103 Israel, Melanie. "Planned Parenthood Sets New Record for Abortions in a Single Year." Heritage Foundation, January 9, 2020.

104 Retrieved from https://en.wikipedia.org/w/index.php?title=David_Daleiden&oldid=951407455 April 21, 2020.

105 Clark, Matthew. "362 Infants Born Alive as Result of Botched Abortions Died in Last Decade," May 13, 2013, https://aclj.org/planned-parenthood/362-infants-born-alive-result-botched-abortions-died-decade, Accessed April 28, 2020.

106 Ibid.

107 Ertelt, Steven. "19 States Allow Infanticide, Let Abortionists Leave Babies to Die Who Survive an Abortion," https://www.lifenews.com/category/statenews/, February 14, 2019, Accessed April 30, 2020.

108 Ibid.

109 Abbamonte, Jonathan. "New York State to Allow Abortion up to Birth," January 29, 2019, https://www.pop.org/new-york-state-to-allow-abortion-up-to-birth/, Accessed May 11, 2020.

110 Ibid.

111 Ibid.

112 Parker, Kathleen. "Abortion Extremism in New York and Virginia paved the way for Alabama and Georgia's laws." *The Washington Post*, May 17, 2019,

113 A"Marc Thiessen: Planned Parenthood defending infanticide," The Washington Post, April 8, 2013, https://www.google.com/search?q=Marc+thiessen+Defending+Infanticide+Washington+

Post&rlz=1C1GCEU_enUS821US821&oq=Marc+thiessen+Defending+Infanticide+Washington+Post&aqs=chrome..69i57.34192j0j8&sourceid=chrome&ie=UTF-8, Accessed April 28, 2020.

114 https://www.congress.gov/bill/116th-congress/senate-bill/311/history, Accessed May 12, 2020.

115 Seitz-Wald, Alex. "Clinton Compares GOP Views on Women to 'Terrorist Groups'." https://www.nbcnews.com/politics/2016-election/clinton-compares-gop-views-women-terrorist-groups-n417061, August 27, 2015. Accessed April 23, 2020.

116 Denison, Dr. Jim. *The Daily Article*, September 20, 2018.

117 "Stats before Roe v. Wade," Georgia Right to Life, www.grtl.org, Accessed April 27, 2020.

118 Ibid.

119 "APA denials of abortion mental health risk contradicted by other studies," Catholic News Agency, August 17, 2008. https://www.catholicnewsagency.com/news/apa_denials_of_abortion_mental_health_risk_contradicted_by_other_studies,Accessed May 19, 2020.

120 Ibid.

121 Ibid.

122 "Jesus Came So We Could Have Abortions, Implies Methodist Pastor," PNP News, September 15, 2018. https://pulpitandpen.org/2018/09/15/jesus-came-so-we-could-have-abortions-implies-methodist-pastor/, Accessed May 19, 2020.

123 Perkins, Tony. "Dems Defend Abortion to the Ends of the Birth," February 11, 2020. https://www.frcaction.org/updatearticle/20200211/dems-abortion, Accessed May 19, 2020.

124 "U.S. Public Continues to Favor Legal Abortion, Oppose Overturning Roe v. Wade," Pew Research Center, August 29, 2019, https://www.people-press.org/2019/08/29/u-s-public-continues-to-favor-legal-abortion-oppose-overturning-roe-v-wade/, Accessed May 11, 2020.

125 https://nhclc.org/nhclc-calls-for-complete-defunding-of-planned-parenthood-federal-government-investigation-condemns-actions-of-national-organization-and-advocates-for-life, Accessed May 19, 2020.

Chapter 10:

126 'Brown v. Board of Education." History.com editors, October 27, 2009;

Updated April 8, 2020. https://www.history.com/topics/black-history/brown-v-board-of-education-of-topeka, Accessed May 21, 2020.

[127] Ibid.

[128] Ibid.

[129] Ibid.

[130] Roe v. Wade, Wikimedia Foundation, Inc. https://en.wikipedia.org/wiki/Roe_v._Wade, Accessed May 22, 2020.

[131] Ibid.

[132] http://landmarkcases.c-span.org/pdf/Roe_Rehnquist_Dissent.pdf, Accessed May 22, 2020.

[133] Gillip, Mandy. "Trump has appointed second-most federal judges through May 1 of a president's fourth year," May 6, 2020. https://news.ballotpedia.org/2020/05/06/trump-has-appointed-second-most-federal-judges-through-may-1-of-a-presidents-fourth-year/, Accessed May 22, 2020.

[134] United States federal courts, Ballotpedia. https://ballotpedia.org/United_States_federal_courts, Accessed May 22, 2020.

[135] United States Court of Appeals for the Ninth Circuit, Ballotpedia. https://ballotpedia.org/United_States_Court_of_Appeals_for_the_Ninth_Circuit, Accessed May 22, 2020.

Chapter 11:

[136] Ur of the Chaldees (Genesis 11:28) has been identified as Urs Kasdim near Nasiriyah in southern Iraq. It was identified in 1862 and excavated in 1927. See https://en.wikipedia.org/wiki/Ur_of_the_Chaldees, Accessed May 27, 2020.

[137] "The Stones of Herod's Temple Reveal Temple Mount History," The Bible History Daily, March 1, 2017. https://www.biblicalarchaeology.org/daily/biblical-sites-places/temple-at-jerusalem/the-stones-of-herods-temple-reveal-temple-mount-history/, Accessed May 28, 2020.

[138] Balfour Declaration, Wikipedia. https://en.wikipedia.org/wiki/Balfour_Declaration, Accessed May 28, 2020.

[139] Ross, Dennis, "Which One of These Presidents Was Toughest on Israel?" The Washington Institute, May 19, 2016. https://www.washingtoninstitute.org/policy-analysis/view/which-one-of-these-presidents-was-toughest-on-israel, Accessed May 28, 2020.

[140] Ibid.

[141] Ibid.

[142] Ibid.

Chapter 12:

[143] Klett, Leah MarieAnn, "India: Hindu extremists rape 4-y-o daughter of pastor who refused to stop sharing Gospel." The Christian Post, September 11, 2019. https://www.christianpost.com/news/india-hindu-extremists-rape-4-y-o-daughter-of-pastor-who-refused-to-stop-sharing-gospel.html, Accessed June 1, 2020.

[144] Smith, Samuel. "Pakistan: School principal abducts 15-year-old Christian girl, forces Islamic conversion." The Christian Post, September 10, 2019. https://www.christianpost.com/news/school-principal-abducted-15-year-old-christian-girl-forced-islamic-conversion-father-says.html, Accessed June 1, 2020.

[145] Ibid., "Indonesian Pastor Sentenced to 4 Years in Prison for Evangelizing to Muslim Cab Driver," May 8, 2018. https://www.christianpost.com/news/indonesian-pastor-sentenced-to-4-years-in-prison-for-evangelizing-to-muslim-cab-driver.html, Accessed June 1, 2020.

[146] Bohon, Dave. "ISIS Terrorists Still Killing Christians, Beheading Children," The New American, August 8, 2014. https://www.thenewamerican.com/world-news/item/18883-iraq-isis-terrorists-still-killing-christians-beheading-children, Accessed June 1, 2020.

[147] Chastain, Mary. "Report: Syrian Christians Cry 'Jesus!' Before ISIS Mass Beheading," Breitbart News, October 5, 2015. https://www.breitbart.com/national-security/2015/10/05/report-syrian-christians-cry-jesus-isis-mass-beheading/, Accessed June 1, 2020.

[148] Mamoun, Abdelhak. "ISIS executes 28 Ethiopian Christians in Libya," Iraqi News, April 19, 2015. https://www.iraqinews.com/arab-world-news/isis-executes-28-ethiopian-christians-libya/, Accessed June 1, 2020.

[149] Open Doors World Watch List 2020. https://www.opendoorsusa.org/wp-content/uploads/2020/01/2020_World_Watch_List.pdf, Accessed June 1, 2020.

[150] All Party Parliamentary Group for International Religious Freedom or Belief, "How Many Christians Are Killed Each Year Because of Their Faith?" October 13, 2018. https://appgfreedomofreligionorbelief.org/how-many-christians-are-killed-each-year-because-of-their-faith/, Accessed June 1, 2020.

[151] Open Doors World Watch List 2020, Op. Cit.

[152] Faust, Michael. "China Persecuted 5,576 Churches in 2019, Climbs to 23 on Worst Persecutors List," Christian Headlines, January 16, 2020. https://www.christianheadlines.com/contributors/michael-foust/china-persecuted-5576-churches-in-2019-climbs-to-23-on-worst-persecutors-list.html, Accessed June 2, 2020.

[153] Ibid.

[154] Three Self Church, BillionBibles.com. https://billionbibles.com/china/three-self-church.html, Accessed June 2, 2020.

[155] Faust, Michael. "China Demolishes 3,000-Seat Megachurch during Worship Service," Christian Headlines, October 21, 2019. https://www.christianheadlines.com/contributors/michael-foust/china-demolishes-3-000-seat-megachurch-during-worship-service.html, Accessed June 2, 2020.

[156] Open Doors World Watch List 2020, Op. Cit.

[157] Klett, Leah MarieAnn, Op. Cit.

[158] "Christian Persecution: Religious Liberty Takes a Huge Hit in India." Election Forum: The Blog, August 9, 2017. https://www.electionforum.org/persecuted-church/india/?highlight=Christian%20Persecution%3A%20Religious%20Liberty%20takes%20a%20huge%20hit%20in%20India, Accessed June 3, 2020.

[159] "Terrifying: Persecution and Oppression of Christians in India Surprises America." Election Forum: The Blog, October 3, 2017. https://www.electionforum.org/persecuted-church/india-2/?highlight=Persecution%20and%20Oppression%20of%20Christians%20in%20India%20Surprises%20America, Accessed June 3, 2020.

[160] "Christians in Southern India Beaten and Detained for Giving Aid to the Poor." Persecution International Christian Concern, March 31, 2020. https://www.persecution.org/2020/03/31/christians-southern-india-beaten-detained-giving-aid-poor/, Accessed June 3, 2020.

[161] Klett, Leah MarieAnn, Op. Cit.

[162] "List of ethnic groups in Myanmar." Wikipedia, https://en.wikipedia.org/wiki/List_of_ethnic_groups_in_Myanmar, Accessed June 3, 2020.

[163] Richardson, Don. *With Eternity in Their Hearts*. Regal House Publishing, Raleigh, North Carolina, 1980.

[164] "Rohingya people." Wikipedia, https://en.wikipedia.org/wiki/Rohingya_

people, Accessed June 4, 2020.

165 "List of ethnic groups in Myanmar," Op. Cit.

166 Wright, David. "1.6 Million Kachin Christians in Myanmar Trapped as Targets in Genocidal War." Stories of Persecution, August 3, 2018. https://www.opendoorsusa.org/christian-persecution/stories/1-6-million-kachin-christians-in-myanmar-trapped-as-targets-in-genocidal-war/, Accessed June 4, 2020.

167 Bohon, Dave. Op. Cit.

168 Hoft, Jim. "The Great Christian Genocide: Mosul Goes From 15,000 Christians to 40 Following Obama's Presidency." Gateway Pundit, August 8, 2019. https://www.thegatewaypundit.com/2019/08/the-great-christian-genocide-mosul-goes-from-15000-christians-to-40-following-obamas-presidency/, Accessed June 4, 2020.

169 "Oppression: The Shocking Truth About ISIS." Election Forum: The Blog, September 12, 2017. https://www.electionforum.org/persecuted-church/isis/?highlight=Oppression%3A%20The%20Shocking%20Truth%20About%20ISIS, Accessed June 4, 2020.

170 Hoft, Jim. Op. Cit.

171 Hoft, Jim. Op. Cit.

172 Showalter, Brandon. "Anti-Christian violence, attacks on churches in Europe at all-time high in 2019: report," The Christian Post, January 22, 2020. https://www.christianpost.com/news/anti-christian-violence-attacks-churches-europe-all-time-high-2019-report.html, Accessed June 2, 2020.

173 Ibid.

174 See the Parable of the Good Samaritan, Luke 10:25-37.

175 Fredericks, Bob and Hicks, Nolan, "Trump promotes religious freedom in UN speech." New York Post, September 23, 2019. https://nypost.com/2019/09/23/trump-promotes-religious-freedom-in-un-speech/, Accessed August 13, 2020.

176 Trainer, Mark. "Pompeo: Religious Freedom is 'a universal human right.' Share America, February 4, 2019. https://share.america.gov/pompeo-religious-freedom-universal-human-right/, Accessed June 6, 2020.

177 Ibid.

178 "Historic Second Annual Ministerial to Advance Religious Freedom." Fact Sheet, Office of International Religious Freedom, July 19, 2019. https://www.state.gov/historic-second-annual-ministerial-to-advance-religious-

freedom/, Accessed August 13, 2020.

179 "Kurdish-Turkish conflict (1978-present)." Wikipedia. https://en.wikipedia.org/wiki/Kurdish%E2%80%93Turkish_conflict_(1978%E2%80%93present), Accessed June 6, 2020.

180 "Free at Last: Andrew Brunson Released by Turkey After Two Years." Christianity Today, October 12, 2018. https://www.christianitytoday.com/news/2018/october/andrew-brunson-free-turkey-court-us-pastor-release-deal.html, Accessed June 6, 2020.

181 "Meriam Ibrahim arrives in New Hampshire, ready to begin new life." Fox News, August 1, 2014. https://www.foxnews.com/us/meriam-ibrahim-arrives-in-new-hampshire-ready-to-begin-new-life, Accessed August 14, 2020.

182 Ibid.

Chapter 13:

183 "McCullough v.Maryland." History.com Editors, June 7, 2019. https://www.history.com/topics/united-states-constitution/mcculloch-v-maryland, Accessed August 18, 2020.

184 "Lyndon B. Johnson." Wikipedia. https://en.wikipedia.org/wiki/Lyndon_B._Johnson, Accessed July 9, 2020.

185 Schwarzwalder, Rob. "Tax Exemption for Churches: An American Value,a Social Imperative," Family Research Council. https://www.frc.org/taxexemptionchurches, Accessed June 7, 2020.

186 Ibid.

187 Ibid.

188 Ibid.

189 Powell, Edward A. and Rushdoony, Rousas John. *Tithing and Dominion.* Ross House Books, Vallecito, California, 1979, pg. 39.

190 "The Supreme Court: The Power to Tax." Time, March 17, 1958. http://content.time.com/time/magazine/article/0,9171,863135,00.html, Accessed June 8, 2020.

191 Schwarzwalder, Rob, Op. Cit.

192 Schwarzwalder, Rob, Op. Cit.

Chapter 14:

193 Wagoner, Jennings L.; Haarlow, William N. "Common School Movement."

Encyclopedia of Education. Encyclopedia.com: https://www.encyclopedia.com/education/encyclopedias-almanacs-transcripts-and-maps/common-school-movement, Retrieved June 6, 2020.

194 Ibid.

195 These are the basic tenets of Deism. Deists believe God created everything and then stepped back and left the created universe to run on its own – and left mankind to fend for itself. Deists agree with Theists on creation, but believe the opposite of Theists regarding everything else.

196 The foundational tenet of Humanism is Darwinian evolution by natural selection. Humanism declares there is no God. It is therefore a man-centered philosophy and religion. Christianity, by contrast, is God-centered.

197 Chen, Grace. "When Teachers Cheat: The Standardized Test Controversies." Public School Review, August 6, 2018. https://www.publicschoolreview.com/blog/when-teachers-cheat-the-standardized-test-controversies, Accessed June 12, 2020.

198 Grant, Billy-Jo, Ph.D., et al "A Case Study of K-12 School Employee Sexual Misconduct: Lessons Learned from Title IX Policy Implementation." National Criminal Justice Reference Service, December 2017. https://www.ncjrs.gov/pdffiles1/nij/grants/252484.pdf, Accessed August 20, 2020.

199 Bustamante, Jaleesa. "K-12 School Enrollment & Student Population Statistics." Educationdata.org, June 9, 2019. https://educationdata.org/k12-enrollment-statistics/, Accessed August 20, 2020.

200 Dotinga, William. "Abuse Victim Says Her School Was a Haven for Predators." Courthouse News Service, October 1, 2012. https://www.courthousenews.com/abuse-victim-says-her-school-was-a-haven-for-predators/, Accessed August 20, 2020.

201 Lambert, Diana. "Rocklin kindergarten teacher caught in firestorm over transgender book named teacher of the year." The Sacramento Bee, March 29, 2018. https://www.sacbee.com/news/local/education/article207214249.html, Accessed June 12, 2020.

202 Adaway, Desiree, "What Exactly is Critical Race Theory?" The Adaway Group, 2020. https://adawaygroup.com/critical-race-theory/, Accessed August 20.2020.

203 A PDF file of the 17-page document can be found here: https://www.utla.net/sites/default/files/samestormdiffboats_final.pdf

204 Ohanian, Lee. "Teacher Union Demands Far-Left Economic Policies

Before Reopening Classrooms." Hoover Institution, July 22, 2020. https://www.hoover.org/research/teachers-union-demands-far-left-policies-returning-classrooms, Accessed August 20, 2020.

205 "The risks of keeping schools closed far outweigh the benefits." The Economist, July 18, 2020. https://www.economist.com/leaders/2020/07/18/the-risks-of-keeping-schools-closed-far-outweigh-the-benefits, Accessed August 20, 2020.

206 Johnson, Scott F. "The 14th Amendment Protects the Right to a Public Education." Concord Law School, April 20, 2017. https://www.concordlawschool.edu/blog/constitutional-law/14th-amendment-protects-rights-education/, Accessed June 15, 2020.

207 Devitt, Rebecca, "Homeschool Vs Public School: Statistics and Test Scores." How Do I Homeschool? July 7, 2018. https://howdoihomeschool.com/2018/07/07/homeschool-vs-public-school-test-scores/, Accessed June 12, 2020.

208 Here are two websites that will help you get started setting up a home school"

[1] http://homeschoolden.com/2020/07/16/starting-to-homeschool/?gclid=Cj0KCQjw4f35BRDBARIsAPePBHzPvhkZYCVuQnMfFKxjANDkFm87u8vOOoWDDeClhwvgV0GxODYYvk8aAntZEALw_wcB

[2] The Home School Legal Defense Association: http://homeschoolden.com/2020/07/16/starting-to-homeschool/?gclid=Cj0KCQjw4f35BRDBARIsAPePBHzPvhkZYCVuQnMfFKxjANDkFm87u8vOOoWDDeClhwvgV0GxODYYvk8aAntZEALw_wcB

209 Ray, Brian D. "Homeschool SAT Scores for 2014 Higher Than National Average." NHERI, June 7, 2016. https://www.nheri.org/homeschool-sat-scores-for-2014-higher-than-national-average/, Accessed June 14, 2020.

210 Quoted in Pratt, David, "Humanism and the Public Schools." Truth Magazine, Fort Wayne, Indiana. http://truthmagazine.com/archives/volume28/GOT028219.html, Accessed June 12,2020.

211 Algar, Selim. "Harvard professor wants to ban homeschooling because it's 'authoritarian'." *New York Post*, April 23, 2020. https://nypost.com/2020/04/23/harvard-professor-wants-to-ban-authoritarian-homeschooling/, Accessed June 15, 2020.

212 Devitt, Rebecca. "The Basis for Christian Homeschooling." Why on Earth Homeschool?, December, 2014. https://whyonearthhomeschool.wordpress.com/2014/12/, Accessed June 15, 2020.

Chapter 15:

[213] "Biblical Worldview in Decline Among Christians in America." MB Missions Box, April 3, 2020. https://missionsbox.org/news/biblical-worldview-in-decline-among-christians-in-america/, Accessed August 5, 2020.

[214] "15M Christians Aren't Registered to Vote: Churches Across US re Participating in 'Voter Registration Sunday.'" CBN News, September 20, 2019. https://www1.cbn.com/cbnnews/politics/2019/september/15m-christians-arent-registered-to-vote-churches-across-us-participating-in-voter-registration-sunday, Accessed August 7, 2020.

☑ **Yes!** I want to discover how to vote for, not against my values ... and strategically limit evil. Please send me my discounted copy of ***The Christian Voter: 7 Non-Negotiables for Voting For, Not Against, Your Values*** — plus my FREE Election Special Report.

TWO PURCHASING OPTIONS (CHECK ONE):

☐ **Save 10%.** Send me_1_copy of ***The Christian Voter: 7 Non-Negotiables for Voting For, Not Against, Your Values*** – valued at $14.99 paperback – for only $13.49 paperback, along with my FREE Election Special Report.

OR

☐ **Save Up to 20%.** Send me ____ copies of ***The Christian Voter: 7 Non-Negotiables for Voting For, Not Against, Your Values*** – valued at $14.99 paperback – for only $11.99 per copy for paperback book *(minimum 10 books),* along with my FREE Election Special Report.

METHOD OF PAYMENT:

____Check or money order made out to **Creative Direct Marketing Agency**

Charge my: ____ VISA ____ MasterCard ____ American Express

Name (as it appears on card) ______________________________

Card Number ______________________________

Exp Date ______________ 3-4 Digit Security Code ____________

Signature ______________________________

Street Address ______________________________

City, State, ZIP ______________________________

Email ______________________ Phone # ______________

☑ Please sign me up for *The Huey Report* and *Reality Alert* – Craig's weekly newsletters on need-to-know news, shocking discoveries and insider insights for politics and economics (*The Huey Report*) and Evangelical Christians (*Reality Alert*).

MAIL THIS FORM TO:

Creative Direct Marketing Group, Inc., Attn: Craig Huey
1313 4th Ave. N., Nashville, TN 37208
Or, visit **www.ChristianVoterBook.com** to purchase a copy online today.

CRAIG HUEY

Craig Huey is author and publisher of *Reality Alert* newsletter, and a frequent commentator on local and national news, TV broadcasts, local and national radio, and podcasts. He is the president of CraigHuey.com and ElectionForum.org.

Craig has spoken to several thousand pastors over the years and in hundreds of churches on how to vote their values and not against them.

Over a million follow his non-partisan recommendations every election, based on a biblical worldview.

Craig is the only expert in the nation who evaluates and recommends judges as either strict constructionists or judicial activists on JudgeVoterGuide.com.

Craig also owns a 94-time award-winning ad agency that utilizes the same advanced marketing techniques used by today's socialists to advance their ideologies (conservative Christians, Libertarians and Republicans, unfortunately, use marketing tools 20 years behind the times). He is one of the top digital and direct response marketers in the United States.

Craig has authored three books, *23 Equity Crowdfunding Secrets to Raising Capital*, *The Deep State: 15 Surprising Dangers You Should Know*, and *The New Multichannel, Integrated Marketing: 29 Trends for Creating a Multichannel, Integrated Campaign to Boost Your Profits Now.*

Craig speaks internationally on politics, Christianity, marketing and advertising.

Christians hold the future to the upcoming election.

The key to national, state, and local victory for turning our nation around is if Christians will vote for and not against their values.

America has found itself torn between the cultural war against Christianity and how government, at all levels, is being used to undermine people of faith, religious liberties, and key issues important to Christians.

This election is about 7 non-negotiables that help determine how Christians should vote.

These 7 non-negotiables are based upon the Word of God.

They are based on a biblical worldview.

They are based on the intersection of faith and politics.

In this new book, *The Christian Voter: 7 Non-Negotiables for Voting For, Not Against, Your Values,* frequent television communicator, author and small business owner, Craig Huey, reveals surprising facts you won't read elsewhere in a roadmap to show you how to vote for and not against your values.